Performing the testimonial

Manchester University Press

theatre
theory • practice
• performance •

series editors
MARIA M. DELGADO
MAGGIE B. GALE
PETER LICHTENFELS

advisory board
Michael Billington, Sandra Hebron, Mark Ravenhill, Janelle Reinelt, Peter Sellars, Joanne Tompkins

This series will offer a space for those people who practise theatre to have a dialogue with those who think and write about it.

The series has a flexible format that refocuses the analysis and documentation of performance. It provides, presents and represents material which is written by those who make or create performance history, and offers access to theatre documents, different methodologies and approaches to the art of making theatre.

The books in the series are aimed at students, scholars, practitioners and theatre-visiting readers. They encourage reassessments of periods, companies and figures in twentieth-century and twenty-first-century theatre history, and provoke and take up discussions of cultural strategies and legacies that recognise the heterogeneity of performance studies.

also available

Performing the testimonial

Rethinking verbatim dramaturgies

AMANDA STUART FISHER

Manchester University Press

Published by Manchester University Press
Oxford Road, Manchester M31 9PL
www.manchesteruniversitypress.co.uk

British Library Cataloguing-in-Publication Data
A catalogue record for this book is available from the British Library

ISBN   978 1 5261 4574 1   hardback
ISBN   978 1 5261 7447 5   paperback

First published 2020
Paperback published 2023

Typeset
by New Best-set Typesetters Ltd

*To Pam Stuart
and Jan Stuart*

CONTENTS

ACKNOWLEDGEMENTS

This book draws on research undertaken over the past eighteen years or so and owes much to the various discussions I have been lucky to have had with many colleagues during this time. However, I am particularly grateful to Derek Paget for his friendship and support of my work during this period and for his role in the organisation of the Acting with Facts conference and the subsequent publications he edited for *Studies in Theatre and Performance*. I would also like to thank Simon Shepherd, Mick Wallis and Gilli Bush-Bailey for their words of encouragement over the years and Joe Kelleher for helping me find my way through the labyrinthine research process that underpins this project. I am also highly appreciative of the help I have received from colleagues at the Royal Central School of Speech and Drama, where I have been supported enormously by Professor Maria Delgado and the research office. Thanks also go to Tanya Zybutz who read my work and offered me much encouragement along the way and to my colleagues who teach with me on the Drama, Applied Theatre and Education course and the Writing for Performance course and covered for me while I was on research leave, particularly: Ben Buratta, Steve Farrier, Farokh Soltani and Gareth White. I would also like to thank Peter Boenisch for reading a draft of Chapter 1, Professor Robert Stern for kindly sharing his research on Løgstrup and the ethical demand with me and Ola Animashawun for our many discussions about dramaturgy over the years. I am also very grateful to Yaël Farber, whose work and dialogue has sparked many of the debates explored in the book. I would like to thank the many undergraduate, postgraduate and research students I have engaged with during the research stages of this book, whose debates and discussions have been critical to my own thinking, in particular Kate Duffy and Karoline Moen, whose research has intersected with my own most directly. I also owe a great deal of gratitude to Sally Baggott who copy-edited this book and provided me with valuable good cheer and optimism throughout, and to Alex Cooke whose friendship and support I have valued greatly. Warm thanks and much love is also extended to my two daughters Beatrice and Matilda for their ongoing patience and encouragement, even when I was preoccupied with the task of writing. Finally, I want to thank Tony Fisher from the bottom of my heart, whose love, support, robust critical interrogation and on-going feedback and good humour have kept me going throughout this project and beyond.

Introduction: Performing the 'promise' of truthfulness: the hybrid practices of contemporary verbatim and testimonial theatre

David: During the process of rehearsals I had concerns about: Why am I saying I instead of we? Where are the stories of the Royal Navy, The Welsh Guards, the Scots Guards, who fought with us? Why are we not talking about the Battles: Goose Green, Tumbledown, San Carlos? Do I have the right to stand here and talk for all those who went to war? Where are the British dead in the play? (Arias, 2017: 42)[1]

About halfway through *Minefield*, a play by the Argentinian theatre maker Lola Arias about the Falklands/Malvinas conflict of 1982, David, one of the three English veterans in the play, reflects on the experience of bearing witness to the events of war. In the production of the play I saw at the Royal Court Theatre, London in 2016, David turned to the audience at this point and addressing us directly, delivered the speech quoted above. It was a halting and poignant moment and was one that flipped the action away from the men's reconstructed memories of the past, bringing us all back to the here and now of watching and making a play in a theatre. The fact that Arias, who wrote and directed *Minefield*, chose to keep these questions within the play text itself is also significant, for it produced an important meta-theatrical moment of self-critique, interrogating the ethics and politics of using other people's lived experiences and testimonies to make theatre. David's questions challenge audiences to actively consider whether or not Arias's dramaturgical process is ethical, asking us to reflect

on whose stories are being remembered in the play and whose are being
forgotten. His questions also draw attention to the issue of appropriation
in this form of theatre, and whether the performance of testimonial
narratives should be viewed as an unethical act of misappropriation or
as a means of recognising the stories and perspectives of Argentinian
and British veterans who experienced this war first-hand. In short, David's
questions are a provocation to the play's audiences to think about what
ethical testimonial theatre making is and what constitutes 'truthfulness'
in these contrasting and contested narratives of the past.

Described by various theatre critics as either a 'documentary play'
(Anthony, 2017), 'a theatrical docu-drama' (Bloodworth, 2017), or simply
as 'verbatim' (Wicker, 2017), like many other examples of contemporary
verbatim or testimonial theatre, *Minefield* resists any simple definition.
While the veterans do tell their own stories within the course of the play,
in an interview, Arias distinguishes her practice from that of a verbatim
theatre maker by pointing out that she 'doesn't simply take people's words
and give them to an actor to say. Rather she returns them to those who
spoke them' (Wicker, 2017). For Arias, the dramaturgical process of
gathering and retelling these stories is akin to the labour undertaken
when creating any new work: 'every word', she explains, 'is as worked on
as any of my poetry or short fiction' (Arias in Wicker, 2017).

Yet while Arias approached the text of *Minefield* by employing her
skills as a playwright, the very fact that the accounts of the war that are
presented derive directly from the testimony of some of the veterans who
fought in it changes the truth claims of this play and the way the audience
becomes positioned within the performance of these truths. The focus
on testimonial accounts of the past makes certain ethical and political
demands upon Arias as the theatre maker, but arguably also on the veterans
who become the actors and conduits of these stories and the audience
who emerge as the addressees of this testimony. Dramaturgically, the
play is constructed so that audiences are made aware that the stories
being told within the play are not fictive but are based on real, personal
accounts of the Falklands/Malvinas conflict. The use of direct address,
the incorporation of testimony and the way the play foregrounds acts of
witnessing therefore become key signifying elements that operate together
to generate a theatre experience that relocates the play away from a fictive
context, framing it instead within the realm of testimonial truth telling.
The positioning of the veterans as the actors who tell their own stories
also provides another layer of authority within the dramaturgy. Their
accounts of their experience of the war become understood by audiences
as testimonial truths, and we assume these men agreed to share their
stories openly and willingly, by participating in an ethical process of

collaboration with Arias. In other words, as an audience, we would probably feel very differently about the production and the truth claims attached to it, if we were to discover that these men were subject to any form of coercion, were somehow deceived into sharing their experiences or if their accounts had been deliberately changed or falsified.

In this sense, testimonial theatre then is determined by its own ethico-political potential. While it can stage a form of ethico-political intervention by revealing stories that have not yet been told or highlighting histories and narratives that have been erased or overlooked by hegemonic, political structural processes, the integrity of testimonial theatre, and therefore its authority, is rooted in its promise of an ethical and honest creative process, established upon relationships of care and trust with the testimonial subjects whose stories it enacts. While Arias is clearly positioned as a theatre maker within the creative process of *Minefield*, she also takes on a facilitative role and is responsible for the way the veterans access and engage with the theatre-making process, how they go about remembering the past and how this is transformed into a dramaturgical text. Unlike a verbatim theatre maker, who establishes the dramaturgical process by working from a predetermined methodological approach, such as only using word-for-word transcribed interview material or pre-existing juridical material, in the construction of the testimonial play, the theatre maker has a degree of artistic autonomy within the process. In *Minefield*, Arias adopted the role of storyteller and auteur while also having a responsibility for the veterans who are witnesses in this process and who must trust Arias with their stories. It is Arias's negotiation of this responsibility and the relationships she establishes with the veterans she works with that ultimately determine how the dramaturgy functions and in what ways testimony contributes to the formation of the play; as such, the dramaturgical process becomes determined by the ethical and political perspectives that Arias invites into the process.

Testimonial theatre-making processes draw on very different ethico-political structures compared to verbatim theatre practices that use a predetermined ethics to negotiate the complex process of making theatre out of real people's stories and experiences. For the testimonial theatre maker, the creative process is determined by the demands of each situation addressed, the particularity of each act of witnessing and also by the performative nature of testimony itself, which is a performative speech act that is generated through representational processes and memory.

In the course of this book, I examine further what distinguishes verbatim and testimonial theatre making and what these different practices might have in common. My analysis is underpinned by a focus on the different dramaturgical structures and approaches adopted within the plays I discuss and an examination of how testimony and acts of witnessing inform the creative development of these plays. My reference to dramaturgy in this context addresses the decisions made about the structural components of a play, such as character, plot, action, but also, where possible, points to the directorial decisions that frame a play's performance. In this sense, my use of the term 'dramaturgy' reflects the creative structure by which the play was created, its use of formal conventions and the way these are realised in performance. In this sense, I agree with Cathy Turner and Synne Behrndt when they describe dramaturgy as 'an overarching term for the composition of a work' (Turner and Behrndt, 2008: 17) but I am also drawn to Adam Versényi's understanding of dramaturgy as 'the architecture of the theatrical event' and the way the different components of a play work together in order to 'generate meaning for the audience' (Versényi quoted in Turner and Behrndt, 2008: 18).

The focus of my examination of verbatim and testimonial theatre centres around a number of contemporary verbatim and testimonial plays that emerged from the 1990s through to the first decades of the twenty-first century in South Africa, Australia, the UK and America. However, I also explore some earlier plays that form a pre-history for this form of theatre. The first part of the book concerns a genealogical exploration of verbatim theatre and its histories, examining how this form of theatre is distinguishable from the documentary theatre that preceded it. In the second part of the book, I move on to focus on testimonial theatre and, by adopting an approach that is informed by philosophical engagements with testimony, witnessing and other forms of truth telling, I consider how different modes of witnessing are enacted in this type of theatre making. In this sense, instead of seeking to establish a finite definition of what constitutes verbatim or testimonial theatre, this book explores the development of a range of different dramaturgical approaches that could be described as verbatim or testimonial and examines what this reveals about the way the truth claims of these forms of theatre are conceptualised, enacted and interpreted.

Verbatim theatre and its limitations

The term 'verbatim theatre' was first established within contemporary theatre scholarship in the late 1980s, when Derek Paget described the emergence of a new form of theatre making influenced by the 'local documentary work' of director Peter Cheeseman at the Victoria Theatre,

Stoke-on-Trent (Paget, 1987: 318). The early verbatim theatre he had in mind was 'predicated upon the taping and subsequent transcription of interviews with "ordinary" people, done in the context of research into a particular region, subject area, issue, event, or combination of these things' (Paget, 1987: 317), resulting in verbatim plays that celebrated local stories and effectively captured the 'vernacular speech' of the region. As Paget points out, these play were often then '*fed back* into the communities (which [had], in a real sense created them), via performance *in* those communities' (Paget, 1987: 317; original emphasis). Much of this kind of theatre work was developed outside of London in areas such as Lancaster, Cheshire and Staffordshire before later being picked up by London-based companies who became more interested in using verbatim and documentary techniques to address issues of 'national' importance. These London-based productions, dubbed by Paget as '"Controversy" Shows', tended to be more 'journalistic' and 'investigative' than the 'celebratory' verbatim plays emerging in Lancaster and Cheshire whose focus was on celebrating and representing 'locality' (Paget, 1987: 322).

This early form of verbatim theatre, Paget argues, offered a new way of creating theatre that democratised the playwriting process by enabling ensembles of actors to engage with communities to gather stories and actively contribute to the writing of the play, giving them 'a greater share in the *means* of production, in the Marxist sense' (Paget, 1987: 318; original emphasis). In an account of the work he produced at this time, and writing some eighteen years after Paget, Cheeseman describes the role of the ensemble of actors, who would work as researchers and devisors, as 'fundamental to the working blueprint' he developed in his documentary theatre work at the Victoria Theatre in Stoke-on-Trent (Cheeseman, 2005: 105). Cheeseman's reflections are presented within a short essay on documentary theatre that accompanied the publication of *Talking to Terrorists*, a contemporary verbatim play by Robin Soans, directed by Max Stafford-Clark in 2005. Commissioned by Out of Joint and the Royal Court Theatre, the play was heralded a success by many critics and was described by *The Guardian* newspaper theatre critic, Michael Billington, as 'the most important new play we have seen this year' (Billington, 2005b). Like the 'controversy' plays described by Paget in 1987, *Talking to Terrorists* was not focused on stories from a specific locality, instead it sought to examine the issue of terrorism by drawing on interviews undertaken with people from around the world who had had some involvement in or been victim of different terrorist attacks. The breadth of terrorist incidents the play covered was therefore vast, with audience members being introduced to a wide range of different characters and stories; one minute encountering Mo Mowlan, ex-Secretary of State for the UK and, in another, an ex-member of the Kurdish Workers Party who was recruited aged fifteen. The play received great praise from theatre critics who described it as 'chilling, moving and mesmerising' (Spencer, 2005) and, as Paola Botham explains, was to become 'unwittingly topical when its London run coincided with the bombings of 7 July 2005' (Botham, 2008: 313). It was also seen as an example of a verbatim play that 'transcends journalism and emerges as a work of art in its own right' (Taylor, 2005). Yet, while *Talking to Terrorists* had much in common with the 'controversy' verbatim plays described by Paget in 1987, significantly it was also structurally very differently from them, as Tom Cantrell's research into the play usefully reveals. Firstly, *Talking to Terrorists* was not dramaturgically constructed by an ensemble of actors, in fact 'only three members of the final cast took part in the production's research stages and were called "actor-researchers"' (Cantrell, 2013: 169). Secondly, instead of using the actors to determine the questions asked, which would ultimately then form the basis of the play's narrative structure, the process was led and determined by the writer and director. As Chipo Chung, one of the actor-researchers in the play points out, the questions the actors asked 'were pre-determined by Stafford-Clark and Soans' (Cantrell, 2013: 170). Yet, while only a few members of the cast ever met the people who were interviewed for the play, Soans, the writer of the piece, 'met all but one of the 29 people who finally appear in the script' (Cantrell, 2013: 170). In this sense, the structure of *Talking to Terrorists*, like many other contemporary verbatim plays, turned away from the 'democratising' collective writing process identified by Paget in the plays of Cheeseman and, significantly, instead used the interviewing process as a mode of research for the playwright.

By adopting a more playwright-led process, the play arguably lost some of the nuances that might have been captured from a wider reaching and less structured interview process. As a consequence, while the play received positive praise from the press, it also attracted criticism from theatre scholars who questioned the truth claims attached to the play, as well as its claims of generating a new and authentic engagement with the issue of terrorism itself. Paola Botham, for example, argued that, in terms of the play's capacity to offer some political acuity on the issue of terrorism, it 'failed to deliver' (Botham, 2008: 313). For Botham, the individual perspectives that the play sought to examine 'got lost in the amalgamation of very different conflicts under the common trait of violence' (Botham, 2008: 314); thus the play ends up 'treating all extremists as the same' and ultimately 'throws politics out of the window' (Sierz quoted in Botham, 2008: 314). Botham is also critical of the way Soans represents some of the verbatim subjects who appear in the play, drawing attention to the repeated representation of 'a misguided "terrorist"' juxtaposed 'alongside an articulate "ordinary person" [...] who could frame the former's behaviour' (Botham, 2008: 314). Similarly, in an article written in 2011, I argued that while Soans's play offers us real stories about real encounters with terrorism, it is difficult to see how the play 'penetrate[s] the act of terrorism itself' or offers any degree of insight into the issues it examines, other than to assert the simplistic message that '"*all terrorism is bad and therefore we shouldn't do it*"' (Stuart Fisher, 2011: 113; original emphasis). These contrasting and critical responses to *Talking to Terrorists* are not unusual in scholarship that examines contemporary verbatim and documentary theatre work where plays are often both watchable, but also ethically and politically problematic. While my focus in this introduction is not to assess whether *Talking to Terrorists* specifically lived up to what it promised audiences, I include the responses the play elicited here in order to lay out the somewhat contested terrain of contemporary verbatim theatre, which I examine and interrogate in the first part of this book.

Verbatim theatre is no stranger to controversy. While its popularity has grown over the past twenty-five years so has the number of its critics. It stands accused of manipulating or misleading audiences, of possessing a 'duplicitous nature' (Martin, 2006: 14) and being a dangerously appropriative art form. Deirdre Heddon describes verbatim theatre as performing an 'act of ventriloquism' with little regard for the values of accountability and responsibility that underpin the act of speaking on behalf of another (Heddon, 2008: 129). She points out that verbatim theatre often 'represents untold stories' and has the capacity to 'give those unheard voices a public place' potentially 'rewriting the dominant narratives in the process (narratives of history, social policy, community)' (Heddon, 2009: 116). However, the emancipatory potential of this form of theatre is underpinned by some important ethical and political questions about 'whose voice is spoken in verbatim procedures and with what other potential effects?' (Heddon, 2009: 116). While, as we shall see in Chapter 1, these critical ethical and political questions have in some form or other always attached themselves to documentary theatre making, and have a long historical provenance, they are also vociferously rekindled in the face of contemporary verbatim practices. The reason for this, I suggest, is that unlike the early 'local' community-orientated verbatim theatre, described by Paget as appearing in the 1970s and 1980s, which tended to be structured around collective representations of social reality, the playwright-led verbatim theatre that emerged in the 1990s and early 2000s focuses instead on

exposing and narrating particular *truth claims*. These 'truth claims' tend
to be formulated through the employment of a wide range of different
dramaturgical devices and strategies. Often forged through an uneasy
alliance of factual, evidential and testimonial material, verbatim theatre
truths are sometimes validated through the performance of newly acquired,
authentic testimony and other acts of witnessing, but sometimes are
verified through the re-presentation of documentary evidence, such as
emails, letters and court proceedings. In some verbatim theatre, certain
'truths' are asserted simply through the dramaturgical structure of the
play, and its construction of character and dialogue, implying some
theatrical narratives and approaches are more 'truthful' and more 'authentic'
than others.

The strategies employed to verify the truth claims of a verbatim play
differ from production to production but are affirmed to audiences through
the performance of a 'promise', which in different ways, sets out to assure
audiences that 'real' people have actively participated in the construction
of the play. Typically, this performed 'promise' is structured around an
assurance that interviews with 'real people' have been undertaken and
used in the formation of the play text. Often this 'promise' is grounded
in some kind of guarantee that 'real stories' have been incorporated in
the dramaturgical development of the play – stories that were narrated
during the creative process and which have probably not been heard
before. Of course, any promise is open to the possibility of it being broken,
and questions of whether certain individuals were actually interviewed,
and whether this was or was not included in the final edit of the play
and the truth of what was actually said in interviews, have become
recurring themes within the many criticisms levelled against verbatim
theatre.

It is arguably because verbatim theatre performs the promise of certain
claims of truth that the ethics and politics of this practice have become
so critical. Much of the scholarship engaging with verbatim theatre has
addressed itself to the complex ethico-political processes of speaking
for others and the responsibility incurred by theatre makers who forge
relationships with verbatim subjects who are often lacking in power and
representational capacity. Mary Luckhurst, for example, uses the term
'ethical stress' to describe the anxiety actors experience when enacting real
people (Luckhurst, 2010: 135). Correlatively, Patrick Duggan considers
'what it means to appropriate the other for artistic means', asking 'what is
at stake in embodying a "real" other (as opposed to a fictional character)'?
(Duggan, 2013: 148). While the process of speaking for another person
can be a form of solidarity and political advocacy, it is also potentially a
source of oppressive appropriation and exploitation: after all, the power

dynamics of the relationship between verbatim subject and theatre maker is structurally unequal and unbalanced. The theatre maker is engaged in a process of speaking for or on behalf of the other, whereas the verbatim subject remains the 'spoken about'. Furthermore, verbatim stories are often sought from people and communities who are in some way marginalised and oppressed and who have been subjected to forms of injustice. These potentially vulnerable individuals are then invited by the playwright, directors and actors to 'speak out' about their experiences in order to address the past and the events they have endured in a creative process that is in some way presented as being 'truthful'. However, while the political dimension of truth telling is vitally important within verbatim theatre practices, this focus on truth and speaking out places pressure on a play's dramaturgical structures, and therefore the foundation of trusting, ethical relationships between the verbatim subject and theatre maker becomes crucial to the ethics of practice of this form of theatre making.

As I will demonstrate in Chapter 2, while the promise of a form of truthfulness remains a central tenet for contemporary verbatim theatre makers, since its inauguration in the late 1970s and early 1980s, verbatim theatre methodologies have shifted and evolved to perform increasingly blurry and fluid truth claims. It is this move away from documentary representations of reality and the shift towards forms of singular truth telling that also arguably heightens the ethico-political aspects of this form of theatre. While most verbatim theatre practices are structured around creative processes that gather stories from 'real' people, the status of these stories within both the writing process itself and in relation to the truth claims performed by the play varies considerably from one play to the next and is often politically troubling. Unlike the documentary plays of Peter Cheeseman, contemporary verbatim plays are rarely constructed through a democratised dramaturgical process and are far more likely to be constructed and/or written by a singular playwright than a collective of actors. It then becomes the writer and the director who drive the authorial process, emphatically determining how the play will be researched and structured, what kinds of people will be interviewed and, crucially, what sorts of questions will be asked. In this sense, rather than locating verbatim theatre within a community of storytellers, as per the 'Stoke Method' described by Paget, verbatim theatre makers today often view the interviewing process as simply part of a research and development process. This approach is exemplified by director Max Stafford-Clark who perceives interviews with verbatim subjects as merely a research tool: 'what a verbatim play does', he writes, 'is flash your research nakedly [...] it's like you're flashing the research without turning it into a play' (Stafford-Clark in Hare and Stafford-Clark, 2008: 81).

Of course, Stafford-Clark's view is not one shared by all verbatim theatre makers. For many other verbatim practitioners, it is the use of personal narratives and the discourse of truth associated with the verbatim form itself than constitutes the potency of these plays. Philip Ralph, for example, who wrote the verbatim play *Deep Cut* (2008), describes verbatim theatre as 'resolutely mediated speech' but also asserts that it 'is certainly as close as we are going to get in the theatre to "truth"' (Ralph, 2008: 23). It is arguably Ralph's recognition of the truth-telling process of verbatim theatre, and the ethical claims this makes on him, that leads him to adopt an almost forensic referencing process in the *Deep Cut*'s published play text. Unlike Soans's *Talking to Terrorists*, which contains no contextual information about the sources used within the play itself, each section of 'verbatim' text in *Deep Cut* is clearly indicated with a reference indicating the origin of each source. Ralph's approach could be viewed as resonant of the early German documentary playwrights of the 1960s. As I describe in Chapter 1, these playwrights, who form an important part of a pre-history for verbatim theatre, tended to produce contextual material to accompany and frame the sources used in their plays, indicating as precisely as possible the play's relationship to fact. In this sense, it is important to note that the debates surrounding the truth claims of contemporary verbatim theatre have a historical precedence. As I discuss in Chapter 1, many of the questions about the tense relationship between a verbatim play's dramaturgical structure and the use of historical fact, fictionalisation and verisimilitude are also evident in the critical debates that circulated around the documentary plays of Peter Weiss and Rolf Hochhuth. These proto-verbatim plays that emerged in Germany in the 1960s are significant to any historical understanding of verbatim theatre practices today. In the dramaturgical approaches adopted by Weiss, Hochhuth and other German fact-based theatre makers of the time, we see a move away from a documentary theatre form rooted in social realism and a shift towards the interrogation of recent history and the need to understand events such as the Holocaust. In this sense, these German documentary playwrights concerned themselves with truth-telling processes in a different way to their predecessors, foregrounding the figure of the witness to stage a trial-like truth process where the audience found themselves implicated within the drama almost as jurors who sit in judgement on the characters they encounter in the course of the play. This focus on witnessing, truth telling and, crucially, on judgement re-emerges as a key element in contemporary verbatim theatre, where the truth claims of verbatim plays are authorised through representations of 'real' people and the reiteration of personal narrative, acts of witnessing and testimonial accounts of lived experience.

Verbatim theatre and personal narrative: Hybrid practices and debated histories

While the re-emergence of verbatim theatre in the 1990s has produced many different forms of verbatim drama, one commonality found within most, if not all, of these plays is a foregrounding of the use of real, personal narratives collated during the research process and reperformed in some way in the course of the play itself. Positioned in plays vicariously as evidence, truth, testimony or sometimes even fact, the use of personal narrative has become a key component of verbatim theatre, as I argue in Chapter 2. In most verbatim plays, these personal narratives are enacted using direct address, which has become a distinctive element of this form of theatre, differentiating it from other documentary theatre practices of the last century. However, as I discuss in more detail later in Chapter 2 and in the second part of this book, the truth claims associated with this use of personal narratives are not always clear. Arguably, the status of personal narrative and testimony becomes all the more complex to decipher and understand in contemporary verbatim theatre because of the way certain dramaturgical structures validate and authorise different kinds of truths. Furthermore, because contemporary audiences are now so familiar with the performative tropes that denote the discourses of truth attached to documentary and verbatim theatre, playwrights can make a play seem more or less 'authentic' simply by the way character and dialogue are constructed. The incorporation of 'errs' and 'umms' from everyday speech and the use of direct address, for example, are both devices that have become familiar indicators of verbatim and documentary theatre. These kinds of tactics are also commonly used in film and television programmes. Here, the use of direct address to camera, hand-held camera footage and the incorporation of subtitles, telling audiences this is 'based on a true story', are adopted to ensure viewers know that what they are watching falls under a documentary as opposed to a fictional genre and to indicate that what they are watching is 'truthful' rather than fictive.

Verbatim theatre makers today draw on numerous dramaturgical and performative strategies to assure audiences that a drama has been constructed through a particular type of researched participatory process, without necessarily having undertaken this in quite the way suggested in the play. The form of verbatim theatre and its capacity to manipulate audience's belief systems is, in many ways, the root cause of many of the accusations of duplicity levelled against it. A good example of the manipulative potential of the dramaturgical form of verbatim theatre is evident in the trickery Dennis Kelly adopts in his pseudo-verbatim play *Taking Care of Baby* (2007). This play is set up to perform the 'promise' of a verbatim play, convincing audiences – initially at least – that they are encountering material that has been derived from interviews with real people and that is being re-enacted by actors. The play uses typical verbatim theatre tropes, such as direct address, stumbling hyper-realistic dialogue replete with 'errs' and 'umms'. As Dan Rebellato explains, when the play opens 'the audience see the words "the following has been taken word for word from interviews and correspondence. Nothing has been added and everything is in the subjects' own words, though some editing has taken place. Names have not been changed"' (Rebellato, 2007: 604). However, as the play progresses, these projected captions, which initially appeared to contribute to the promise of truthfulness, become corrupted and appear as unreadable gobbledygook as audiences gradually realise the play is actually fictional. As Kelly's play artfully illustrates, an audience's engagement with a verbatim theatre play is arguably determined not simply by the presence of factual truth, but by the 'promise' of some sort of authenticity, though what grounds this promise is often somewhat blurred and difficult to pin down. Furthermore, within many verbatim plays, different promises of truthfulness co-exist alongside each other. While audiences might have been told that the actors performing before them met and interviewed the people they are portraying, this might not always be entirely true for each and every character presented in the play. Furthermore, while a play's dialogue might appear to be an accurate reiteration of 'word-for-word' transcribed interviews, some verbatim writers, such as Robin Soans, admit to '[using] a notepad and a pencil' and eschew the use of any recording device when interviewing verbatim subjects (Soans quoted in Cantrell, 2013: 169). This suggests that while dialogue might sound as if it has been reproduced faithfully from a transcription, this may not actually be the case. Some verbatim theatre practitioners take the promise of the use of accurately recorded text in an entirely different direction. UK-based verbatim playwright Alecky Blythe and Australian Rosyln Oades perform a certain form of authenticity in their plays by interviewing verbatim subjects and relaying this live recorded text through headphones or ear pieces worn by actors. Of course, audiences of this kind of verbatim theatre have no access to the editorial process that selected certain interviewees and certain elements of the recorded text, but the reperformance of 'natural' speech becomes an important element of the apparent promise of truthfulness and authenticity that emerges in these plays. Correlatively, other practitioners, such as Australia's Alana Valentine, use blended research approaches when creating verbatim dramas, drawing together interviews with real people and incorporating this within fictionalised scenes to tell real stories about real issues. Taken together, these different hybrid practices illustrate just how diverse contemporary forms of verbatim theatre have become and how very different types of truth claims are being attached to this form of theatre making. Arguably, however, it is precisely this promise of truthfulness and authenticity that tends to draw audiences and theatre makers to this type of theatre work. Contemporary verbatim practices not only carry certain pre-histories with them, they engage in a constant process of hybridity and adaption. This hybridity relates not only to the *form* of verbatim theatre and the way these texts are performed, but also to the way truthfulness is conceived and promised by the various dramaturgical strategies that are adopted to construct these texts.

Contemporary verbatim theatre arguably owes its hybridity both to the wide range of different dramaturgical practices that get incorporated under the label 'verbatim theatre' but also to the way the influence of verbatim and testimonial theatre emerged in different parts of the world and in different cultural contexts. In the UK, we might look to the influential Tricycle Tribunal plays that grew out of a collaboration between the journalist Richard Norton-Taylor and Nicholas Kent, who in the early 1990s was the artistic director of the Tricycle Theatre in Kilburn, North London. Commencing with a series of plays that set out 'to present a public inquiry on stage' (Kent in Kent, Norton-Taylor, Slovo and Edgar, 2014: 17) the tribunal plays '[consisted] of the meticulous re-enactment of edited transcripts of state-sanctioned inquiries that address[ed] perceived miscarriages of justice and flaws in the operations and accountability of public institutions' (Megson, 2011: 195). The first of these tribunal plays, *Half the Picture* by Richard Norton-Taylor, premiered in 1994 and restaged the 1992 Scott Inquiry, a juridical process that examined claims that British companies had sold arms to Iraq in the 1980s. This was followed in 1996 by *Nuremberg* (Richard Norton-Taylor) and *Srebrenica* (Nicholas Kent) and several years later in 1999 by *The Colour of Justice* (Richard Norton-Taylor), which is discussed in detail in Chapter 4 of this book.[2] However, as I go on to argue in the course of this book, while tribunal theatre re-enacts spoken testimony (through its re-enactment of an inquiry) and is often described as verbatim theatre, the dramaturgical structure of this kind of theatre differs considerably from other forms of what might be described as 'testimonial' verbatim theatre. In 'testimonial' verbatim theatre, the construction of the play emerges from specially commissioned interviews that are sought out and undertaken by the writer, director or actors in order to tell a person's story or examine a particular issue.

In other parts of the world, verbatim theatre is framed by different historical dramaturgical approaches and histories. In Australia, verbatim theatre also arrived in the 1990s, although various documentary plays had been performed in the 1950s and 1960s (Garde, Mumford and Wake, 2010). The most notable verbatim play of this era appears to have been created in 1991, when Paul Brown who worked with the Newcastle Workers Club in New South Wales wrote *Aftershocks* (1993), a play 'based on interviews, with members of the Club about their experiences and memories of the Newcastle earthquake' that hit the area in 1989 (Garde, Mumford and Wake, 2010: 15). At about the same time, in 1992, in the United States of America, actor and professor Anna Deavere Smith drew on oral history and verbatim theatre techniques to create *Fires in the Mirror: Crown Heights and Other Identities* and *Twilight: Los Angeles*. In these solo performance plays, Smith takes on multiple roles, drawing on interviews with different individuals from various cultural backgrounds who were caught up in 'race riots' in New York and Los Angeles in 1991 and 1992 respectively, to recreate numerous characters who talk directly to the audience about their experiences of this time.

What these examples of the different forms of verbatim theatre begin to reveal is how the recent re-emergence of verbatim practices draws on many diverse dramaturgical strategies and processes. These various dramaturgical approaches in different ways also seek to reinvent the claims of truthfulness and authenticity associated with this form of theatre. In his account of Smith's performance in *Fires in the Mirror*, for example, Richard Schechner draws attention to the almost shamanistic process by which Smith 'incorporates' another person's identity into her performance, '[absorbing] the gestures, the tone of voice, the look, the intensity, the moment-by-moment details of a conversation' (Schechner, 1993: 64) with the person she is emulating. The truthfulness of Smith's testimonial verbatim plays, then, emerges not from a use of word-for-word accurate transcriptions of interviews but from her capacity to capture the mannerisms, voice and perhaps something of the actual 'essence' of another person, which feels in performance to be authentic and real. I return to Smith's work, which I discuss in more detail, in Chapter 4.

What we understand as being the truth claims of a verbatim theatre play, however, differs from play to play and even from one character to the next within the same play text. This means that the truth claims associated with this form of theatre are constantly in a process of being reconstructed and redefined. For example, in Ralph's verbatim play *Deep Cut*, the bereaved parents of Private Cheryl James, Des and Doreen, are generated from material gathered from interviews with the writer, however, the dialogue of the journalist Brian Cathcart and the lawyer Nicholas Blake, is taken from pre-existing published journalistic articles and the Deepcut Review (Blake, 2006) itself. Similarly, in a play such as Soans's

Talking to Terrorists, the staging of each character subtly determines the mode by which we verify the truthfulness of what each character says. In this play, the ex-Secretary of State, for example, is presented to us at home, and we encounter her very much within a domestic setting where she is also in conversation with her cleaner. Correlatively, the ex-members of the Kurdish Workers Party, the National Resistance Army, Uganda and the other 'terrorists' presented in the play emerge within a more placeless, abstract setting where they speak only of the past and the violence they were involved in. The lack of familiarity in the setting subtly reframes the truth claims we attach to the text. While it seems likely that the ex-Secretary of State was indeed interviewed in the research process of the play and, it appears, shared some personal reflections on the issue of terrorism, the status of the testimonies of the 'terrorists' remains more ambiguous. Without any context to the testimony, audiences perhaps have less empathy for the various viewpoints reflected in what the 'terrorists' say. Furthermore, as I go on to discuss in Chapter 2, the different forms of dialogue and different forms of characterisation within verbatim theatre also suggest different modes of acting, producing different forms of realism. The promise of truthfulness associated with verbatim theatre is in a constant process of flux and reinvention within the dramaturgy of contemporary verbatim practices. Ultimately, while we are witnessing more and more contemporary 'theatre practices and styles that recycle reality' (Martin, 2013: 5), we are also having to negotiate very different kinds of truths being performed in these forms of theatre.

'What people say': shifts in the positioning of personal narrative in contemporary verbatim theatre

This book reframes the standard interrogation of verbatim theatre, by shifting the focus of debate away from discourses of the real that have tended to dominate scholarship in this area (see: Forsyth and Megson, 2011; Martin, 2013). Instead, through an examination of how testimony and personal narrative operate in verbatim theatre, I consider how the blending together of documentary fact and testimonial text creates complex and, at times, troubling promises of truth telling. The tendency to use more testimonial text in verbatim theatre is also considered by Derek Paget who argues that 'what people say has acquired a new level of significance' in contemporary verbatim theatre where '[t]estimony expressed through verbatim material has re-emerged as a basis for the claim of documentary truth' (Paget, 2011: 176). Arguing that 'the idea of "bearing witness"' should be understood as a 'key ethical concept and claim' in new forms of verbatim theatre, Paget suggests that theatre that enacts forms of witnessing 'must be subject to careful scrutiny' (Paget, 2011: 190). By examining how contemporary verbatim theatre engages with practices of truth telling and witnessing, this book, in many ways, responds to Paget's call for scrutiny, but develops this further by also interrogating the political potential of this kind work.

Forsyth and Megson argue that the 'ongoing diversification' of documentary theatre has led to the incorporation of 'a more varied range of "evidence" (including testimony, orature and anecdote)'. This approach, they suggest, represents 'a self-conscious acknowledgment of the complexity of "reality"' and reflects a move away from 'propounding a mono-dimensional truth claim' (Forsyth and Megson, 2011: 3). However, this perspective does not take account of the ethical and dramaturgical implications of incorporating factual, documentary material and anecdote alongside other forms of testimonial material. This leads me to argue that a growing emphasis on testimony within verbatim theatre, and its often un-troubled relationship of adequation with other forms of factual evidence, cannot be fully understood through an interrogation of the real and theatre's capacity to represent reality. Instead, I suggest, we need to better understand how the 'promise' of truthfulness operates within verbatim theatre and how an engagement with this 'promise' and what it discloses both ethically and politically helps us to understand how the appropriation of reiterated personal narrative and testimonial truth functions in this type of theatre work. The emerging focus on personal testimony in verbatim drama also opens up important questions about how the demands of truth, fact and drama are to be negotiated in the dramaturgy of these plays. This requires a rethinking of the way truthfulness and fact are negotiated in a play that strives to be structurally dramatic, how testimonial truth relates to other truths such as historical and politics truths in this form of theatre work, and what kinds of ethical, political and dramaturgical imperatives inform the use of testimony and witnessing as a form of authorisation and veracity within contemporary testimonial and verbatim theatre. This book addresses these concerns by focusing specifically upon the truth claims attached to the performed reiteration of 'what people say', looking closely at what testimony is and how it is used to generate ethical and politically nuanced verbatim and testimonial theatre today. Moving on here to consider what testimonial performance is and how it ethically implicates both theatre makers and their audiences, I consider some definitions of witnessing and testimony and introduce some of the key problematics that are examined in the second part of the book.

Testimonial truths: Staging promises and the ethical demand of testimony

Etymologically, the word 'verbatim' derives from the Latin term *verbum*, meaning 'word' and today denotes the spoken repetition of a written or spoken phrase repeated precisely and word-for-word. When coupled with the word 'theatre', 'verbatim' describes the way certain play-making processes are undertaken, pointing to a set of dramaturgical processes that are both iterative and appropriative, where real stories are researched, recorded and/or transcribed and used as the material for a play. 'Verbatim' also has a juridical connotation and is often used in legal proceedings as a guarantor of accuracy. Witnesses, for example, who are asked to give evidence, might be asked to reiterate what they heard 'verbatim', meaning they repeat something they have heard or read by including every detail. However, while the term 'verbatim' denotes the accuracy with which particular forms of evidence are represented and repeated, 'testimony' on the other hand refers directly to the truth claims associated with and performed by a particular type of text. As I go on to discuss in Chapter 3, an etymological account of the term 'testimony', as Jacques Derrida (2005) and Giorgio Agamben (1999) both explore, reveals a derivation that points both to the presence of the witness at an event as a 'third' party and as the one who has lived through something from beginning to end and survives. Witnessing and testimony therefore evoke claims of presence but also perform a certain mode of (testimonial) truthfulness. However, bearing witness is constitutively bound not to objective or factual truth, but to an oath or a 'promise' to '[engage] a responsibility before the law' (Derrida, 2005: 75). To testify, therefore, is not the same as offering a proof or a fact – a point that Derrida forcefully advocates when he writes: 'Bearing witness is heterogeneous to producing proof or exhibiting a piece of evidence. In the case of a statement under oath, bearing witness appeals to the act of faith [*acte de foi*], and thus takes place in the space of pledged or sworn word [*foi jurée*] ("I swear to tell the truth")' (Derrida, 2005: 75).

In this sense, while the term 'verbatim' describes the accuracy with which certain sources are reiterated and represented for an audience in the course of the play, conceptually, it is not a term that can discern whether or not a play is *testimonial*. Furthermore, the term 'verbatim' points to an engagement with a specific creative process, but one that is not, however, available to audiences in the moment of performance itself. The audience for verbatim and, for that matter, for testimonial theatre, must rely on a sense of trust in the creative team and the promises of truthfulness and accuracy that become manifest and performed through the dramaturgy of the play itself, and through what Susan Bennett describes as the 'pre-production elements' (Bennett, 1997: 142) of verbatim and testimonial theatre, such as marketing materials and digital content on websites.

In her theorisation of the audience's engagement with theatre, Bennett distinguishes between the 'outer' and the 'inner' frame of the theatre event. The outer frame, she argues, is 'concerned with theatre as a cultural construct through the idea of the theatrical event, the selection of material for production, and the audience's definitions and expectations of a performance' (Bennett, 1997: 1–2); whereas, 'the inner frame' contains 'the event itself and, in particular, the spectator's experience of a fictional stage world' (Bennett, 1997: 2). Bennett is particularly interested in the way an audience's experience of theatre is framed by the social, economic and cultural contexts in which different kinds of theatre take place. However, if we import her idea of the 'outer frame' of the theatre event into a reading of how theatre audiences encounter verbatim and testimonial plays, we can see how certain promises of truth and authenticity are communicated to audiences well before a ticket is even bought; for instance, through the way the play is advertised as a 'verbatim' play. In this sense, audiences do not go to a verbatim and testimonial theatre play expecting fiction. The very premise of this kind of theatre is a promise of veracity, fidelity to the real and an authenticity not found elsewhere in the theatre – in short, a promise of truthfulness which is first introduced to audiences through the way a play is marketed and sold to them. These truth claims are also often then reaffirmed through carefully chosen programme material that informs audiences about the 'real' people involved, the nature of the 'real' events they are about to encounter and the real issues that the play purports to be examining. Taken together these pre-production elements 'contract' audiences into the 'truth' of the experience by establishing in them the firmest belief that the play they are about to watch has been created through a process that indeed 'promises' – through its very form – a kind of veracity not found in any other genre of theatre; it is a promise which is constructed through the direct involvement of actual individuals, whose stories are being told within the text itself. When these 'real' stories address moments of violence, disempowerment and the lived experiences of injustice, the performance of testimony can enact a mode of speaking truth to power, grounded in an appeal for the testimony of the witness to be listened to and approved in some way by the audience.

As I have indicated above, testimony is constitutively structured around the promise to speak truthfully – it is, in Derrida's terms, an 'appeal' to the listener, the addressee of testimony (Derrida, 2005: 77). However, as Derrida goes on to examine, the promise is 'always open to betrayal' and to the 'possibility of perjury, infidelity, or abjuration' (Derrida, 2005: 75). In the performance of testimony the actor who reperforms the witness's testimony becomes ethically and politically implicated in some crucial way in this act of attestation – firstly, in relation to the actual event that is being testified to and, secondly, in relation to the original, primary witness whose testimony has become the actor's script. In the performance of testimony, it is the integrity of the witness that is at stake as opposed to the accuracy of the transcription. As Derrida argues elsewhere, testimony is not the same as a narrated text, it is an act in which the witness 'offers himself' (Derrida, 2000: 38) and places his or her integrity on the line. Consequently, when a testimony is disbelieved, it is not simply a case of disputing what was said: rather, it is a turning away from having any sense of faith in the witness. The accusation of perjury or lying in this context, therefore, is not simply about a lack of veracity within the testimony itself but is an accusation addressed to the *person* who bears witness and whose lived experience has produced this testimony. While the term 'verbatim' might indicate an accurate mode of repetition, testimony's promise is – for the subject who speaks – far more profound and binds both the witness and the addressee of the testimony together in a dialogical relationship framed by both trust and by the possibility of denial and betrayal. The performance of testimony, in other words, is bound by an invitation to the audiences to listen and to believe what is being attested to and not to turn away or disavow this act of witnessing.

While this close examination of testimonial and verbatim texts begins to reveal some significant differences between these various terms, such distinctions are not always entirely clear in the moment of performance itself. In contemporary verbatim theatre, audiences can sometimes find themselves encountering different characters speaking testimonial and verbatim text within the same play. This means the distinctions between the different types of truth claims performed in a play can become blurred and are more difficult to decipher. This becomes all the more difficult because the style of performance adopted by an actor plays such an important role in the way verbatim and testimonial text is encountered by audiences. This melding together of testimonial and verbatim text in contemporary performance is also evident in the discussions about these types of plays that emerge in the scholarship that accompanies it, further highlighting the slipperiness of the truth claims associated with this type of work and the complex ways these contemporary dramaturgies play around with concepts of the real, the actual and the mimetic. In order to begin to think about what distinguishes the term 'verbatim' from 'testimonial' in contemporary dramaturgy, then, we must take account of some of the different connotations associated with these terms and look at how these shift within different cultural contexts. While my examination of this mode of theatre making primarily draws on practices that have emerged in European, American and Australian contexts, in Chapter 3 I expand this approach to consider other cultural engagements with testimonial performance and the different formations of truthfulness that are associated with it. In the following part of this introductory chapter, however, I want to shift focus in order to lay out some proposals about how we might most usefully think about the ethical dimensions of performing and making testimonial work. I will then move on to examine the political potency of this kind of theatre work and consider how contemporary performances of witnessing reconfigure the Euro-American models of testimony that have dominated scholarship in performance studies and the humanities since the inauguration of trauma studies in the 1980s.

In order to think through the challenges of making theatre using other people's stories and the ethical implications of this, in Chapter 4, I establish an ethical framework that draws on what some moral philosophers have called 'the ethical demand' (see Løgstrup, 1997; Critchley, 2007). Building on theorisation of the ethical experience as developed by Simon Critchley and Knud Ejler Løgstrup, I develop an account of what I describe as the 'ethical demand of testimonial practice' and consider how theatre making drawing on testimonial text places certain ethical demands on theatre makers and their audience. In order to introduce here what the 'ethical demand of testimonial practice' means and how it shapes dramaturgical processes, I return to consider the performance of *Minefield* introduced at the outset of this chapter.

Responsibility and dramaturgy: Some ethical questions for testimonial theatre

Developed with six veterans who fought in the conflict that took place in the Falklands/Las Malvinas in 1982, Lola Arias created *Minefield* by drawing on the testimonies, memories and lived experiences of the six veterans who enact themselves in the play. Performed in both Spanish and English, the play explores what combat in this war meant to those who fought in it and how the events of this time are remembered both personally and culturally in Britain and Argentina. David's questions, quoted in the epigraph at the start of the chapter, highlight the paradoxical stance of the witness who occupies a relatively privileged position and who speaks on behalf of others, including those who lost their lives. His reflections also pertinently draw attention to the challenges of collectively remembering the Falkland/Malvinas conflict. For British and Argentinean combatants, the process of talking about and remembering this conflict is metaphorically a political and ethical 'minefield', not least because, as the play reveals, the memory of this war means something very different in the British and Argentinian contexts. At the point that David asks these questions, we have just witnessed Lou, another British veteran-actor, describe how he shot and killed an Argentinian soldier, and how he then stayed with him – talking to and consoling the dying man. Lou goes on to tell us how the image of this soldier's death has remained with him long after the end of the war and 'keeps popping into [his] head' (Arias, 2017: 42). The account of the dying Argentinian solider also remains with us as David speaks, serving to remind us of what is at stake when these veterans bear witness on behalf of others. David's reflections also invite us to think further about how the play's dramaturgy might in some way contribute to the historiographic telling of the conflict and the political and ethical challenges of placing one history over or alongside another. The use of direct address adopted throughout *Minefield* also draws attention to the function of witnessing within the play and arguably to the dialogical structure of testimony itself. In this sense, the performance of testimony places different ethical demands on audiences and theatre makers compared to the reiteration of verbatim and documentary text that is drawn from juridical processes or from 'orature and anecdote' (Forsyth and Megson, 2011: 3). Furthermore, as we see in *Minefield*, the ethics of the encounter between audience and actor in the performance of testimony becomes even more critically nuanced when the actor is bearing witness to an event that they personally lived through.

   It is clear from the play that the lived experience of the war was deeply troubling and, at times, a source of trauma for those who fought within it. Yet the individual testimonies that emerge in the course of the play are not presented as individualised encounters with the traumatic. However, these are certainly accounts of suffering and hardship, and it is clear that, for both the Argentinian and British veterans, the war and the challenge of transitioning back into civilian life afterwards presented certain psychological difficulties and in some instances led to a diagnosis of post-traumatic stress disorder. The testimonial accounts presented in the play are not framed as narratives of trauma, and the process of remembering and bearing witness to these events is not constituted around what trauma theorist Cathy Caruth has described as forms of 'belatedness' (Caruth, 1996: 92), where any memory of the event is framed by an 'inability to know it' (Caruth, 1996: 92). Rather than witnessing being presented as a psychological endeavour in which the testimonial subject returns to the past in order to retrieve some memory of it and to understand it more fully, the veterans in the play narrate past experiences with a sense of alacrity and a self-conscious awareness of the form and depth of their own individual suffering and how it connects with the experience of others. In this sense, Arias structures the dramaturgy of the play to move beyond the pathology of trauma and suffering. Instead, she frames her participants as protagonists with agency, who have the capacity through the play to critically reflect both on the dramaturgical structure of Arias's dramaturgy and their own role within this. In this sense, in common with many of the other plays examined in the course of this book, *Minefield* moves beyond the psychoanalytic framing of testimony and witnessing as developed by Shoshana Felman and Dori Laub in their seminal book on the subject: *Testimony: Crises of Witnessing in Literature, Psychoanalysis, and History* (1992). In so doing, Arias reimagines the act of attestation by generating performances of witnessing that have become untethered from any expectation of healing or other ameliorative benefit. Rather than being structured around some sort of transformative or emancipatory function, the play is framed as a collective reflection on the act of remembering itself. As such, the past events of the war are not positioned as belonging to the dimension of individual psychopathology but emerge as part of a collective history that comes to be narrated in a dialogic process of bearing witnessing and remembering it.

The capacity for testimonial theatre to move beyond the psychoanalytic framework of witnessing is addressed more broadly in Chapter 3, where I explore conceptualisations of witnessing and testimony that can be best understood as contributing in some way to the process of decolonising trauma studies and testimonial practices. Like other theorists who are developing work in this area from other disciplinary contexts, such as Andermahr (2016a), Craps (2015) and Bennett and Kennedy (2003), I seek to destabilise the centralisation of the Euro-American subject within debates of witnessing and testimony. As such, in the second part of this book, I explore performance processes that reimagine the act of witnessing and which step beyond the Eurocentrism of the psychoanalytical framework of testimony.

The transition this book makes from an interrogation of verbatim theatre practices towards an engagement with testimonial performance is therefore one that is also accompanied by a shift in focus towards the interrogation of the political potency of this form of theatre making. The political possibilities of testimonial performance are, I suggest, more critical than ever, as we find ourselves living in a context where it is becoming vitally important to be able to speak out against injustice in order to counter the populist, right-wing rhetoric emerging with increased frequency in a number of public and political contexts across the globe. Drawing on Foucault's account of *parrhesia*, which he characterises as a speech activity in which the speaker (the *parrhesiastes*) 'says what he *knows* to be true' (Foucault, 2001: 140; original emphasis) and, at great risk to him or herself, finds the courage to speak out, I examine examples of testimonial theatre in which the witness engages in a process of speaking truth to power. In these plays, the act of witnessing becomes highly politicised, and the dramaturgical structure positions the testimonial subject as a *parrhesiastes* who speaks out against the violence and social injustice that they encounter within their community and their day-to-day existence.

Underpinning the discussions of the testimonial performance examined in the course of this book is a desire to move beyond the limits of verbatim theatre and its reliance on a predetermined dramaturgical form. The shift towards testimonial performance in the second part of this book signals a move towards a more fluid and responsive form of theatre making that foregrounds the witness, drawing on testimonial practices to enact new and potent forms of truth telling. I position testimonial performance as a practice that is constituted by the ethico-political demands of the testimony and the truth-telling processes that emerge within each situation and every event it addresses. In this sense, rather than being determined through a pre-formed set of practices and approaches, testimonial dramaturgy is constantly evolving and adapting as it shifts and responds to the changing political landscape, the demands of each event it addresses and the lived experiences of the witnesses who come forth to speak out.

The structure of the book

As discussed above, this book is developed through two interconnected areas of inquiry. In the first part, I focus on verbatim theatre and, by examining the wide range of heterogeneous practices that are gathered under this term, I explore the changing role of direct address in verbatim and documentary theatre and consider what authenticates the truth claims attached to this form of dramaturgy. The genealogy of contemporary verbatim theatre practices, I argue, is framed through a foregrounding of witnessing, the use of direct address and a focus on personal narrative as a means of authorising the truth claims of the play. However, while the structure and format of verbatim theatre have been widely adopted by many different theatre makers, the use and status of testimony within this form of dramaturgical practice vary considerably from play to play. As such, the authority attributed to testimony in this form of theatre is a much debated problematic and continues to be a source of much criticism of the form.

In the second part of the book, I turn to consider testimonial modes of performance and the way witnessing comes to be reimagined by contemporary theatre makers working in this form of theatre. Through an analysis of the ethico-political possibilities and problematics of performing testimony, I consider how different modes of witnessing emerge within different testimonial practices that have been developed in different parts of the world. My central concern within this part of the book is the positioning of the testimonial subject within the dramaturgy of these plays and the possibilities for forms of testimonial performance that can address acts of injustice and enact political forms of witnessing.

The first chapter in the book establishes a pre-history of verbatim theatre by exploring the evolving approaches to documentary theatre evident in the theatre making of Erwin Piscator and precipitated, in part, by his exile to the United States as a result of the Second World War. Drawing attention to the shift from the spectacular, largely devised projects Piscator developed in the early decades of the twentieth century, to the more playwright-centred documentary theatre emerging in the post-war context of Germany in the 1960s, I argue that these new German documentary plays were highly influential to the development of the contemporary verbatim theatre form. I develop my argument through an examination of two key plays from this time: Peter Weiss's *The Investigation* and Ralph Hochhuth's *The Deputy*, which premiered in 1965 and 1963 respectively and were both directed by Piscator. In different ways, these plays both foreground the figure of the witness and establish forms of truth telling that interrogate the role of the individual and the collective in the decision-making processes that led to the events of the Holocaust.

In Chapter 2, I focus more directly on the recent resurgence of documentary, verbatim and testimonial theatre that has occurred over the past twenty-five years or so in the United Kingdom, the United States and Australia. By examining some of the different historiographies of these forms of verbatim theatre, I identify a range of practices that in different ways draw on individual and collective narratives to enact forms of truth telling that address real events and real people's lived experience. Through an exploration of the dramaturgical approaches adopted by an international range of verbatim playwrights and directors, such as Alana Valentine, Roslyn Oades, Alecky Blythe, Anna Deavere Smith, Robin Soans, Peter Cheeseman and Max Stafford-Clark, I consider the evolution of the verbatim theatre form as it developed from the late 1980s through to the first decades of the 2000s. By focusing specifically on the changing use of dramatic character within these plays, I argue that contemporary verbatim theatre draws on a range of different dramaturgical processes to produce different forms of truth telling, which ultimately direct the audience towards certain types of empathic forms of response to the issues examined by these plays.

Chapter 3 marks the commencement of part two of the book and focuses more specifically on testimonial performance and what we can learn from it about the act of bearing witness and the ethics of creating theatre that draws on real people's stories about real events. Beginning with an examination of the constitutively performative nature of testimony, this chapter examines three different modes of dramaturgical performance developed in different cultural and geographical contexts and considers how the 'promise' of testimonial work is differently interpreted. Drawing on philosophical engagements with witnessing and theorisation that troubles the domination of psychoanalytic accounts of testimony in trauma and literary studies, this chapter examines a range of testimonial theatre from South Africa, Australia and from the indigenous native communities in America and explores how, in different ways, these new dramaturgical approaches move towards a decolonised engagement with testimony and witnessing.

In Chapter 4, I move the debate forward to consider how testimonial performance has the political potential to stage a mode of speaking truth to power by enacting what Michel Foucault aptly describes in his Berkley lectures in 1983 as *parrhesia* (Foucault, 2001). Drawing on three plays that deal with the violence of racism in the UK and North America (*The Colour of Justice* by Richard Norton-Taylor, *The Hounding of David Oluwale* by Oladipo Agboluaje, and *Notes from the Field* by Anna Deavere Smith, 2016), this chapter examines how the performance of testimony can position the witness as a *parrhesiastes* who speaks out about racism and the social injustice they are subjected to on a daily basis. This chapter concludes with a discussion that draws on the ethical theorisation of Critchley (2007) and Løgstrup (1997) to further develop my account of the ethical demand of testimonial practice. In order to establish ethical forms of testimonial theatre making, I argue, the encounter between the testimonial subject and theatre maker must be one that both places the testimonial process of truth telling at its heart and which is constituted by relationships of care and trust.

The book concludes with an examination of the role of testimonial performance within a post-truth era, arguing that, with its capacity to enact forms of truth telling and speak truth to power, testimonial performance can provide critical counter-narratives to the populist discourses of the time, challenging the tendency towards political viewpoints that seek to erase or silence minoritarian perspectives (Kondo, 2000: 82). The testimonial theatre form, I argue, is constitutively always in a process of evolving and changing, not least because it is an approach that responds and adapts to each situation it addresses. Today, new developments in testimonial performance are emerging that move the form on and further rethink witnessing and its relationship to performance. In this final part of the book, I reflect on the performance of *And the Rest of Me Floats*, a new play that was presented at the Bush Theatre, London in 2019. Created and performed by a group of actors who self-identify as trans or queer, the play draws on testimonial narratives to collectively bear witness to the lived experience of socially oppressive, heteronormative structures that regulate gender and sexuality. Drawing on dance, song and music, the actor's narratives dialogically engage with the other performative elements of the play, creating a mode of witnessing that is constructed upon and which attests to the actors' corporeal presence as trans or queer subjects and their experience of growing up and coming of age. In this performance, like other performance practices that incorporate dance, testimony and performance, the act of witnessing becomes reconfigured away from individualised, lived experience and instead is reconstructed performatively and collectively in dialogue with an audience, who are invited to attend to the testimonies of these young people and recognise moments of potential alliance and solidarity with them. In the new forms of testimonial performance emerging today, I argue, individual lived experience is becoming increasingly configured in dialogue with questions of alliance, *communitas* and the possibility of identifying and activating new, performative modes of resistance.

Notes

1 The play was performed at the Royal Court Theatre in 2016 and the text published in 2017.
2 These tribunal plays are published in Brittain, Kent, Norton-Taylor and Slovo (2014) *The Tricycle Collected Tribunal Plays: 1994–2012*

Part I

Verbatim theatre and its histories

1

Germany and the pre-histories of contemporary verbatim theatre: Piscator, Hochhuth and Weiss

Forms don't die, they change and reappear. (Weiss in Munk, Weiss and Gray, 1966: 110)

When asked in an interview about the dramaturgical approaches he adopted when writing his Auschwitz play *The Investigation* Peter Weiss responded by arguing that certain historical situations and events required particular forms of dramatic response. In order to write a play about Auschwitz, Weiss suggests, he had to move away from 'individualistic characters', turning instead to the structure of 'ancient tragedy' and the use of a chorus of voices and blocks of testimonial text (Weiss in Munk, Weiss and Gray, 1966: 108–10). Rather than framing his approach around processes of replication and reiteration, as is common within the dramaturgy adopted in contemporary verbatim and tribunal theatre, Weiss describes shaping 'blocks' of testimony in a way that is reminiscent of an artist transforming raw material into a work of art. This reflects Weiss's interdisciplinary arts background, for, along with being a playwright, he was also an experimental film maker and surrealist painter. As a consequence, the dramaturgical approach he adopts in *The Investigation* is framed by formal experimentation, which Weiss compares to sculpture: 'The enormous amount of material I gathered from the Frankfurt trial was concentrated into eleven big blocks of testimony, presented one after another. Each block was a closed complex. Some modern sculpture is neither abstract nor figurative, it's only a thing which stands there – a sense of this imbues the play' (Weiss, in Munk, Weiss and Gray 1966: 108).

When Weiss speaks of forms that 'change and reappear', then, as quoted in the epigraph at the outset of this chapter, he refers to the way that *The Investigation* draws on documentary theatre techniques but, in so doing, both changes and transforms them. By constructing this play around blocks of testimonial text and eschewing the use of individualised characterisation, Weiss reimagines documentary theatre, rethinking its use of character and what character means in this play. For the characters in *The Investigation* do not depict a recognisable social reality nor are they constructed with a psychological coherence or with individual motivation. Like some other key documentary playwrights emerging in post-war Germany at this time, such as Rolf Hochhuth and Heinar Kipphardt, Weiss reframed his approach to documentary theatre around forms of truth telling. This new generation of German playwrights moved beyond representations of collective realities and instead foregrounded the figure of the witness through dramaturgical approaches in which truth telling becomes authorised by testimonial accounts of the past and key historical protagonists are interrogated and called to account.

In this chapter, I explore some of the formal innovations developed in Weiss's play and in Hochhuth's *The Deputy*, which makes use of a very different dramaturgical approach from the one adopted by Weiss. What these dramaturgical innovations reveal, I suggest, is a move away from collective, social reality and a focus on individual action, moral decision making and culpability. These dramaturgical approaches were arguably symptomatic of the time, for the plays were created by a generation of post-Holocaust artists and playwrights who were struggling to come to terms with Germany's history, seeking to identify and call to account those who were responsible for the atrocities of the past. This turn towards a dramaturgical theatre engaged in acts of bearing witness and truth telling is particularly significant to the arguments developed within this book, because this shift towards an excavation of the truth of the event became a key approach adopted by the new forms of verbatim theatre emerging in the 1990s and early 2000s. Of course, the plays emerging at the end of the twentieth century were addressing a very different age, yet the 1990s was arguably also to some degree characterised by a sense of loss and what Andreas Huyssen describes as 'a deepening sense of crisis' (Huyssen, 1995: 1). While the impending arrival of the new millennium might have represented a moment of celebration and optimism, it was instead culturally framed by a sense of nostalgia for what had been lost from the past, along with a growing, pervasive anxiety about what the 2000s would bring. This was encapsulated by the public anxiety surrounding the 'Millennium bug' and the fear that, as the year 2000 dawned, the data on computers everywhere would be wiped out, leaving populations vulnerable to cyber-attacks and unable to function in their day-to-day lives. The rapid expansion and growth of information technology, Huyssen argues, led to a 'chaotic, fragmentary, and free-floating' engagement with cultural memory and a 'virus of amnesia that at times [threatened] to consume memory itself' (1995: 7). It is perhaps this amnesiastic quality of the era that Shoshana Felman also addresses, when, in *Testimony: Crisis of Witnessing in Literature, Psychoanalysis, and History*, she describes the contemporary moment as being marked out by a 'crisis of truth', precipitated by the legacy of the contemporary trauma of the Holocaust and the failure of history to adequately recall and transmit these events (Felman, 1992: 6). It is the failure of facts to adequately historicise the past, she suggests, that has led to the turn towards testimonial practices as a form of cultural and individual remembering. The crisis of truth telling arguably deepened in the UK as a result of the Iraq war in 2003 and was precipitated further by the death of David Kelly, a UK government scientist who was sent to Iraq to unearth the presence of the kinds of weapons of mass destruction (WMD) that the Prime Minister, Tony Blair, had used to justify Britain's involvement in the war. Kelly's inability to find any such WMD and his subsequent untimely death ultimately brought about not only the collapse of Tony Blair's government, but also a radical decline of faith in the trustworthiness of UK politicians. Many of the different forms of documentary and verbatim drama produced at this time addressed this loss of faith through dramaturgical narratives that aimed to investigate and expose the undisclosed truths of specific historical events or issues. As I shall go on to argue in Chapter 2, rather than being centred around the representation of the real, these contemporary plays are best understood as engaging in new forms of truth telling. To do so, verbatim and tribunal playwrights turned to testimonial and documentary text, seeking to identify and represent key witnesses who could authenticate certain political narratives by revealing untold truths about these events. This approach, I suggest, was largely rooted in the influence of the post-war German documentary plays of the 1960s, many of which were directed by Erwin Piscator (1893–1966), a founding figure in the field of documentary drama.

Through an examination of the changing dramaturgical shape and function of the documentary character, I consider some key innovations that emerged in documentary theatre, as it developed through two critical moments within the twentieth century. The first part of the chapter concerns the early forms documentary theatre developed in Germany in the 1920s that were directed and produced by Piscator, and the second examines two influential plays that were written by Peter Weiss (1916–66) and Rolf Hochhuth (b. 1931) in the 1960s, which were also directed by Piscator. This period of documentary theatre history between the 1920s and the 1960s should be viewed as forming a pre-history for the contemporary verbatim theatre that appeared in the 1990s onwards. While the use of character in contemporary verbatim theatre tends to be somewhat fluid and at times inconsistent, what these verbatim plays have in common is a desire to use the figure of the witness to draw out new and previously untold narratives, in order to expose new truths about a key political event or issue.

Reconfiguring documentary character: Moving beyond dramatic character

Character is a central element in classical forms of dramatic structure and tends to be understood as being intrinsic to the play's action. However, this configuration has to be rethought when creating documentary and verbatim theatre, because the action of the plot in these types of plays is determined not by a fictive world but by real events and real people. Of course, this is a challenge confronted by many dramatists dealing with historical material. However, in documentary and verbatim plays, the representation of real people arguably becomes more politically and ethically acute, not least because often it is the actual, personal narratives drawn from living people that are used as a basis of the dramaturgical text itself. As such, deciding what motivates a character to act and determining how an audience will engage with the ideas a character represents determines the means by which character is constructed and what function character serves within a play.

The relationship between character and action in classical dramatic structure is discussed by Aristotle in *The Poetics*. Framed by a unity of plot, character and action, Aristotle presents an account of the structure of drama that appears to subordinate the importance of character to plot, while maintaining that within classical tragedy these two elements remain 'closely linked' (Janko, 1987: 109). Describing 'plot' as being the 'soul of tragedy', Aristotle positions character as a 'secondary' element (Aristotle, 1987: 8). Yet, it is this apparent conjoining of character and action that has probably been most influential in the development of dramatic structure in Western theatre, leading to the widely held view that 'character is action' and the playwright's job is to 'show not tell'. On the subject of the relationship between character and action, Aristotle suggests that actors 'do not act in order to represent the characters, but they include characters for the sake of their actions' (Aristotle, 1987: 9). This leads him to argue that '[c]onsequently the incidents, i.e. the plot, are the end of tragedy, and the end is the most important of all [...] without action a tragedy cannot exist, but without characters it may' (Aristotle, 1987: 9). However, when character and plot are determined not by the playwright but by history itself, then the form of character and character's relationship to action must be rethought. Of course, the structure of any character within the dramaturgy of a play is itself always somewhat fluid and contingent because the structure and function of character shift and change from one genre of theatre to the next, and, as such, the claims of truth associated with each dramaturgical structure also shift and change. Trying to determine how to make a real person into a documentary character becomes a complex dramaturgical task and, as I will argue in this chapter, often has an ethico-political dimension to it.

Aristotle's account of character in relation to action and plot in *The Poetics* has also been a source of much debate, not least because the vision of character being grounded in action has been very influential to the way the structure of character has evolved in many forms of classical drama from Shakespeare onwards. To make matters more complex, while connecting character with plot, Aristotle also suggests that it is character 'which reveals decision' (Aristotle, 1987: 9), and this belief in an intrinsic relationship between character, motivation and decision has tended to imprint itself onto classical dramaturgical structures of characterisation. However, this is not to suggest that Aristotle's vision of character as being connected to action, plot or decision automatically produces psycho-social forms of characterisation, determined by individual desires or wants. Elinor Fuchs points out that 'character' in classical Greek theatre was not determined by any concept of an 'individual psychology' and certainly 'the tragic actions' of Greek tragic heroes were not 'anchored in recognizable contexts of psychological and material life' (Fuchs, 1996: 24). This contrasts to the construction of Shakespearean characters, such as Hamlet, who emerges not only through his outward actions, but through his expression of an 'interior' life comprised of personal desires and motivations. As such, when we encounter Hamlet, he seems to be a completed 'whole', and, as such, we envisage him existing as a whole person, exceeding beyond 'the only partially visible Hamlet' we encounter within Shakespeare's play (Fuchs, 1996: 25).

In her carefully traced historical account of the development of dramatic character in *The Contemporary Political Play* (2017), Sarah Grochala examines how changing social and cultural understanding of the human subject contributed to key shifts in the way dramatic character was viewed and constructed. The 'Renaissance commentators on the *Poetics*', Grochala argues, 'recast playwrights as teachers of moral conduct' (Grochala, 2017: 194), and this led to characters being 'split into predominantly good or bad types' with their fates being 'determined by their moral condition' (Grochala, 2017: 194–5). However, by the late eighteenth century, characters became unleashed from their moral status and were expected to have a 'life of their own' (Hazlitt quoted in Grochala, 2017: 198). By the late nineteenth century, there followed 'a shift in characterisation towards an understanding of human behaviour in terms of socio-psychological causation' (Grochala, 2017: 196), and characters were constructed as increasingly complex beings whose choices and motivations were determined by different social and psychological factors. The sense of a character's action being determined by a social and psychological 'causation' continued, in many ways, to dominate the different dramatic constructions of character that appeared within the various forms of naturalism and psychological realism at the commencement of the twentieth century. Here, as Grochala indicates, '[c]haracters were positioned as both the products of their experiences and their social circumstances' (Grochala, 2017: 197).

However, the documentary plays of the 1960s, as Hans-Theis Lehmann argues, move beyond the tradition of dramatic theatre, for in these plays 'little depends on the outcomes of the process of investigation' (Lehmann, 2006: 55). As such, Lehman therefore positions Weiss's *The Investigation* as part of the pre-history of post-dramatic theatre. By moving beyond dramatic structure, these documentary plays also collapsed the structures of 'socio-psychological causation' which, as Grochala has argued, dominated the formation of dramatic character in many naturalistic social realist plays (Grochala, 2017: 196). Indeed, underpinning the structure of the documentary character is a paradox of the real versus the dramaturgical. On the one hand, documentary characters are based on 'real' people who are determined by intrinsic motivation and socio-psychological wants and needs, but, on the other hand, these 'real' people are transformed into characters within a play who must act according to external goals that emerge from the historical facts of the event being written about. As such, the documentary character is caught in between the representational process of playwriting and the actuality of the real events themselves.

Furthermore, the question of what grounds action and what motivates a character to act is arguably not only a dramatic question, but also a profoundly philosophical and ethico-political one. The history of the documentary character is one that is constituted through debates and contestation around the relationship between history, social reality and the human subject, while also being rooted in the historical context of the playwright. Erwin Piscator is an influential figure in this regard. In a theatre career spanning some forty years and crossing the two World Wars of the twentieth century, Piscator's approach to characterisation also shifted and changed, not least as a result of his enforced exile to the United States in 1939, a move which introduced him to the Dramatic Workshop and led him to embrace new, psychologically nuanced approaches to characterisation and acting.

Erwin Piscator's early German documentary theatre

Widely acknowledged as 'the founding father of the genre' (Irmer, 2006: 19), Piscator made a highly significant contribution to the documentary form. In his youth, prior to becoming a theatre producer and director, Piscator worked as an actor before being seconded to the army with the arrival of the First World War. Like many others who lived through the First World War, Piscator was profoundly affected by what Eric Hobsbawn (1995) describes as the historic 'catastrophe' precipitated by the outbreak of the conflict. The advent of the First World War signalled a break with all that had gone before, throwing Europe into crisis and bringing about a 'breakdown of the (western) civilisation of the nineteenth century' (Hobsbawn, 1995: 6). According to Judith Malina, who studied under Piscator at the Dramatic Workshop at the New School, New York, it was as a result of his experience of fighting on the battlefields in Ypres that Piscator experienced some kind of '*crise de conscience*' and resolved 'to make the work of theatre meaningful' (Malina, 2012: 4). Malina asserts this came about when a sergeant noted Piscator's clumsiness as a soldier and 'asked him mockingly what he did for a living in civilian life' (Malina, 2012: 4). In this moment, Piscator felt great shame in having to explain that he was an actor, and it was this that ultimately led him to seek 'to redeem the art [of acting] from its degraded state' (Malina, 2012: 5) and to 'enlist in the political struggle for permanent peace' (Piscator quoted in Malina, 2012: 5).

By 1924, Piscator had become a stage director at the Freie Volksbühne Theatre where he experimented with forms of agit prop and revue-based theatre. Taking its name from 'agitation' and 'propaganda', agit prop was a highly political form of theatre that aimed for 'emotional involvement as well as rational communication' with audiences (Innes, 1972: 23). Emerging out of the work of the Blue Blouse, 'a Soviet Union-based theatre collective that operated from 1923–1928', agit prop was a 'make shift' and 'mobile' art form where 'the agitation [was] the vibrant theatricality and the propaganda [was] the conscious desire to represent a specific ideological position with a focus on a particular theme such as workers' rights' (Gale and Deeney, 2010: 300). While Piscator's work was influenced by the political performance work of the Blue Blouse, he soon began to adapt these early experimentations into professional theatre productions that drew on a revue-style structure to address contemporary political issues of the time. It was this approach he adopted when developing his first documentary theatre play *Trotz alledem!*

Translated into English as 'In Spite of Everything!' or 'Despite All!', *Trotz alledem!* was created by invitation of the Community Party of Germany and was presented at the Groβes Schauspielhaus, Berlin in 1925 as part of the party's conference there. Using a revue format, *Trotz alledem!* 'grew out of a mammoth historic review' Piscator had mounted 'in the Spring of that year for the Worker's Cultural Union', which included '2000 participants [and] twenty gigantic spotlights […] to light up the natural arena, massive symbolic props [to] illustrate the separate passages' and '[a] sixty-five-foot battleship' to 'represent British Imperialism' (Piscator, 2014: 271). Directed by Piscator with a text written by Felix Gasbarra and stage sets designed by John Heartfield (Favorini, 1995: 1), *Trotz alledem!* took its title from a phrase by Karl Liebknecht which was adopted 'to show that the social revolution continued to take place, event after the terrible disaster of 1919', when Liebknecht and Rosa Luxemburg, two leading communist revolutionaries, who feature in the play, were assassinated in Germany (Piscator, 2014: 272).

Incorporating many dramaturgical elements associated with contemporary documentary drama such as 'a scenic montage of authentic speeches, newspaper articles, flyers, photographs and film footage of the war and the November Revolution' (Jestrovic, 2005: 361), the play is considered the first example of documentary theatre because 'the text and staging were based solely on political documents' (Piscator, 2014: 271). Drawing on devised elements, *Trotz alledem!* was 'a collective effort' where '[t]he separate tasks of writer, director, musical director, designer and actor constantly overlapped' (Piscator, 2014: 272). As a consequence perhaps, the construction of the piece was not undertaken in any linear fashion and '[d]ifferent scenes were put together simultaneously in different parts of the theatre, sometimes even before a definite script had been worked out' (Piscator, 2014: 272). This collective mode of working stands in stark contrast to the more playwright-driven documentary theatre that Piscator was to stage some forty years later, at Berlin's Freie Volksbühne Theatre where, in plays such as *The Investigation* and *The Deputy*, it is the authorship of the playwright, as opposed to the director, who determines the play's dramaturgical structure.

Describing *Trotz alledem!* as drawing on 'a montage of authentic speeches, essays, newspaper cuttings, appeals, pamphlets, photographs, and film of the War and the Revolution, of historical persons and scenes' (Piscator, 2014: 274), Piscator argues that his play reached out to the working classes in a way unseen before in the bourgeois classical works usually presented at the Großes Schauspielhaus. However, he stresses, the play 'had exactly the same moments of tension and dramatic climaxes as literary drama, and the same strong emotional impact' (Piscator, 2014: 276). In this sense, this early form of documentary theatre still maintained a sense of the dramatic and used both politics and empathy to communicate its message. According to the critic Otto Steinicke, writing in the communist paper *Die Rote Fahne*, *Trotz alledem!* was a great success and opened the way for a theatre to be 'staged by and for the proletariat [...] in Germany' (Steinicke, 1995: 13). However, Steinicke was also critical of Piscator's reluctance to depart from historical fact, arguing that the production remained 'too true to history' (Steinicke, 1995: 13) and suggesting it would benefit from a finale that exhibited 'more excitement among the masses on the stage' (Steinicke, 1995: 13). Steinicke, it seems, would have been happier if Piscator had been less 'literal' and the production had included more theatrical gestures. This leads him to argue, somewhat provocatively, that there was 'no reason to get so hung up about "how it was"' (Steinicke, 1995: 13).

However, it was this commitment to showing 'how it was', coupled with the stylistic use of montage, that was to become the defining feature of the documentary theatre that appeared in the twentieth century. Derek Paget, for example, positions Piscator's use of montage as a key element in what he dubs, 'The "Piscatorian Tradition"' (Paget, 1990: 61), an approach which, he argues, influenced many future documentary dramatists, including Joan Littlewood and the Theatre Workshop's production *Oh What a Lovely War* in 1963. Piscatorian montage operated to enhance the audience's critical engagement with the performance and to communicate the political message of the play. It is an approach that incorporated various dramaturgical and performative devices, including the use of '*projections of actualities*', a text created 'from printed "documentary" sources', actors addressing '*the audience directly* from the stage', the incorporation of 'music and song' and the adoption of what Paget aptly describes as 'that "cool" acting style associated with Brecht's *Verfremdungseffekt*', which enables actors 'to play several roles, rather than a single naturalistic "character"' (Paget, 1990: 61; original emphasis). In his adoption of these kinds of montage techniques, Piscator used documents and other sources of evidence, not to authenticate the truth claims being asserted by the play, but to establish a direct connection with the actual lived experience of everyday life, encouraging audiences to seek out connections, incongruities and dissonances within the very different material placed together through the course of the play.

Alongside this use of montage and the deliberately non-dramatic narrative structure of the play text, Piscatorian theatre was also marked out by the ambitious use of innovative stage technology. Unlike most contemporary documentary and verbatim theatre staged today, these early forms of documentary theatre made great use of stage machinery, film and screened projections, which were used to illustrate the social and material conditions of the working classes and to convey the political message of the play. For *Trotz alledem!*, for example, Piscator employed 'a terraced structure of irregular shape with a raked platform on one side and levels on the other' that 'stood on a revolving stage' (Piscator, 2014: 274). Similarly for his production of *Fahnen* (Flags) in 1924, he 'used a complicated divided set on a revolving stage with a treadmill street running through it, and images of the characters and documentary material projected on either side of the stage' (Malina, 2012: 6).

While these elaborate stage designs were highly spectacular, Piscator was also criticised for allowing his pursuance of a political message and his penchant for complex mechanistic stage machinery to overshadow the theatre-making process itself. Brecht, for example, who was a long-time collaborator of Piscator, suggested that for Piscator, theatre became 'a parliament' and, while not being entirely indifferent to applause, Piscator 'preferred a discussion' and was 'even ready to do wholly without actors' (Brecht, 2015b: 136). For Brecht, Piscator's elaborate and technical experiments threatened to dominate or perhaps even replace the process of acting itself. These productions, Brecht argued, 'began by causing complete theatrical chaos' turning 'the stage into a machine shop' while 'the auditorium became a public meeting' (Brecht, 2015b: 136).

The evolving uses of character in documentary theatre

One of the challenges confronting Piscator and also, to a large extent, Brecht was how to create a political theatre that presented a dramatic hero whose situation was not determined by personal circumstances or psychology, but by the social and material conditions of the age and the lived experience of the proletariat. Both Piscator and Brecht, in different ways, turned away from the psychologically coherent characterisation adopted by earlier 'naturalistic' dramatists such as Henrik Ibsen (1828–1906) and August Strindberg (1849–1912). Instead of seeking an individualised protagonist, Piscator wanted to generate representations of what might be described as a communist hero. As Innes points out, Piscator 'labelled himself a "historical materialist"' (Innes, 1972: 123), and saw his theatre making as 'an *absolute* historical-philosophical recognition' of '*Marxist doctrine*' (Piscator quoted in Innes, 1972: 123; original emphasis). For Piscator, as for other Marxist theatre makers of the time, the proletariat was positioned as a 'mighty I' (Piscator quoted in Innes, 1972: 123), and 'the individual lacked personal freedom of decision' (Innes, 1972: 123) and was viewed as being 'inseparably integrated with the great political and economic factors of [the] age' (Piscator quoted in Innes, 1972: 123). This new form of political drama sought to completely overturn the conventions of the traditional Aristotelian concept of the classical dramatic paradigm and to uncouple character from the concept of a social subject whose decision to act was determined by individualistic 'socio-psychological causation' (Grochala, 2017: 196). As Innes points out, Piscator rejected the 'concept of the individual as a moral being' (Innes, 1972: 121) and instead wanted to create a theatre that revealed the social conditions which acted upon the proletariat and which enabled them to represent the plight of the working classes. For Piscator, the concept of man as an autonomous individual determined by individual desires and wants belonged to a bygone age. Reflecting on his experiences of war and the economic depression in Germany, he wrote that 'Man as an individual being, independent […] of social bonds, focusing egocentrically on the concept of his self, rests in reality beneath the marble plaque of the "Unknown Soldier"' (Piscator quoted in Innes, 1972: 121).

This perspective is echoed by Brecht, who in his essay, 'The Street Scene: A Basic Model for an Epic Theatre' (2015c), describes a style of performance in which the actor can be critically distant from the role he or she is enacting. For Brecht, this form of acting is more like a 'demonstration' of a set of actions than the pursuance of a psychological connection of truth between the actor and the character being portrayed. This leads him to write:

> [T]he demonstrator should derive his characters entirely from their actions. He imitates their actions and so allows conclusions to be drawn about them. A theatre that follows him in this will be largely breaking with the orthodox theatre's habit of basing the actions on the characters and having the former exempted from criticism by presenting them as an unavoidable consequence. (Brecht, 2015c: 179)

As David Barnett points out, Brecht – and, I would argue, also Piscator – did not want to focus the audience's attention 'on characters' and 'their desires, their struggles', but 'on situations and on how situations inform, affect and transform characters' (Barnett, 2014: 27).

These innovations in the way political and documentary theatre is constructed and performed were not simply a result of Piscator's (or Brecht's) personal political belief systems. Rather, these innovations in the theatre form were determined by the political, historical context in which Brecht and Piscator were making theatre; a period in which conflicts between left- and right-wing political factions were beginning to become increasingly critical. This was a period in Germany's political history not only dominated by the rise of the far right, but also characterised by a major split on the political left between Germany's Communist Party (the KPD) and the Socialist Democratic Party. It was this split within the politics of the left that ultimately led the way for fascism to take hold in Germany and, in 1933, enabled the Nazi party, led by Adolf Hitler, to be elected. With the emergence of the rule of the Nazi party, came increased levels of violence against left-wing political parties and activists. As German historian Florian Wilde points out:

> Brutal attacks and murders of well-known anti-fascist activists followed immediately after Hitler's ascension to power. Hit most quickly and most heavily by Nazi repression was the Communist Party (KPD). Nazi thugs stormed and closed the KPD headquarters, the Karl Liebknecht House, on 23 February 1933 and banned their newspaper, *Die Rote Fahne*, a few days later. (Wilde, 2013)

At this point, Piscator had already left Germany to work in the Soviet Union and, after 'many nomadic years', in 1939 he arrived as an exile in New York 'to become the head of the New School's Dramatic Workshop' (Arjomand, 2016: 52). The move to New York was to make a big impact on the kind of theatre work Piscator was to be interested in. Not only did this period in exile bring him into contact with new forms of acting and theatre making, but the cultural context of New York and the impact of the war on Piscator himself opened up new political challenges and new pressing questions and concerns. As Arjomand indicates, '[t]he spectacles of Fascism and Stalinism unsettled Piscator's faith in the transformative power of theatre and the creation of mass audiences' and it was this, she argues, that ultimately led him to '[turn] against the ideals of a unified mass audience' (Arjomand, 2016: 52). Furthermore, as we have seen, the move to New York also exposed Piscator to some very different theatre-making processes. While in Germany, Piscator had largely been involved with making large-scale epic and semi-devised theatre, but in New York he found himself '[staging] plays, many of them canonical' (Arjomand, 2016: 52). During the years that followed, Piscator was able to combine the political theatre practice he developed in Germany and the Soviet Union with the ideas he encountered while working with 'teachers committed to psychological realism and the Stanislavski Method' (Arjomand, 2016: 52) such as 'Stella Adler and Raiken Ben Ari' (Arjomand, 2016: 52). A close look at some of the teachers Piscator taught with in New York at this time reveals the extent of the impact his experience at the Dramatic Workshop would have on his future engagements with political theatre making, with several of his fellow teachers going on to become future collaborators of Piscator. Chouteau Dyer, for example, became Piscator's 'assistant and assistant director', and Leo Kerz went on to design 'Piscator's production of Hochhuth's *The Deputy* in Berlin' (Malina, 2012: 4).

This period of exile in New York also impacted on Piscator's own political interests as he moved away from the espousal of a particular political doctrine and ideology and became increasingly concerned about the prevalence of anti-Semitism. As a consequence, his approach to theatre making shifted away from narratives of class-struggle, dominated by political ideology, and instead embraced what might be characterised as the adoption of a somewhat 'humanist attitude towards the audience' (Saal quoted in Arjomand, 2016: 52). What is evident in these shifts and transitions in Piscator's approach is not so much a loss of faith in political theatre, I would argue, but an evolution and development of his engagement in the documentary form. As Arjomand's assessment of Piscator's work of this period makes clear, Piscator began to recognise a potency in theatre making that was more dramaturgically nuanced and less structured around spectacle and representations of social reality, as Arjomand aptly explains: 'Piscator, along with his many students and collaborators, began to develop a new sort of documentary theatre whose political impact would rely not solely on the content of the documents or the collective effervescence of a mass rally but rather on the conventions of theatre itself' (Arjomand, 2016: 52).

The emergence of a new form of documentary character

It wasn't until 1951 that Piscator finally returned to Germany. However, this return from exile was not an easy one, and it took over ten years for Piscator to be re-established as a director of a theatre. Finally, in 1962,

Piscator once more returned as the artistic director of the Freie Volksbühne theatre in Berlin. One year later in 1963, he directed Ralph Hochhuth's controversial play *The Deputy*. It is this play, I suggest, that signals a significant shift towards new structures of documentary character where personal decision and individuated character play a more decisive role. While the dramaturgical structure of *The Deputy* was in many ways flawed, the play itself effectively draws together questions of personal moral responsibility, exploring the ethical and political implications of the decision-making process of specific characters. It was also an important and timely play to be staged at this time: indeed, as Piscator indicates in an essay he wrote about the play when it came out, the form and the content of *The Deputy* enabled it not only to represent this particular historical moment in Germany's recent historical past but also to interrogate it. *The Deputy*, Piscator argued, aimed 'not at the "interesting," at making the point, at constructing the plot […] rather it [aimed] at objectivising, exploring the total human attitude not in story but in history' (Piscator, 1964: 13). As Piscator notes here, in the writing of *The Deputy*, Hochhuth combined documentary evidence with the conventional tropes of dramatic writing to generate a potent examination of the moral faltering of Pope Pius XII and his failure to speak out against the mass deportation and murder of the Jews.

While *The Deputy* is often positioned, alongside *The Investigation* and *In the Matter of J. Robert Oppenheimer*, performed in 1964, as being formative to the development of the new documentary theatre that emerged in Germany the 1960s (Herzfeld-Sander, 2001; Irmer, 2006), Hochhuth's dramaturgical approach is very different from Weiss's and Kipphardt's. Firstly, Hochhuth draws far more extensively on fictional characters in the course of his play and, secondly, there are also moments when the dramaturgical action of the play is informed by the desires, wants and moral decisions of the play's individuated characters. In this sense, while Hochhuth's play is formative to the development of the German documentary theatre tradition, it also draws innovatively on non-documentary dramaturgical approaches, using character not only as a reference to 'real' people but to determine the dramatic structure of the play.

The Deputy

Written in free verse by first-time playwright Ralph Hochhuth under the German title *Der Stellvertreter: Ein christliches Trauerspiel* (The Deputy: A Christian Tragedy), *The Deputy* examines the role of the Catholic Church and Pope Pius XII specifically in the events of the Holocaust. Described by many as one of the most controversial plays of its generation (see

Arendt, 1964; Bentley, 1964), *The Deputy* premiered at the Freie Volksbühne theatre in 1963 under the direction of Piscator. Critically, at the same time, the text itself was also published with an accompanying essay by Hochhuth entitled 'Sidelights in History', contextualising the material presented in the play and the sources he drew on. The play text of *The Deputy* was also quickly translated into English and soon productions were taking place across Europe where it attracted riots and protests by supporters of the Catholic Church, and, in 1964, a version of the play opened on Broadway, New York.

When writing *The Deputy*, Hochhuth made use of various research strategies and dramaturgical processes that would be familiar to many scholars, audiences and practitioners of documentary theatre makers today. In 'Sidelights on History', for example, he describes drawing extensively on a range of documentary evidence that had 'already been made [publically] available' including: 'memoirs, biographies, diaries, letters, records of conversations and minutes of court proceedings which bear on the subject' (Hochhuth, 1964: 287). Stating that 'as far as possible [he] adhered to the facts', Hochhuth saw his role as a documentary dramatist as one in which he would 'transform the existing raw material of history into drama' (Hochhuth, 1964: 287). To do this, he incorporated both real and fictional characters into the play, generating a documentary theatre style that blended together both factual and fictive dramaturgical devices. Out of the thirty-eight characters only the Pope, the Nuncio, Gerstein, Hirt and Eichmann were not fictitious. The play's protagonist Riccardo is a fictional character, but based on Provost Bernhard Lichtenberg of Berlin Cathedral who, Hochhuth explains, 'came forth and prayed publicly for the Jews, was sentenced to jail, and asked Hitler's henchmen to let him share the fate of the Jews in the East' (Hochhuth, 1964: 14).

Despite this use of fictional characters and the riotous responses the play received, it seems that the facts themselves, as presented in Hochhuth's text, were never called into question. As Hannah Arendt explains:

> [t]he facts themselves are not in dispute. No one has denied that the Pope was in possession of all pertinent information regarding the deportation and 'resettlement' of Jews. No one has denied that the Pope did not even raise his voice in protest when, during the German occupation of Rome, the Jews, including Christian Jews (that is, Jews converted to Catholicism), were rounded up, right under the window of the Vatican, to be included in the Final Solution. (Arendt, 1964: 86)

It seems, then, that the controversy that the play stirred up and the protests the play attracted were more concerned with how these facts were presented to audiences and how the dramaturgy of the play itself dealt with the historical events it represented. Trying to understand the relationship between the text itself and its performance is a complex process, however, because the text was edited and therefore changed each time it was performed. Furthermore, due to the lengthiness of Hochhuth's text, performances of the play tended to draw on extracts that had been cut or edited from the original. This meant that when the play was performed in different parts of the world, the material presented was quite different and was cut and reshaped not by Hochhuth but by whoever directed it. Interestingly, this did not seem to detract from the potency of the play itself or the truth claims associated with it. However, as Clara Winston argues, 'the personalities of the directors, their talents and their assessment of their audience […] governed to more than the usual degree what [was] seen on the stage' (Winston, 1964: 425). In the version of the play directed by Piscator in Berlin, for example, the action 'stops short of the daring last act set in Auschwitz' (Winston, 1964: 425) and therefore did not show the arrival of the Jews at Auschwitz nor the scenes of confrontation between Riccardo, Gerstein and the doctor that follow. The reason for this somewhat drastic edit is largely unknown. Winston suggests that the final act was perhaps cut because 'this was considered too strong for the German audience', however, as she points out, '[t]his may or may not be true' (Winston, 1964: 425).

There are, of course, many reasons why Piscator might have decided not to stage the scenes of the play set in Auschwitz. Perhaps he was mindful of the challenges of representing the atrocities of the concentration camps on stage or was aware of Adorno's essay, written some twelve years before in 1951, in which Adorno stated that '[t]o write poetry after Auschwitz is barbaric' (Adorno, 1983: 34). The cutting of the final act might also have been in part simply determined by pragmatics, for as Mark Edward Ruff points out, Piscator cut Hochhuth's play from 'seven hours to two and a half' – a decision that rendered this somewhat unwieldly and lengthy play into a far more watchable experience (Ruff, 2017: 168). Either way, these cuts were clearly a point of contention between the playwright and director and 'the two men fought bitterly over the cuts right up until the premiere' (Ruff, 2017: 168).

While the collaborative process between Hochhuth and Piscator seems to be one that was, at points, marked by a degree of antagonism and robust debate, it also evidences the formation of a new politics that began to shape the form and content of documentary theatre. Within this new form of documentary theatre, the dramaturgical structure of documentary character moved away from representations of the proletariat and the communication of a particular political ideology, instead seeking out characters that were positioned 'as authentic protagonists from history'

(Irmer, 2006: 17). While, arguably, the characters in *The Deputy* were somewhat one-dimensional, they are people who have an internal world and who are confronting moments of great moral and political decision. A good example of this can be found in the character of Riccardo, the play's protagonist, who embodies what individual choice and personal morality can achieve in the face of a politics of oppression. It was the bringing together of personal moral decisions with the political and ethical issues of the event that arguably made *The Deputy* so successful and also so controversial: a point Piscator himself made, when he stated '[o]nly in rare instances is the view of individual destiny comprehensive enough to be symbolic, exemplary in the original meaning of the word, "deputized" for the generality, as it were' (Piscator, 1964: 12).

By dramaturgically placing individual decision making and morality at its centre, *The Deputy* also placed more attention upon the labour of the actor and the individuated characterisations that the play demanded. While in 1936, Brecht had suggested that Piscator's approach to theatre had been so focused on technology such that it seemed he 'was even ready to do wholly without actors' (Brecht [1936] 1964: 131), in *The Deputy*, personal character is placed at the centre of the drama, making the play far more focused on the dramatic actions and decisions of individuals than on the aesthetics of a spectacle. The structure of *The Deputy*, like many of Piscator's other post-war dramas, also invites the audience not to sign up to a particular politics, but requires them instead to sit in judgement on the morality of individual others. *The Deputy* has a public juridical quality to it and, through its dramaturgical structure, places certain characters on trial. Arjomand argues that after the Second World War, '[m]ost of Piscator's […] documentary productions fall into one particular genre: the documentary trial play, based on the transcripts of a historical trial' (Arjomand, 2016: 51). In these plays, she notes, 'Piscator restaged trial transcripts to show how atrocity can be presented and understood differently in theatres than in courtrooms' (Arjomand, 2016: 51). While *The Deputy* is not strictly speaking a 'trial play', the play certainly places the Catholic Church 'on trial' and, by restaging real historical characters in this way, the Hochhuth–Piscator collaboration invites the audience to believe (or disbelieve) the truth claims that are asserted within the play and the people represented with it. In this sense, I argue that in *The Deputy* the authority of the play is not to be located within the social or political reality depicted, but instead is found in a search for truthfulness and a desire for theatre to excavate the truth of a profoundly traumatic historical event.

Following the success and controversy of *The Deputy*, a number of other documentary plays opened on the stages of Germany in the 1960s, many (such as Kipphardt's *In the Matter of J. Robert Oppenheimer*) were also directed by Piscator. Some have argued, as Mary Herzfeld-Sander does, that it was Piscator's return to Germany that led to this revival of 'political theatre and documentary technique' (Herzfeld-Sander, 2001: vii). However, it seems likely that the political and social context of post-war Germany also played a part in the return to the documentary form. Many playwrights and artists of this time were trying to come to terms with the events of the Second World War and Germany's role within it. Furthermore, many of this generation of documentary theatre playwrights had been personally affected by the events of the Holocaust. The father of Heinar Kipphardt, for example, 'was prisoner in the concentration camp Buchenwald' (Herzfeld-Sander, 2001: xiii–xiv); similarly, Peter Weiss's father was 'a Czech Jew' (Hilton, 1970: 12), and so much of Weiss's life was determined 'by crises, wars and persecutions' (Hilton, 1970: 12). Arguably, the German documentary theatre of the 1960s could be seen as a response to a collective desire to account for the recent events of the past, to arm theatre with the means of excavating historical truths of what occurred and in some way to call the perpetrators to account. In fact, as I shall now go on to explore in my discussion of Weiss's *The Investigation*, underpinning many of these new documentary plays was not only a process of interrogation and representation of the facts of an event, but also an attempt to generate revelatory truths of why these events occurred in the first place, and who should be held accountable. The dramaturgical documentary approaches adopted at this time emerged precisely because it was 'the dramatist's preferred strategy for communicating with a public unable and unwilling to face its recent past' (Cohen, 1998: 51). Only five years before the premier of *The Deputy*, Theodor Adorno had published his essay 'What Does Coming to Terms with the Past Mean?' (Adorno, 1986). In this essay, as Yasco Horsman argues, Adorno 'draws the by-now familiar picture of postwar West Germany as a country firmly in denial of its Nazi past' (Horsman, 2011: 1). Horsman goes on to argue, while the German government of the time 'had officially recognised the nation's responsibility for the Holocaust and had agreed to pay reparations to survivors, Germans privately sought to side-step the question of the Holocaust as much as possible' (Horsman, 2011: 1). The German documentary plays of the 1960s were therefore speaking difficult truths to an audience that was reluctant to hear them.

It is within some of these documentary plays, with their focus on truth telling and on personal judgement, that we begin to glimpse a form of documentary theatre that I suggest becomes a prototype for verbatim plays. What is noticeable in this pre-verbatim, documentary theatre is the growing emphasis on the performance of witnessing and the authority bestowed on testimony. It is this emerging faith in the testimony of the witness, I suggest, that marks out these plays as different from the documentary theatre that preceded them. For example, *In the Matter of J. Robert Oppenheimer*, while Heinar Kipphardt indicates that the text draws on 'documents and reports concerning the investigation' against Oppenheimer (Kipphardt, 1968: 5), his play largely centres around the reiteration of court proceedings where Oppenheimer, who is placed on the stand, is ultimately judged by the audience. The stage directions in Kipphardt's play tell us that the scenes are punctuated by projected text, reminiscent of early Piscatorian documentary theatre, but here, rather than representing social reality, the projections are used to authorise the source of the text presented on the stage. For example, Scene 2 commences with the following projected lines:

> *The following text is projected on the hangings*:
> EXCERPT FROM THE PROCEEDINGS ON THE SECOND DAY:
> GUILT THROUGH ASSOCIATION? (Kipphardt, 1968: 22)

In his introduction to the play, Kipphardt foregrounds the role of testimony and reiterated spoken text in the play, but reflects on the challenges of relying solely on 'verbatim' text, pointing out that the length of the inquiry and number of witnesses called made 'it was impossible to achieve the required concentration with a verbatim reproduction of statement and counterstatement' (Kipphardt, 1968: 6). A 'verbatim' approach also seemed to Kipphardt to be something of a distraction from the dramaturgical demands of the play structure itself and was not therefore perceived to be 'in the interests of the unity of the play' (Kipphardt, 1968: 6). Stating that in his play he presents 'a version which lends itself to being staged and which does not distort the truth' (Kipphardt, 1968: 5–6), Kipphardt reflects on the complex relationship between verbatim text, factual truth and dramaturgical structure that would ultimately, several decades later, become the subject of much discussion in relation to contemporary verbatim theatre.

The Investigation

Several years after the premier of Kipphardt's *In the Matter of J. Robert Oppenheimer*, another important documentary play – also directed by Piscator and making use of the dramaturgical structure of a trial – was staged at the Freie Volksbühne theatre. *The Investigation*, written by Peter Weiss in 1965, drew on material from the Frankfurt Auschwitz Trials (1963–65), adopting a courtroom structure and staging witnesses and defendants to interrogate the conditions that made Auschwitz a possibility. Unlike the characters in Hochhuth's and Kipphardt's plays, the documentary characters that emerge in *The Investigation* are almost devoid of any individuality and any distinguishing features. While structurally very different from *The Deputy*, Weiss's play also became the subject of much contestation and debate. Underpinning these criticisms levelled against Weiss's play are some critical ethico-political questions about the singularity of the witness vis-à-vis the communicability of testimony, which continue to frame the use of testimonial text in performance. Weiss's critics also raised some complex and penetrating questions about how theatre might be understood as participating in historiographical processes and how the collapsing of dramatic conventions were viewed by some as being ethically problematic.

Like Hochhuth, who drew on 'free verse' in the construction of *The Deputy*, Weiss similarly turned to poetic form in order to address the events of the Holocaust in *The Investigation*, by adopting an Oratorio structure for the play, which he presents in eleven Cantos '[paralleling] the numeric canto structure of Dante's Commedia' (Berwald, 2003: 23). However, despite the commonality of this adoption of a poetic structural approach, the form and structure of *The Deputy* and *The Investigation* differ considerably. *The Deputy* is structured around specific and named characters that, broadly speaking, are defined by their own morality and the individual choices they make. However, in *The Investigation*, Weiss strips back all sense of subjectivity within the characterisation. With all the witnesses presented in the play anonymised, Weiss only includes the names of the defendants as they appear in witness statements or the address of the judge. The only exception to this is Lili Tofler, a young woman who does not appear in the play but whose story is told in Canto Five 'The End of Lili Tofler'. In this part of the play, we learn that Tofler was working as a typist at the camp when she wrote a letter to one of the male prisoners there. On discovery of the letter, she 'was taken into custody' and 'interrogated' before being made to stand 'naked several times before the wall'. She was then tortured until finally being shot by Boger, one of the defendants in the play (Weiss, 2010: 95–107). One reading of the scenes with Lili Tofler is that in some way she represents or draws attention to 'the courage and death of an individual Shoah victim' (Berwald, 2003: 24). However, as Gene Plunka argues, 'the death of Lili Tofler emerges not to demonstrate an act of courage or individual responsibility, but as a *fait accompli* that removes individual choice as an option' (Plunka, 2009: 125). For while Weiss includes the name of Lili Tofler in his text, her positioning within the dramaturgy of the play serves only to reveal the anonymity of suffering within the camp system. In the final part of Canto Five, when the judge asks: 'Can anyone tell us where Lili Tofler came from', it becomes clear that no one knew who she really was or her history. Viewed in this way, the story of Lili Tofler seems only to highlight the irrevocable process of suffering the camp wrought on those incarcerated there. The actual Lili Tofler and the nature of her suffering remains unknown and unknowable. She is presented in the play only as someone forgotten and overlooked – simply another victim of the murderous mechanisms of the camp.

As I indicated above, Weiss argues that the stylistic form he adopts in *The Investigation* was a necessity that enabled him to find a way in which to deal with the atrocity of Auschwitz. A similar point is made by Hochhuth who, in a preamble to Act 5, reflects on the challenges of presenting Auschwitz on stage, arguing that the staging of this final act should set aside what he describes as a 'documentary naturalism' and instead embrace an 'altogether surrealistic' feel (Hochhuth, 1964: 222–3). However, unlike Weiss who introduces his play by calling for all 'personal experiences and confrontations' to be 'softened into anonymity' (Weiss, 2010: 10), in *The Deputy*, Hochhuth seems to fall back into representational forms of drama and depicts both the cattle trucks transporting prisoners to Auschwitz and the camp itself. Hochhuth opens the final act of the play with a series of monologues set 'in the interior of a freight car', a setting that is further elaborated by stage directions indicating that the actors 'crouch on the floor […] jammed in tightly among suitcases and bundles' (Hochhuth, 1964: 223–4). In a series of monologues that follow, Hochhuth recreates some of the deportees who were transported to Auschwitz, positioning the audiences as spectators to their suffering:

THE OLD MAN:
Not to die in the car, with my grandchildren watching,
Fear has long since rubbed out the shape of their faces,
Quelled their questions. They sense what I know:
The journey's end will be our end as well. (Hochhuth, 1964: 224)

In later scenes in this act, Hochhuth presents a confrontation between the play's protagonist Riccardo and the doctor. However, while this con-frontation is written as a dialogue, it is structured through a somewhat simplified two dimensional use of characterisation where the SS guards and the doctor become positioned as thoroughly evil and are pitted against the play's moral protagonist, the good Riccardo. The effect is arguably neither surrealistic, nor a form of documentary naturalism. Furthermore, by presenting the perpetrators as excessively evil, this characterisation overlooks the fact that these acts were perpetrated by ordinary men and women and, in this sense, does not capture what Hannah Arendt aptly describes as the 'banality of evil' (Arendt, 2006) that made the camp system operative. A similar point is made by Lawrence Langer, who argues that:

> [W]hen Hochhuth shifts from setting to character, he lapses into figures so conventional that he sacrifices any surrealistic effect achieved by the vague movements of the doomed toward the gas chambers in the dim recesses of the stage. The Priest and the Doctor are so clearly defined as adversaries in the context between Good and Evil that they dwindle into allegory, a finale fatal to *any* adequate representation of Auschwitz in art. (Langer, 1995: 96; original emphasis)

In writing *The Investigation*, Weiss, like Hochhuth, draws on documentary material relating to the German concentration camps, however, his approach to characterisation and dramaturgy is very different. By adopting the structure of the trial in the dramaturgy of *The Investigation*, Weiss does not need to engage in any direct representation of Auschwitz. Furthermore, the juridical setting of *The Investigation* serves to refocus the audience's attention away from a restaging of the past and instead reflects on the testimony of witnesses in the present and how we should view the defendants who stand before us, defending their actions and decisions. In this way, Weiss shifts the focus back to the present day and a contemporary process of calling to account. Thus, *The Investigation* interrogates what connects the historical events of the past with the present moment of bearing witness. According to early proofs of the play, it seems that Weiss was in two minds about what to call his play. As Berwald explains, 'Weiss's handwritten margins on the galley proofs' reveal that he considered alternative titles such as '"Das Lager" (The Camp), "Die Deweisaufnahme" (Taking Evidence), "Das Tribunal" (The Tribunal) and "Die Besichtigung" (The Inspection)' (Berwald, 2003: 23). By opting for the title *Die Ermittlung* (The Investigation), Weiss seems to point to a process that is not solely concerned with the representation of historical fact, but with the interrogation and analysis of these truths. As Berwald argues, the evocation of the word 'investigation' 'provides access to a wider spectrum of connotations, from the concrete trial to a more comprehensive philosophical examination of the fragility and possibility of truth' (Berwald, 2003: 23).

By choosing not to recreate individualised representations of survivors, *The Investigation* is able to shift the audience's focus away from the suffering of individualised victims and from potentially simplistic questions of good versus evil and instead interrogate how the mechanisms of a modern capitalist society enabled Auschwitz and the concentration camp system to occur. Weiss's decision to create largely non-individualised characters also breaks away from a characterisation structure rooted in 'socio-psychological causation', where '[c]haracters [are] positioned as both the products of their experience and their social circumstances' (Grochala, 2017: 197). By uncoupling any sense of personal identity from the witnesses and defendants, Weiss's play also recalibrates the audience's engagement away from questions of personal and individual culpability and encourages an examination of the political and economic structures that made the conditions of Auschwitz a possibility.

This dramaturgical approach also, in some way, reflects the brutal objectification and dehumanised treatment encountered by those interned within the camps. Weiss draws attention to the stylistic quality he seeks to generate in *The Investigation* by indicating within some opening remarks in published play text that the play 'can contain nothing but the facts as they came to be expressed in words during the course of the trial' (Weiss, 2010: 10). The effect of this, as Andreas Huyssen highlights, is a description of Auschwitz that is presented 'in a grey, matter-of-fact, curt prose' (Huyssen, 1980: 131). In this way, Weiss focuses the audience's attention on the disjuncture between the horror of the camp and the response of post-war Germany in relation to this history; a response which Huyssen suggests was marked by denial and inadequacy. 'The reality of Auschwitz', Huyssen argues, 'comes alive' in the language of *The Investigation*, 'especially in the speeches of the accused which exemplify the language of denial and apology so characteristic of post-war Germany in general' (Huyssen, 1980: 131).

The stripped back, stylised and anonymous characterisation lends a collective, choric quality to the text, evoking an aesthetic resonant of a Greek Chorus, which comments on the action of a play while remaining separate, or outside of it. Similarly, the voices of the witnesses merge together to form a collective choral force creating a 'dreamlike' quality where the '[c]haracters [seem] to be caught up in some fatalistic limbo reminiscent of Beckett or the nightmares of surrealist writers' (Ellis, 1987: 48). The event of Auschwitz emerges then not as a personification of evil, but as an inevitable outcome of increasingly instrumentalised economic and social systems in which everyone is a participant. This perspective is summed up effectively in the play by witness 3 who says:

> We must get rid of our exalted attitude
> That this camp world
> Is beyond our comprehension
> We all knew the society
> Which had produced the regime
> That could bring about such a camp
> We were familiar with this order
> From its very beginnings. (Weiss, 2010: 88)

However, while this stylised approach to character enabled Weiss to shift away from personal, individual tragedy and to focus more on the hegemonic political structures that brought Auschwitz into existence, his play also attracted much criticism. Robert Cohen identifies three categories of criticism of Weiss's play. Firstly, there is the accusation that *The Investigation* is undramatic, offering audiences only a simple and 'condensed version of the proceedings of the trials' (Ezrahi quoted in Cohen, 1998: 46). Secondly, the play was seen by some as failing to address the specificity of Jewish losses and suffering that was a fundamental element of the Holocaust. As Cohen indicates, the fact that 'in *The Investigation* the word "Jew" is never mentioned' was something that 'scandalised' many of the critics (Cohen, 1998: 53). It was felt that Weiss had generalised the atrocity of Auschwitz and, by doing so, had overlooked the specificity of the anti-Semitism which pre-empted it and the events of the Holocaust. Associated with this criticism of an apparent disavowal of anti-Semitism was also the suggestion, from some quarters, that Weiss himself was 'denying his Jewishness' (Cohen, 1998: 53). This accusation overlooks the fact that in his other literary and autobiographical work, Weiss often 'reflected on his Jewish side' and was, as Cohen explains, arguably 'obsessed' with it because 'according to Weiss's own narrative of his life it had prevented him from joining the perpetrators, as his half-brothers and many of his childhood friends had done' (Cohen, 1998: 54). The third element of criticism Weiss received in relation to *The Investigation* relates to his seeming use of the testimony from the Frankfurt Auschwitz Trials to make a wider political point about the morality of capitalism. As Cohen explains, for Alvin H. Rosenfeld and Sidra DeKoven, '*The Investigation* reduces fascism to a form of capitalism', which was perceived as a 'most unacceptable transgression' (Cohen, 1998: 60).

There is no room here to fully consider how we might defend Weiss's play from these criticisms, but certainly Cohen's article offers an insightful and convincing response to Weiss's critics, the implications of the accusations that are levelled at his play and how the play can be read as a counter-argument to these criticisms. Dramaturgically, underpinning these different criticisms is a desire to see the Holocaust rendered as something knowable and accessible through the use of familiar dramaturgical structures which would make use of identifiable characters and a plot that offered some kind of redemptive narrative. A dramaturgy, in other words, that would make use of 'individually drawn, fully rounded characters who invite audience-identification, naturalistic dialogue, a recognisable dramatic structure with a beginning, middle and end, a story-line presumably built around issues of personal guilt, fate, punishment and redemption, and resolution' (Cohen, 1998: 46). This type of dramaturgical approach, as Cohen insightfully points out, could be more readily found in Hochhuth's *The Deputy* (Cohen, 1998: 46). The contrasts between documentary characters that represent certain historical realities and the reconstruction of fully rounded, coherent 'real' people remains an unresolved tension within contemporary verbatim theatre and will be discussed further in Chapter 2 when I consider the legacy of Weiss's play and the new verbatim theatre plays emerging in the 1990s and 2000s. In the final section of this chapter, however, I turn to consider the foregrounding of witnessing within the German documentary plays of the 1960s and how these playwrights distinguished facticity from any form of objectivity.

Repositioning truth telling: Rethinking the documentary form

What the arguments, controversies and debates surrounding *The Deputy* and *The Investigation* usefully expose is how this second wave of German documentary theatre shifted both theatre makers' and audiences' understanding of what documentary theatre was capable of being and what constituted 'truthfulness' in these new types of political plays.

In different ways, both *The Deputy* and *The Investigation* evidence how post-war German documentary drama began to reconfigure the voice of the witness more centrally within the documentary form leading to new conceptions of character and rethinking what authorises the truth claims of this form of theatre making. It is this that leads me to suggest that the socio-political context of these two plays and the influence of Piscator as their director, began to lay the ground for a pre-history for the emergence of a contemporary verbatim theatre that would take place three decades later. While in some ways both *The Deputy* and *The Investigation* were very specifically rooted in a particular time and place, their influence certainly exceeded this; not least because both plays were performed widely and in different countries.

What is perhaps most noticeable in the dramaturgical structure of both of these plays is the move away from the devised agit prop style of performance and the representations of a social reality that were so prevalent in Piscator's earlier documentary works. Perhaps more significant, at least for the future history of verbatim theatre, is that both Weiss and Hochhuth refocused the audience's attention away from a representation of a collective social reality and instead foregrounded a historical witness who is then, in some way, placed on trial by the dramaturgical structure of the play itself.

Interestingly, while Weiss attended some of the proceedings of the Frankfurt Auschwitz Trials himself, much of the text of the play is, as Cohen explains, 'based almost to the letter on documentation of the Auschwitz trial in Frankfurt' as relayed in 'newspaper articles by Bernd Naumann published during the trial and later as a book' (Cohen, 1998: 46). As such, when writing *The Investigation*, Weiss was not making use of the verbatim strategies that would become so prolific some three decades later. Furthermore, as Cohen points out, Weiss and many of the other documentary dramatists emerging in Germany at this time make an important distinction between the *'facticity'* of their plays and any claims of 'objectivity' of truth (Cohen, 1998: 53). This distinction 'between factuality and objectivity is crucial' as Cohen goes on to argue, 'for as its lineage would indicate [documentary theatre] takes sides, it is designed to intervene in the political reality of the day' (Cohen, 1998: 53) as opposed to simply represent it. While much verbatim theatre is criticised for manipulating or leading its audiences towards certain kinds of truths, both Hochhuth and Weiss had no interest in affirming an objective account of these historical events. Furthermore, in different ways, both playwrights saw their role as writers not to accurately replicate certain juridical processes from the past but to offer an analysis and an interpretation of key historical events. While in the writing of *The Investigation*, Weiss shifts the focus away from factual evidence and instead foregrounds the testimony of the survivors. In so doing he established a creative process that irrevocably tied together documentary theatre with the performance of witnessing, placing the testimony of the witness and documentary evidence perpetually in an uneasy alliance. In this sense, both *The Investigation* and *The Deputy* also, in some critical way, recalibrate the way that truthfulness and the truth claims of theatre are dramaturgically established and interpreted by audiences.

In her essay 'Reflections on *The Deputy*', Susan Sontag argued that what makes *The Deputy* 'an important play' (Sontag, 1964: 120) is its capacity to tell the truth. Refuting Piscator's claims that *The Deputy* should be seen as 'a successor to the historical dramas of Shakespeare and Schiller and the epic theatre of Brecht', she suggested instead that 'Hochhuth's play stands or falls by its fidelity to the complete historical truth' (Sontag, 1964: 120). Yet interestingly, Sontag's account of the play is also haunted by the trickery of the dramaturgical sleight of hand of the playwright and the opacity of authorship that is so pervasive in documentary theatre. While her reading of *The Deputy* focuses almost entirely on the play's fidelity to historical truth, this interpretation does not fully take account of Hochhuth's own methodological, dramaturgical approach. Certainly, it is clear that the historical facts in the play were carefully researched and, where possible, assiduously followed, but in his 'Sidelights on History' essay, Hochhuth explains that some 'condensation' of these truths was 'necessary in the interests of drama' (Hochhuth, 1964: 287). Furthermore, as I have discussed, unlike many of the documentary dramas on our stages today, *The Deputy* is constructed through a number of fictional scenes, populated with fictitious characters and was often performed by editing or cutting certain scenes altogether. This places pressure on Sontag's faith in the play's fidelity to historical truth, or rather, it exposes how a sense of truth in theatre has shifted at this historical point towards a faith in the truth telling of the witness and a 'fidelity' in the playwright's dramaturgical process. In *The Investigation* and *The Deputy*, we begin to see the formation of verbatim theatre's promise of truthfulness, for as Sontag's response to Hochhuth's play reveals, the new forms of documentary dramaturgy emerging at this time were structured not only to affirm certain truths but to convey a faithful commitment to a research process that was rooted in factual research and a forensic examination of certain documentary evidence and certain historical truths.

The legacy of the German documentary theatre of the 1960s: Towards a verbatim character

In her account of what she calls 'theatre of the real', Carol Martin positions *The Investigation* as 'arguably the most important documentary play of the twentieth century' (Martin, 2013: 89). I agree: there is much to suggest that *The Investigation*, along with plays such as *The Deputy* and *The Matter of J. Robert Oppenheimer*, played an important role in the development of new forms of documentary theatre. In these plays, we see evidence of a development of the documentary and verbatim theatre form that would, once again, as Susan Sontag suggested, position 'theatre as a forum for public, moral judgement' (Sontag, 1964: 120). Chris Megson makes a similar point to Martin, arguing that structurally, *The Investigation* 'clearly establishes a template for the Tricycle's [tribunal theatre] approach' (Megson, 2011: 196). Drawing a comparison between *The Investigation* and Richard Norton-Taylor's first tribunal play *Half the Picture*, Megson suggests that the 'interpolated monologues' written by John McGrath that appear in *Half the Picture*, share some commonality with Weiss's approach to the dramaturgy of the documentary. This leads him to argue that McGrath, like Weiss, 'espouse a commitment to devising a contemporary theatrical aesthetic that restores a social-critical dimension to the staging of documentary material' (Megson, 2011: 196).

Arguably, there are many connections to be made between the documentary theatre developed by Weiss and Kipphardt in the 1960s, and the new forms of documentary theatre that would later appear in the 1990s. However, I suggest that in the structure and form of *The Investigation* and *The Deputy* we can also begin to identify particular dramaturgical strategies that become influential to the development of a set of verbatim theatre practices that sit *beyond* the 'template' of the tribunal play that Megson points to, with its emphasis on the reactivation and redramatising of juridical processes. While Hochhuth's and Weiss's plays signal important developments in documentary theatre, what is also significant is how these plays refocus the audience's attention towards processes of truth telling and the authority of the witness. While the role of documentation and source material clearly played a significant role in the development of *The Deputy* and *The Investigation*, it is noticeable that the dramaturgy of these plays, in different ways, hinges around the centrality of the witness as an authorising element of the play and various dramaturgical structures of individual choice and institutional and personal culpability. In Weiss's critical writing around documentary theatre, he projects an image of a documentary theatre derived from a wide range of different fact-based sources, such as:

> Minutes of proceedings, files, letters, statistic tables, stock-exchange communiqués, presentations of balance sheets of banks and industrial undertakings, official commentaries, speeches, interviews, statements by well-known personalities, press-, radio-, photo- or film-reportings of events and all the other media bearing witness to the present. (Weiss, [1968] 1995: 139)

Yet the dramaturgy of *The Investigation* itself is formed around a trial-like structure that places the voices of witnesses and defendants at its centre such that it revolves around acts of witnessing as opposed to representations of documentary evidence. Weiss is also clear that the documentary theatre he was seeking to create was different from what, today, we would describe as 'tribunal theatre' – a dramaturgical process predicated upon the re-enactment of a transcribed juridical inquiry process. For Weiss states that while '[t]he documentary theatre can take the shape of a tribunal', it does not 'pretend to vie in authenticity with the Nuremberg trial, with the Auschwitz trial at Frankfurt, with a hearing before the United States Senate or with a session of the Russell Tribunal', the documentary play moves beyond a word-for-word representation of judicial proceedings and instead takes 'the questions and the litigious points raised in the real courtroom and treats of them (*sic*) in a novel manner' (Weiss, [1968] 1995: 142).

A similar point is made by Hochhuth who, while describing his research materials as deriving from 'memoirs, biographies, diaries, letters, records of conversations and minutes of court proceedings' (Hochhuth, 1964: 287), argues that any dramatic process that addresses a historical event must negotiate the way fact sits within and negotiates around a play's dramaturgical structure. For Hochhuth, then, the transformation of factual evidence into the dramaturgy of a play is a process of art making, 'not scholarly work' (Hochhuth, 1964: 288), where individual facts must be harnessed in some way to serve a broader, more epic truth. For dramatists such as Hochhuth, the playwright is seen as retaining some sense of artistic integrity and 'must hold fast to his freedom which alone empowers him to give form to the matter' (Hochhuth, 1964: 288).

What is also noticeable about the positioning of the playwright in the different dramaturgical approaches of Weiss and Hochhuth is a marked shift away from the documentary play, as described by Piscator, constructed as 'a collective effort' where the tasks of the 'writer, director, music director, designer and actor constantly overlap' (Piscator, 2014: 92). Rather, for both Hochhuth and for Weiss, the documentary dramaturgical process is led by the vision and authorial positioning of a singular playwright who seeks out specific structures and modes of characterisation in order to excavate and perform particular truth-telling processes. Instead of using documentary evidence to construct historical fact via placards and projections and generating performances in which '[t]heatre [is] a reality' (Piscator, 2014: 276), the dramaturgical structures of *The Investigation* and *The Deputy* are more centred around the construction of truths that are determined by the particular research and political ambitions of the playwright. Furthermore, the integrity and authenticity of these truths occupy a central position within the play where they are placed under scrutiny. In *The Deputy*, Hochhuth constructs a dramaturgy that places Pope Pius XII personally, and the Catholic Church more broadly, on trial. The structure of the play invites audiences to sit in judgement not on the veracity of the events that are presented in the course of the play, which as Arendt pointed out 'are not in dispute' (Arendt, 1964: 86), but on the moral ambiguity of the decisions made by the Pope and his representatives. Correlatively, in *The Investigation*, Weiss's stylistic response to the Frankfurt Auschwitz Trials is not an endeavour to objectively recreate the trials themselves. Weiss uses language and voice to frame how the evidence presented at the trials should be interpreted. He adopts various dramaturgical tropes to convey a sensation that resonates with a classical tragedy, drawing choric structures to reconstruct the almost surrealistic, nightmarish world of Auschwitz. I would therefore suggest that the tendency in contemporary documentary theatre scholarship to view *The Investigation* as a template or prototype for tribunal or verbatim theatre overlooks the authorial role of the playwright within these early German documentary plays and does not therefore take account of the importance these dramatists place upon the witness as a loci of authenticity and truth telling.

Arguably, instead of heralding a turn towards a theatre of the real, these German documentary plays can be better understood as both developing and anticipating a form of theatre that seeks to establish a process of 'dramaturgical' truth telling that emerges from a fidelity to the figure of the witness. In different ways, Hochhuth and Weiss represent the voice of the historical witness on stage. They did so in order to use the stage as a means of interrogating the historical events of the Holocaust and the veracity of its representation – specifically revealing what had been overlooked by the legislative processes of the time. In these approaches to the documentary form, character becomes either a function of the playwright's line of inquiry – in *The Deputy* – or is positioned as an intermediary dramaturgical device that in some way enables the audience to locate an authentic and profound truthfulness that they are invited to bear witness to and to sit in judgement upon – as in *The Investigation*.

In these German documentary plays, the dramaturgical character comes to be intimately tied to both moral decision making and truth telling. In the verbatim drama that would appear some thirty years later in the 1990s, this triadic structure of character as a site of historical witnessing, moral decision making and truth telling is – I argue – central to the way verbatim theatre came to be dramaturgically constructed and how it is received. It is also this sustained focus on truth telling, witnessing and the trial-by-audience positioning of the character-as-witness that opens up the verbatim theatre form to accusations of duplicity, falsity and betrayal. In the following chapter, I consider the more recent histories of verbatim theatre and how, within these plays, the promise of truth telling and the performance of witnessing returns, becoming once again a site of considerable controversy.

2

The genealogy of contemporary verbatim theatre: shifting dramaturgies and performances of truthfulness

In the previous chapter, I examined how some key German documentary plays of the 1960s, *The Deputy*, *In the Matter of J. Robert Oppenheimer* and *The Investigation*, should be understood as forming a pre-history for the contemporary verbatim theatre that appeared in the UK, Australia, the United States and in other parts of the world in the 1990s. Written by a post-war generation of playwrights, with many of them directed by Erwin Piscator, these documentary plays addressed Germany's recent history and sought to account, in some way, for its past. However, in contrast to Piscator's earlier documentary work, these plays were not driven by a political ideology, but were more focused on processes of truth telling and a collective desire to call the nation of Germany to account for its involvement in the Second World War and the events of the Holocaust. The dramaturgical construction of these documentary dramas 'demanded a thorough knowledge of German history' and aimed to 'enlighten the present' (Herzfeld-Sander, 2001: viii) by raising critical questions in the course of the play about participation in and responsibility for the realisation of the Nazi project and the individual and institutional culpability for the atrocities wrought as a result. Foregrounding testimonial text, and placing individual decision making and questions of personal accountability at the heart of the play, this new generation of post-war German playwrights adopted innovative and influential approaches to the dramaturgical construction of a documentary theatre that set out to bear witness to the truth of certain historical events, putting historical protagonists 'on trial'.

Suggesting that these German documentary plays of the 1960s form a *pre-history* to contemporary verbatim theatre is not, however, to suggest that verbatim theatre's relationship to documentary theatre is one determined by a conventional historical 'lineage' (Nelson, 2013). What I am arguing is that there is a transmission of ambition and a cross-hatching of practices that is detectable between the plays of Hochhuth, Kipphardt and Weiss and the new forms of verbatim theatre that were written in the 1990s. In this sense, these German documentary theatre plays, along with Piscator's early documentary theatre, form part of what might be better termed as verbatim theatre's *genealogical* development. I borrow the concept of 'genealogy' from Foucault's reading of Nietzsche's theorisation of history, and it is adopted in this chapter not to stand in opposition to any historical account of verbatim theatre, but to signal a methodological approach that eschews a search for 'origins' (Foucault, 1991: 80). In this chapter, I explore influences, moments of transmission from one tradition to another and historiographical accounts of this emerging form. By adopting this genealogical approach to the development of verbatim theatre, I do not 'pretend to go back in time to restore an unbroken continuity that operates beyond the dispersion of forgotten things'; nor is this an attempt to 'demonstrate that the past actively exists in the present, that it continues secretly to animate the present, having imposed a predetermined form to all its vicissitudes' (Foucault, 1991: 81). The construction of a genealogical account of verbatim theatre is an attempt to establish an engagement with the multitude of different histories and different discourses (and practices) that have collectively contributed to the development of this form of theatre and how it is understood today. In this sense, while I am drawn to moments of potential historical influence, I am also interested in the various historiographical moments of myth, mis-step and mis-recognition that surround verbatim theatre's histories. In following Foucault's account of a genealogical approach, I want to take account of 'the accidents, the minute deviations – or conversely, the complete reversals – the errors, the false appraisals, and the faulty calculations that gave birth to [verbatim theatre]' and which 'continue to exist and have value for us' (Foucault, 1991: 81, 146). One such myth or mis-step concerns the influence of Weiss's play, *The Investigation*, and how it has come to be positioned within accounts of verbatim theatre's history.

A number of commentators have described Weiss's play as part of the historical development of contemporary documentary and verbatim theatre (Edgar, 2008; Filewod, 2011; Megson, 2011; Martin, 2013) with Alan Filewod describing it as 'perhaps the most famous verbatim documentary in an increasingly crowded field' (Filewod, 2011: 61). Along with plays such as Kipphardt's *In the Matter of J. Robert Oppenheimer* and Hochhuth's *The Deputy*, *The Investigation* is considered a key example in a new movement of theatre, emerging in the 1960s and 1970s that came to be called, 'theatre of fact'. However, in the same way that verbatim theatre often finds itself described as 'documentary theatre', 'theatre of fact' also became a label that tended to generalise, rather than distinguish the very different dramaturgical processes adopted in the plays that were described by this term. As Dan Isaac points out, 'theatre of fact' plays were often 'very different from one another in both aesthetic style and ideological argument' (Isaac, 1971: 119). Perhaps because of this, Isaac formulates a somewhat broad and nebulous definition of the 'theatre of fact' genre, describing it as a 'theatre whose complex form and concentrated function raise ethical questions that cannot easily be separated from the claims of the aesthetic' (Isaac, 1971: 119). Looking back on the historiography of documentary and verbatim theatre, it is clear that there is also some confusion informing the historical discourses about the actual dramaturgical approaches adopted within the construction of documentary and verbatim plays and what people have said about this. Historical accounts of Weiss's *The Investigation*, for example, often merge with readings of Weiss's influential essay 'Fourteen Propositions for a Documentary Theatre' ([1968] 1995). In the essay, as discussed in the previous chapter, Weiss describes documentary theatre as 'a theatre of factual reports', defining it as being constructed from evidence such as '[m]inutes of proceedings, files, letters, statistic tables' and so on (Weiss, [1968] 1995: 139). However, while Weiss indicates that *The Investigation* contains 'nothing but the facts as they came to be expressed in words during the course of the trial' (Weiss, 2010: 10), this does not mean that *The Investigation* was written by drawing only on transcribed material taken verbatim from the Frankfurt Auschwitz Trials themselves. As the previous chapter argued, a close reading of the play itself and research around the historical context in which it was written soon reveals that, like many other documentary theatre makers at the time, Weiss understood his incorporation of factual evidence in the writing of *The Investigation* as an approach that did not preclude his own dramaturgical interventions. Importantly, there is no suggestion from Weiss that his documentary approach sought to establish an objective account of the trials themselves.

However, in scholarship that addresses the historical provenance of verbatim theatre, there is a tendency to view *The Investigation* as an example of a play that is written by simply reiterating the juridical processes of a trial. Viewing *The Investigation* in this way suggests that the historical development of verbatim theatre is rooted in a set of practices in which the playwright was omitted, where verbatim theatre becomes positioned as a form of theatre that eschews any form of dramaturgical intervention in the formation of the text itself. One such example of the mis-historicising of the legacy of *The Investigation* appears in an article written for *The Guardian* newspaper by the playwright David Edgar who, in a somewhat critical account of the re-emergence of verbatim theatre in the 1990s and 2000s, examines what he describes as '[t]he rise of a theatre of reportage rather than enactment' (Edgar, 2008). In this much-cited essay (see Lane, 2010; Megson, 2011; Cantrell, 2013), Edgar connects contemporary verbatim theatre with the 'theatre of fact' movement of the 1960s, arguing that writers, such as Weiss and Kipphardt, focused on documents and facts as a 'conscious evasion' of 'dramatic invention' (Edgar, 2008). Accordingly, Edgar suggests, '[t]he theory behind these works was not [...] to explain the phenomena they described' but to establish a dramaturgical approach that would allow audiences to freely interpret the material they were being presented with. Referencing Kipphardt's *In the Matter of J. Robert Oppenheimer* and Weiss's *The Investigation*, Edgar explains that:

> the playwrights were saying that, after the enormities of Auschwitz and Hiroshima, the old concepts of cause and effect no longer apply. All the playwright can do is present the documents for the audience to make of them what it will. In this sense, Theatre of Fact is the other side of the coin of 50s and 60s absurdism. Both forms sought to express phenomena they could no longer explain. (Edgar, 2008)

While this account of the 'theatre of fact' movement certainly captures the challenges of representing events such as the Holocaust and the bombing of Hiroshima, Edgar's suggestion that playwrights, such as Weiss and Kipphardt, sought to *evade* a dramaturgical interpretation or explication of the events being examined in these plays does not take account of the different ways these writers crafted and shaped the material they used. In their book, *The Political Theatre of David Edgar* (2011), Janelle Reinelt and Gerald Hewitt also draw attention to Edgar's characterisation of verbatim theatre emerging from the fact-based theatre of the 1950s and 1960s. Reinelt and Hewitt explicate Edgar's viewpoint by suggesting that the documentary playwrights of the 1950s and 1960s engaged in '"a kind of abdication"' (Edgar quoted in Reinelt and Hewitt, 2011: 156), in which they evaded 'putting forth an argument or interpretation of reality in dramatic form' (Edgar quoted in Reinelt and Hewitt, 2011: 156). Edgar, as Reinelt and Hewitt go on to point out, 'charges this type of theatre with only presenting documents and allowing the audience to do all the interpretative work' (Edgar quoted in Reinelt and Hewitt,

2011: 156). However, as my earlier discussion in Chapter 1 reveals, this account of Weiss's and Kipphardt's dramaturgical processes fails to take account of the political approaches adopted by these playwrights in relation to the source material they were working with, nor does it acknowledge the dramaturgical innovations these plays initiated. If, by way of an example, we return for a moment to the criticism levelled against Weiss in the 1960s, addressing the way he used material from the Frankfurt Auschwitz Trials in *The Investigation*, we see that Weiss's critics at the time actually spoke out against Weiss precisely because of how he chose to structure the material his play examined. As mentioned in Chapter 1, Weiss was criticised for using the Frankfurt Auschwitz Trials to develop a Marxist critique of the economic and political structures that made Auschwitz possible. This again points not to an 'evasion' of the playwright, but to the particular stance that was adopted by Weiss when framing and reworking this material. Furthermore, as Robert Cohen argues, the criticisms levelled at Weiss's play arguably emerged because of a failure to acknowledge the stylistic dramaturgical conventions explored by Weiss in the writing of *The Investigation*. Unable to interpret the tropes of epic theatre and the references to surrealism that Weiss incorporates, much of the criticism the play received was 'driven by a normative impulse' (Cohen, 1998: 46), motivated by a desire for a dramaturgy that made use of 'individually drawn, fully rounded characters who invite audience-identification, naturalistic dialogue' and the use of 'a recognizable dramatic structure with a beginning, middle and end' (Cohen, 1998: 46). By failing to acknowledge the way Weiss intervened and shaped the material garnered from the Frankfurt Auschwitz Trials, Edgar also seems to disavow the formal innovations in Weiss's play, appearing also to reinstate the very form of dramatic theatre that Weiss wanted to distance himself from. By adopting this position, Edgar arguably also forecloses the political interpretation that Weiss wishes to bring to *The Investigation*, relegating the dramaturgy of the play to a simple reiteration of juridical processes.

The mis-recognition and mis-stepping in the historicising of verbatim theatre is by no means limited to this one example. The history of verbatim theatre is peppered with historiographical moments of self-forgetting and mis-reading, which draw attention not only to the context of the debates surrounding its historical development, but to the different ways verbatim theatre is appraised and understood. In this chapter, I examine some of the different histories of verbatim theatre and the differing, and at times competing, truth claims that subsequently become attached to this form of theatre. While often addressing itself to collective political situations, contemporary verbatim theatre, I argue, foregrounds the individual witness, focusing in on the authenticity of spoken testimony. Unlike the political documentary theatre that was developed in Germany in the 1960s, contemporary verbatim theatre tends to use personal narrative to authenticate a particular truth process or to validate the narrative the play seeks to establish, often incorporating testimony alongside other forms of documentary truths and the performance of fact. What the various histories of verbatim theatre reveal then is not simply a diversity of dramaturgical form but a contested array of truth claims that are performed by verbatim theatre practices. I turn now to examine some of the more recent historiographical accounts of verbatim theatre and consider how these different histories, and the discourses around them, determine the way this form of theatre frames the truth-telling processes with which it engages.

Waiting Room Germany (Pohl, 1995): A new form of verbatim theatre

My own initial encounter with verbatim theatre was at the Royal Court Theatre watching *Waiting Room Germany*, a translation of *Wartesaad Deutschland*, a German documentary play by Klaus Pohl, which ran for just two weeks due to an unexpected delay to the production that was due to open in the Royal Court Theatre downstairs. Opening just eighteen months after the premier of the first tribunal play at the Tricycle Theatre, North London, *Waiting Room Germany* was not described as verbatim theatre in any of its publicity materials. Consequently, like me, I suspect many audience members did not know what to expect when they came to see this play. Based on a series of interviews and observations undertaken by Pohl as part of a project for the German magazine *Der Spiegel*, the play explored the impact of the reunification of Germany through a series of monologues by real people who lived in both East and West Germany. In the published play text that accompanied the opening of the play at the Royal Court, David Tushingham, the play's translator, explains that Pohl's original text was comprised of an extensive series of monologues, which made use of an 'unusually open […] form' with 'no prescribed cast or order of speeches' (Tushingham, 1995: 1). Pohl's original text was too long to 'be performed in a single evening' (Tushingham, 1995: 1) and, consequently for the Royal Court production, the material was cut back to twenty-two speeches, enacted by a cast of five with each actor playing several characters. The staging consisted of the five actors sitting in chairs in a line, performing their monologue directly to the audience and barely engaging with the other characters on stage.

While the dramaturgical structure was extraordinarily simple, the play was extremely watchable and made a strong impression on me. The dialogue seemed fresh and authentic and appeared to have been taken directly from original interview material, creating the impression that as audience members we were getting access to the daily reality of those East and West Germans living through this key historical event. Looking back on this performance today, however, I realise there was nothing in the play's programme to suggest that the play text was based on actual interview material, and I wonder now if I was actually encountering re-enacted, transcribed material or simply, what Thomas Irmer refers to in his description of the play, as 'a series of well-made monologues' written by Pohl himself (Irmer, 2006: 24). Regardless of how Pohl constructed the text, the performance felt very different from other forms of new writing I had seen at the Royal Court. The inclusion of the vocal tics and the 'errs' and 'mmms' of everyday speech gave the monologues a hyper-real and almost un-actorly feel, producing the uncanny sensation that it was real people, rather than actors, emerging on the stage before us. As a result, like the audiences described by Robin Soans – who acted in this production and later wrote about it in Hammond's and Steward's *Verbatim Verbatim* (2008) – I found myself 'not just listening, but really listening' (Soans, 2008: 22). After all, the stories told in the play offered an insight into the reality of an event I had, until that point, only read about in newspapers. Like many other young people in the 1980s, the tearing down of the Berlin Wall and the reunification of Germany seemed to signify a politics of liberty that was obviously an emancipatory event. Yet, as I watched *Waiting Room Germany*, a wholly different and more complex historical reality emerged. I witnessed disturbing stories of East Germany's recent past: imprisonment, restriction and surveillance, but, in between the euphoric stories of escape to the West, another more complex situation was exposed. The characters talked about an enduring prejudice towards the *Ossis* (the 'Easties'), and for some a growing nostalgia for a lost era in the East and a longing for a return to the sense of solidarity of a more community-orientated way of life. In this sense, *Waiting Room Germany* provided a powerful counter-narrative to media reports of the events of reunification, and I soon found myself recalibrating what I thought I understood about this historico-political moment. Today, I would describe the dramaturgical structure and style of performance adopted in *Waiting Room Germany* as a 'typical' example of verbatim theatre; it was constructed only from what appeared to be reiterated interview material, it incorporated a style of acting that made the text

seem hyper-real and precisely transcribed, and it used this edited material
to interrogate a specific cultural and historical event. Yet it would be a
further decade, not until 2005, when Robin Soans's *Talking to Terrorists*
opened, that the Royal Court would stage a play that would be described
explicitly as verbatim theatre.

The distinctiveness I noticed in the performance of *Waiting Room
Germany* was clearly not only the result of the particular dramaturgical
structure of the play, rather it was created through the style of performance
adopted by the actors. This was resonant of what Paget has defined as
the "'cool" acting style associated with Brecht's Verfremdungseffekt' (Paget,
1990: 60). Described by Paget as characteristic of Piscatorian theatre, this
style of acting continues to be adopted today in verbatim theatre when
actors must 'play several roles, rather than a single naturalistic "character"'
(Paget, 1990: 60). In *Waiting Room Germany*, this style of acting seemed
almost to disavow the process of acting itself, generating understated but
very 'real' enactments that felt almost as if we were watching a talking
heads interview on a television documentary rather than actors on a
stage. The careful replication of vocal hesitations and repetitions that
were written into the script itself also contributed to a mode of enactment
that was caught somewhere between imitation and re-enactment. These
different stylistic acting elements worked together to produce a style of
performance that felt very new, fresh and particularly true and authentic.
Characterisation was established through the reiteration of transcribed
text rather than through any psychological desire or internalised motive
generated by the actor. As Robin Soans explains, it was an approach that
lacked 'a geographical [...] emotional and psychological shape' (Soans,
2008: 21), and consequently it produced a detached style of performance
that was further heightened by the lack of interaction with other characters.
While in fictional theatre, as Soans points out, actors tend to interact
with one another, in *Waiting Room Germany*, like the new forms of
contemporary verbatim theatre that would soon appear, 'ninety per cent
of the time [the actor's] attention is directed towards the audience' who
become 'a key, if silent, character in the performance' (Soans, 2008: 21).
It is this use of direct address – and this tendency to, in some way, *cast*
the audience – coupled with the 'cool' acting style that ultimately became
recognisable as the characteristic features of the new forms of verbatim
theatre that would emerge in the late 1990s and early 2000s.

Irmer positions Pohl's play as part of a wave of 'new German documentary theatre' that was created in the 1990s, which was interested in
exploring multiple perspectives on 'contemporary sociological issues'
(Irmer, 2006: 24). However, as he goes on to argue, unlike other experimental documentary theatre emerging in Germany at this time, the success

of *Waiting Room Germany* is arguably due to the fact it was written by 'a well-known playwright' and structured around 'well-made character monologues' (Irmer, 2006: 24) rather than because of the innovative approach to documentary theatre it adopted. While other more experimental documentary theatre makers, such a Hans-Werner Kroesinger, explored the use of 'multidimensional, multimedia presentation' to examine 'multiple perspectives on the issues under discussion' (Irmer, 2006: 24), Pohl's play relied on single perspectives that were communicated through carefully crafted monologues.

The commissioning of Pohl's *Waiting Room Germany* by the Royal Court was a result of an exchange between the Royal Court and the Deutsches Theater in Berlin (Dodgson, 1995), and it is therefore unsurprising that it was *Waiting Room Germany*, and not one of the more experimental multi-perspective documentary dramas, that was selected as part of the Royal Court's *New German Voices: Plays from a Changing Country* season. After all, as a new writing theatre, the Royal Court foregrounds the role of the playwright in new writing, and the focus on discovering new voices has tended to play an important role in its commissioning and development processes. As I shall go on to discuss, the historical evolution of verbatim theatre is one that straddles both playwright-based and more ensemble-driven approaches to theatre making. Consequently, while certain historical accounts of verbatim theatre centre around writer-led dramaturgical processes, other histories tell a story of a practice rooted in collaborative writing processes. Correlatively, while for some the history of verbatim theatre is located firmly within a new writing tradition, others view the emergence of this form of theatre as developing in relationship with oral history and other community-orientated and ethnographic story-telling practices. This type of community-orientated approach to verbatim theatre is evident in another important genealogical thread of its historical development that can be traced not in Germany but in Stoke-on-Trent in England. For Derek Paget, it was this communal and democratised approach to the creation of verbatim theatre that was critical to its formal development.

The influence of community documentary practices

In his discussion of how a desire for 'true stories' dominated the new forms of documentary drama that emerged in radio, screen and stage in the late 1970s and early 1980s, Derek Paget historicises the early forms of British verbatim emerging at this time as being influenced by the Stoke documentary method, pioneered by Peter Cheeseman in the 1960s (Paget, 1987). Inspired by the 1950s radio ballads of Charles Parker and the 'didactic Left Wing theatre brilliantly extended by Joan Littlewood out of the German and American documentary traditions' (Cheeseman, 1970: xi), Cheeseman's documentaries, like Littlewood's *Oh What a Lovely War*, had a strong focus on documentary and verbatim theatre practices but were rooted in collective authorship and ensemble performance.

Opening at the Theatre Royal Stratford East on 19 March 1963 and directed by Joan Littlewood, *Oh What a Lovely War* drew on traditional documentary theatre practices as developed by European directors such as Piscator and Brecht and made use of photographs, projections, as well as 'a ticker-tape "Newspanel"' above the proscenium arch providing 'often statistical accounts of the "cost" in human lives of the battles on the Western Front' (Paget, 1990: 64). Under Littlewood's direction, the production made use of a collective devising process that directly contrasted with the more playwright-driven, new writing that was being produced at the time by theatres such as the Royal Court. As Steve Nicholson explains, while the Royal Court Theatre 'believed in placing the playwright at the heart of creation', the Theatre Workshop 'saw the written script as a starting point for actors and director to develop their performance' (Nicholson, 2012: 32). In this sense, the 'collectivist principle' that Paget identifies as emerging with the development of the work of the Theatre Workshop (Paget, 1990: 67) was grounded in a dramaturgical approach rooted in a desire for multiple perspectives, rather than the singular viewpoint of a writer.

This ensemble style of theatre making, combined with the different styles of performance employed within the play, meant that *Oh What a Lovely War* also drew on a 'mix of acting styles' (Paget, 1990: 65). While some of the parodic moments in the play required a more emblematic, Brechtian mode of acting, which might be described as acting as 'demonstration',[1] other more poignant, 'realistic' scenes, such as the depictions of 'the arrival at Waterloo station of the first British wounded of the war', drew on a more psychologically nuanced mode of characterisation (Paget, 1990: 65). As a consequence 'a two-dimensional comic scene' was placed alongside 'a "realistic" scene' (Paget, 1990: 65) and while some characters were created by drawing on the 'performer's skills of instant characterisation, often at the kind of emblematic level which was the hallmark of the Blue Blouse or FTP [Federal Theatre Project] groups', others were depicted with a 'Stanislavskian "psychological reality"' (Paget, 1990: 64). As I shall later go on to discuss, this collision of performance styles, which was an important element of Littlewood's use of juxtaposition within *Oh What a Lovely War*, also became a characteristic element of verbatim theatre and continues to be used in verbatim plays today.

For documentary theatre makers, such as Peter Cheeseman, the collective theatre-making approaches of the Theatre Workshop also opened up what Gillette Elvgren describes as new ways of 'binding the theatre to the community through the presentation of local subject matter' (Elvgren, 1974: 90), enabling the stories explored within the play to remain rooted in the concerns of the local area. This was exemplified by Cheeseman's approach, which he describes as emerging as a consequence of having to create theatre without the use of a playwright. This leads him to explain that 'If we had no writer amongst us, we must assume the function collectively, as a group, shape our own material out of documentary research into the history of this community' (Cheeseman, 1970: xi).

The connections Cheeseman draws here between locality, community and ensemble theatre highlight the historical relationship verbatim and documentary theatre has with ethnography and oral history practices. It is perhaps therefore somewhat unsurprising that Paget's account of the verbatim theatre work emerging in the 1970s and 1980s is rooted in a theatre that was developed in community contexts and which owed much to the influence of folk traditions and other community-based arts practices. In addition to this, Cheeseman's documentary theatre work also drew influence from 'the practices of Charles Parker's "Radio Ballads"' (Paget, 2008: 131), a form of narrative radio documentary that appeared in the late 1950s, in which 'the story [was] told entirely in the words of the actual participants themselves as recorded in real life; in sound effects which [were] also recorded on the spot, and in songs which [were] based upon these recordings, and which [utilised] traditional or 'folk-song' modes of expression' (Parker quoted in BBC2, 2006). Following in the spirit of Parker's folk-orientated practices, Cheeseman's documentary plays not only sought to democratise the dramaturgical processes of production by exploring the history and cultural context of a region, but were also created with local audiences in mind and for 'quite particular and deliberately local motives' (Cheeseman, 1970: viii). Yet while foregrounding locality and democratising the creative process was clearly an important element of the Stoke documentaries, Cheeseman was also keen to incorporate writers within these collaborative, creative processes. Nevertheless, it is somewhat significant that the dramaturgical process did not begin with the production of a script; rather, the writers became 'true partners in the creative enterprise' with a script being developed only during the rehearsal process itself (Cheeseman, 1970: ix).

Verbatim theatre and the playwright: From local to national contexts

As Paget suggests, the collective plurality inherent in verbatim theatre practices became dissipated when 'London-based companies' began to be interested in this form of theatre (Paget, 1987: 322) and verbatim theatre moved out of the regions and into the metropolitan context of the city. This shift precipitated a new focus to verbatim, where 'issues of "national" importance' led the development of 'another kind of verbatim play', one that would 'address some *present* national "controversy"' (Paget, 1987: 322; original emphasis), such as the Royal Court Theatre's play *Falkland Sound/Voces de Malvinhas* (1983). Directed by Max Stafford-Clark and presented in the Royal Court's theatre upstairs, *Falkland Sound* was structured around two parts, with the first drawing on a series of published letters and poems written by David Tinker, a Royal Navy officer who fought and died in the war in 1982 and the second half 'based on verbatim transcripts of interviews' undertaken 'by the company' (Stafford-Clark, 1983).[2] While the creative process made use of collective research processes undertaken by the cast and other members of the creative team, 'key decisions had been taken before the company first met' (Stafford-Clark, 1983). This meant that while the cast contributed to the gathering of the verbatim material to be included within the script, the writing process itself was led mainly by the director with perhaps some input from the playwright, Louise Page, who is credited in the published script as the play's 'editor'. In Stafford-Clark's early approach to verbatim theatre making, then, interviews formed part of the research and development of the play, rather than being a structural element of it. In this sense, Stafford-Clark's approach to *Falkland Sound* resonates with his much later account of verbatim theatre-making process, where he positions verbatim theatre simply as a form of research, arguing that '[w]hat a verbatim play does is flash your research nakedly. It's like cooking a meal but the meat is left raw, like a steak tartare. It's like you're flashing the research without turning it into a play. The hard thing is to turn it into dialogue, to make the transition between somebody talking to the audience and drama' (Stafford-Clark in Hare and Stafford-Clark, 2008: 51).

Stafford-Clark's engagement with verbatim theatre-based practices signals a move away from region-orientated, oral history-type performances to an approach more closely determined by the singular perspective of a director or writer and this, I suggest, represents an important transitional moment in the historical development of verbatim theatre in the UK. For in this moment, verbatim theatre shifts away from collectively devised processes and is relocated firmly within new writing traditions. As a result, dramaturgically, verbatim theatre, in the UK at least, began to evolve away from the use of multiple perspectives and collective narratives and instead began to adopt singular authorship practices. By this I mean, what emerged was a form of verbatim theatre where the narrative is supported rather than informed by documentary and verbatim material. This shift in practice meant that UK verbatim theatre became defined not so much by its capacity to recognise and validate local voices, but by its co-option of interview material and other personal narrative to tell a predetermined story and to authenticate certain arguments and perspectives.

This writer-led and director-led development within verbatim theatre is reflected on by Stafford-Clark who presents a somewhat different historical account from the one presented by Paget (Stafford-Clark in Hare and Stafford-Clark, 2008). Rather than positioning the history of verbatim theatre within community-orientated, documentary processes and oral history traditions, Stafford-Clark argues that the first 'verbatim' play was *Eleven Men Dead at Hola Camp*, which opened at the Royal Court in 1959 (Stafford-Clark in Hare and Stafford-Clark, 2008). Running for 'one Sunday night only', this play was created by Bill Gaskill and Keith Johnstone (Robbins Dudeck, 2013: 59) and responded to events that had taken place earlier that year at 'a colonial prison camp established in Hola Kenya, during the Mau Mau anticolonial guerrilla campaign' where '11 detainees were beaten to death' (Robbins Dudeck, 2013: 59). Through a series of improvised short scenes and songs interspersed with extracts from Hansard, recounting some of the facts of the case, the play was performed by an ensemble of actors, comprising mainly of 'ten back actors including [Wole] Soyinka and Bloke Modisane, a celebrated South African actor/writer/journalist who had just fled to England' (Robbins Dudeck, 2013: 47). A press release for the play described it as using improvisation, but incorporating 'a man in charge of the facts to say what actually happened' while drawing on 'dramatized excerpts from the Inquiry and songs by Royal Court writers written for the occasion' (English Stage Company quoted in Robbins Dudeck, 2013: 47).

Highly political, the play, it appears, broke down midway through, disintegrating into a 'wild, heated discussion between the black actors and the audience' (Robbins Dudeck, 2013: 47). While the play was highly experimental in its form, it also activated its audience into what was an unprecedented level of debate at that time, leading the theatre's manager George Devine, to tell Keith Johnston that 'it was the first time he had heard an audience so vociferous in the theatre' (Robbins Dudeck, 2013:

46). The formula of using real text and ensemble improvisation to explore and research a real and topical event was an approach that Bill Gaskill therefore perceived as having much potential. Consequently, some seven years later, when he co-founded the Joint Stock theatre company with Max Stafford-Clark, it would be a co-directed documentary play, *The Speakers* (1974), that was chosen to be the 'inaugural production' (Cantrell, 2013: 16). Directed by Gaskill and Stafford-Clark, the production was based on an adaptation of a novel by Heathcote Williams that drew on 'actual conversations and speeches recorded by Heathcote' with 'the speakers in Hyde Park' (Gaskill quoted in Cantrell, 2013: 16) and, like *Eleven Men Dead at Hola Camp*, it again involved an ensemble of actors in its development. Subsequently, for their third production, Joint Stock went on to stage *Yesterday's News* (1976). Also directed by Stafford-Clark and Gaskill, the play is described by Stafford-Clark as being his first encounter with 'verbatim theatre' (Stafford-Clark in Hare and Stafford-Clark, 2008: 47). Based on the events surrounding 'Costas Georgiou, aka "Colonel Callan"', who was a 'mercenary who shot his own people in Angola' (Stafford-Clark in Hare and Stafford-Clark, 2008: 47), *Yesterday's News* was devised by the cast, drawing on interviews with several ex-soldiers who had been in Angola. However, while the research underpinning it was collectively generated by the company, Stafford-Clark explains that after an initial research process had taken place, the play was then developed through a 'conventional rehearsal period' (Stafford-Clark in Hare and Stafford-Clark, 2008: 48). As Cantrell indicates, this collaborative approach to researching with a company of actors in order to create fact-based plays became a key element of Stafford-Clark's working methodology and was adopted in many of the other verbatim-based dramas Stafford-Clark went on to direct. However, the input of the actors in these productions tended to be tightly controlled by Stafford-Clark, who did not always 'share the actors' preoccupations about their roles' (Cantrell, 2013: 50). In this sense, the new mode of verbatim theatre innovated by Stafford-Clark's prolific engagement with this form of theatre could be understood as being centred around an approach where interview material, and other research material, forms the basis of a *research process*, but does not necessarily determine the dramaturgical development of the play, which tends to remain instead within the purview of the director and/or playwright.

The evolution of verbatim theatre in other parts of the world, however, has followed a somewhat different trajectory. In Australia, for example, where verbatim theatre also emerged in the early 1990s, the development of the form was closely associated with a tradition of 'community plays that utilised oral history' (Garde, Mumford and Wake, 2010: 15), and it is significant that the key verbatim play to be produced at this time drew only on interview material, gathered from the local community. *Aftershocks* (1993) by Paul Brown and the Workers Cultural Action Committee (WCAC) was created in response to the earthquake that hit Newcastle, in New South Wales, Australia in 1989. The development of the play owes much to the work of the WCAC, an organisation that had affiliations with a number of groups and individuals across Newcastle that established 'a network concerned with cultural development among Newcastle workers and their families' (Brown, 1993: viii). Closely associated with the trades union movement, the WCAC was an organisation dedicated to the democratisation of cultural production and, in 1990, 'proposed a play about the earthquake, to put on stage the perspective of people involved with the collapse of the Newcastle Workers Club' (Brown, 1993: viii). At this point, Paul Brown was already employed as Community Writer in Residence at the WCAC, and, working together with a research team and a 'steering group of ten trade unionists and club personnel', he drew together the transcripts of interviews 'into dramatic form' (Brown, 1993: ix–xiv). Centred around the collapse of the Newcastle Workers Club, the play captured the building's collapse, the rescue of some of those trapped inside, the lives that were lost and the impact of this earthquake on a local community for whom the social club played such a significant social and communal role. One of the central thematics of the play was its commitment to community ownership both in relation to the disaster of and recovery from the earthquake itself and the writing of *Aftershocks*. As Brown argues, after the earthquake, there was 'a desire for closure in Newcastle – for the story of the earthquake to end, for it to be filed away and forgotten, for rebuilding to proceed quickly' (Brown, 1993: viii); yet for many reasons this didn't happen, and the play addresses the painful aftermath of the earthquake on the local community and the fact that 'for some people, a "normal life" would not be achieved for ten years' (Brown, 1993: viii).

The possibility for verbatim theatre to enhance or develop community alliances or to forge and strengthen community life is a thematic that has been influential to the many contemporary Australian verbatim plays produced since *Aftershocks* first appeared in 1991. For example, the verbatim theatre work of Australian playwright Alana Valentine, whose play *Parramatta Girls* (2007) is discussed in Chapter 3, often addresses questions of community identity and formation. She argues that verbatim theatre has 'transformative' and community building properties that enables community members to 're-experience their connection to other people', strengthening community bonds (Valentine, 2010: 107–8). Similarly, Australian playwright Roslyn Oades, whose headphone theatre plays are discussed in more detail below, often uses oral history and ethnographic approaches in her writing, creating plays that are embedded within community and local lived experience. Furthermore, in recent years a number of verbatim plays have emerged in Australia, created by and drawing on the lived experiences of refugees and asylum seekers (see Wake, 2010). Here, the material that is used as the basis for the dramaturgical development of the play is developed in collaboration with refugees and asylum seekers rather than being edited or written by a writer. It seems therefore that the historical development of Australian verbatim theatre has maintained a closer sense of commitment to the community-orientated practices described by Paget and has in some way resisted being co-opted entirely by the shift towards 'national "controversy"' type plays (Paget, 1987: 322). By viewing the historical development of verbatim theatre in Australia, alongside the historiographical accounts of its development in the UK, it becomes possible to recognise the many different histories and intersections of this form of theatre. These interconnecting histories also go some way to explaining the different kinds of discourses that have become associated with this form of theatre, particularly in relation to how verbatim theatre engages with acts of truth telling and how the truths of this form of theatre are verified and authenticated through the different forms of dramaturgies adopted. While, community-orientated verbatim theatre practices and playwright-led processes have been influential to the development of this form of theatre, many historical accounts of verbatim theatre centre on the influence of the Tricycle tribunal plays of the early 1990s (see Reinelt, 2006; Lane, 2010; Carlson, 2018), in which the playwright, and any sense of collective authorship, is structurally replaced with the reactivation of documentary material. However, while tribunal theatre is often viewed as playing a highly significant role in the development of verbatim theatre practices, it is a form of theatre that arguably produces very different modes of truth telling when com-pared to community-led verbatim practices or even to the writer-led verbatim plays that explored national controversies and wider political issues.

The Tricycle tribunal plays: Juridical verbatim performance

Rooted in a collaboration between theatre and journalism, the Tricycle tribunal plays addressed 'perceived miscarriages of justice and flaws in the operations and accountability of public institutions' (Megson, 2011: 195) by reanimating juridical processes and drawing on documentary evidence to interrogate key political events and the legalistic processes that investigated them. Many of the Tricycle tribunal plays were created by *The Guardian* newspaper journalist Richard Norton-Taylor and Nicholas Kent, the Tricycle's artistic director at that time. However, the tribunal form was also adopted by other journalists-cum-playwrights, such as Gillian Slovo and Victoria Brittain who wrote *Guantanamo* (2004) together, with Slovo writing *The Riots* (2011) independently. The tribunal format proved to be a highly productive mode of theatre making and, between 2004 and 2012, ten tribunal plays were written and produced at the Tricycle Theatre.[3] Although these plays are often all grouped together as 'tribunal theatre' (see, for example, Brittain, Kent, Norton-Taylor and Slovo, 2014), some plays drew on a different dramaturgical approach to the one adopted in the Norton-Taylor/Kent collaborations. For example, both *Guantanamo* and *The Riots* draw from spoken evidence taken from a series of interviews researched in the process of writing of the play, rather than from transcribed text from court proceedings (see, for example, Brittain, Kent, Norton-Taylor and Slovo, 2014). By editing together interview material and placing this alongside the reiterated speeches of politicians, these two plays arguably inaugurate their own tribunal process by interrogating different witnesses who have some experience of the events the plays examine. The claims of veracity associated with these plays tend to be framed by debates about what kind of juridical material is reiterated, how sources are sought and elicited and what kind of editorial work has been undertaken by the writer. While some have accused these plays of lacking dramatic invention and being too iterative in their form, others have praised the editorial skill of the writer, viewing the process of selecting and editing material as a form of dramaturgy itself. While acknowledging the success and timeliness of the tribunal play *The Colour of Justice* (1999), Janelle Reinelt is critical of the way the play so closely reiterates the juridical material it presents, arguing that the 'dialogue was based strictly on the transcripts, and the acting was representational and understated in style and function' (Reinelt, 2006: 80). Correlatively, writing about the same play, David Hare praises Norton-Taylor's editorial skills describing his approach as accomplishing 'precisely what an artist does' (Hare, 2007: 77). These somewhat paradoxical responses to the use of reiterated juridical texts in tribunal theatre are illustrative of the criticisms of anti-theatricalism that are often levelled at verbatim theatre in general and at tribunal theatre specifically. For while tribunal theatre is understood as providing a potent form of dissemination of key issues and new facts relating to a specific current event, like verbatim theatre, it is also perceived as lacking drama and is thus accused of simply re-presenting pre-existing material.

Historically, however, the tribunal theatre form was not always under-stood in these terms. While the Tricycle tribunal plays that emerged in the early 1990s were widely regarded as a new form of political theatre, this was not the first time theatre making had engaged with these kinds of tribunal processes. As discussed in Chapter 1, many of the German documentary plays emerging in the 1960s had centred around investigatory processes of real political and historical events, and many of these plays also drew on material gathered from trials and other juridical processes. Writing about the documentary plays emerging at this time, Laureen Nussbaum argues that the tribunal form owes its efficacy to the fact that it operates simultaneously on two levels. Firstly, it presents factual material about the case being examined by the play '[constituting] a history lesson for the young uninitiated'; secondly, and concurrently, it engages audiences with the 'tribunal's dealing with [the] case', encouraging the audience 'to evaluate the pronouncements of the witnesses, attorneys, and judges along with those of the accused' (Nussbaum, 1981: 240). In this sense, the tribunal theatre of the 1960s sought to interrogate rather than simply represent the juridical processes it examined. In so doing, these tribunal plays could offer a new perspective not only on the juridical processes examined in the course of the play, but on the events that were examined by the inquiry itself.

In his discussion of documentary theatre, Peter Weiss argues that although 'documentary theatre can take the shape of a tribunal', plays based on trials and other legalistic procedures do not 'pretend to vie in authenticity' with the actual juridical inquiries themselves (Weiss, [1968] 1995: 142). Similarly, while today's documentary theatre can call historical and political protagonists to account and interrogate real events, its potency, I suggest, does not rest on its capacity to faithfully reproduce the juridical processes that it represents. Rather, when documentary theatre enacts a form of tribunal examination, as Weiss suggests, it explores the juridical process itself – firstly, by critiquing the legal process, showing 'the hearings from points of views which were not presented at the original trial' (Weiss, [1968] 1995: 142), and, secondly, by penetrating and further examining the events that are debated within the actual trials. In this way, tribunal theatre '[introduces] the public into the heart of the proceedings, which is impossible in the real courtroom; it places the spectator on an equal footing with the accused or the accuser; it can enable him to sit on a Commission of Inquiry; it can contribute to the understanding of inter-related phenomena or else provoke an attitude of maximum opposition' (Weiss, [1968] 1995: 142).

In this sense, I would suggest, it is the focus on an interrogation and examination of both the juridical process itself and the events the play examines, through the incorporation of forms of dramatic invention, that marks a distinction between the tribunal theatre of the 1960s and the tribunal plays that emerged in the 1990s. While the German tribunal plays of the 1960s intervened within the material that was represented in the course of the play, contemporary tribunal plays tend to be structured around the promise of an edited but word-for-word replication of a juridical process. While *Half the Picture* (1994) made use of some additional material and monologues written by the playwright John McGrath, the dramaturgical construction of the play – like most of the other tribunal plays created by Nicholas Kent and/or Richard Norton-Taylor – centres around a faithful reiteration of inquiry transcripts. In this sense, while the tribunal plays of the 1990s make use of verbatim theatre-making strategies, by reproducing every vocal hesitation and every 'err' and 'mmm' recorded in the transcript, the dramaturgical process underpinning the writing of these plays centres crucially on the reanimation of a *pre-existing* document (i.e. an inquiry transcript). This, I would suggest, positions this form of tribunal theatre as part of the documentary tradition, rather than as a form of verbatim theatre. Furthermore, by establishing its dramaturgy on the replication of pre-existing transcripts of a trial or public inquiry, unlike verbatim theatre, contemporary tribunal theatre ultimately does not establish its own narrative trajectory. Instead, it reconstructs a pre-existing structure that was first established by the juridical process, just as they were originally transcribed. While it is true to say that the reiteration and reanimation of a transcribed juridical process can imbue the re-enactment of a juridical process with a certain poignancy and criticality, arguably this approach delimits the scope for a critical interrogation of the material by the playwright, and this sets contemporary tribunal theatre apart from the tribunal theatre of the 1960s. It is this important distinction between the dramaturgical approaches adopted in the tribunal plays of the 1960s, as exemplified by Weiss's *The Investigation*, and the use of reiterated material from public inquiries in contemporary tribunal theatre that Edgar fails to recognise when he conflates verbatim and documentary theatre practices together and characterises verbatim theatre as evidencing a 'conscious evasion' of the playwright to intervene dramatically within the issues examined (Edgar, 2008).

As suggested above, the use of spoken evidence as opposed to transcribed juridical material in Slovo's and Brittain's tribunal plays establishes a different dramaturgical approach to Norton-Taylor's and Kent's plays, arguably locating *Guantanamo* and *The Riots* in the realm of a verbatim theatre-making tradition. However, by conflating different types of tribunal dramaturgies together under the term 'verbatim', the distinctive features of these two tribunal dramaturgical processes are lost. We see evidence of this in the introductory essay to the anthology of tribunal plays edited by Brittain, Kent, Norton-Taylor and Slovo (2014). Here, *The Guardian* newspaper theatre critic Michael Billington focuses his attention not on contemporary forms of tribunal theatre, but on the growing popularity of *verbatim* theatre, a genre which he traces back to Peter Weiss's *The Investigation* in 1965 and Eric Bentley's *Are You Now or Have You Ever Been?* in 1971, a documentary play that examines the anti-communist 'showbusiness' investigations of the Un-American Activities Committee from 1947–56. Furthermore, in the transcribed roundtable discussion that follows, Kent, Norton-Taylor, Slovo and the playwright David Edgar again focus on a discussion of verbatim rather than tribunal theatre practices. Other than a casual reference by Edgar to 'interview plays', 'Tribunal plays' and 'trial plays' (Edgar in Brittain, Kent, Norton-Taylor and Slovo, 2014: 38), there is little other distinction made between the different dramaturgical approaches that have created the plays included within this edited collection. This conflation of verbatim and tribunal theatre is not limited to this publication and reveals the way these different dramaturgical forms tend to get gathered together and described using the same kinds of labels and definitions. However, by failing to recognise the distinctiveness of verbatim and tribunal theatre, the truth claims associated with these different dramaturgical approaches also become conflated and, as such, are subjected to generic criteria that renders these claims somewhat ambiguous and fluid. For while certain dramaturgical approaches are established upon the word-for-word reiteration of pre-existing text, this approach does not necessarily affirm the testimonial truth or the factual truth of a text. Correlatively, the re-enactment of courtroom proceedings does not necessarily interrogate or offer new insight into the events examined in the course of the trial or inquiry.

Of course, on one level, the categorising of plays as either tribunal or verbatim could be viewed as a simple semantic process, where these two terms are used interchangeably to describe the same sorts of practices. However, such a move ultimately obscures the important differences in these forms of theatre. This kind of conflation of terminology emerges in Carol Martin's account of 'verbatim theatre', which appeared in a *TDR* special issue on documentary theatre in 2006. Here, Martin argues that 'verbatim' is simply a British term used to describe what elsewhere is more commonly known as documentary theatre: '[i]n the U.K., she writes, 'documentary theatre is known as "verbatim theatre" because of its penchant for direct quotation' (Martin, 2006: 12). However, this account of the verbatim form not only overlooks the specific historical evolutions of verbatim theatre and its departure from documentary theatre, it also fails to acknowledge how contemporary tribunal theatre has evolved from the tribunal documentary plays of the 1960s. Martin's engagement with the semantics of verbatim and documentary theatre also reveals her somewhat dismissive attitude towards the verbatim theatre form itself, which she describes as having a 'duplicitous nature' and being 'akin to the double-dealing of television docudramas' (Martin, 2006: 14). The grounds for this accusation is that verbatim theatre – and by association, therefore, some elements of documentary theatre – fails to 'display its quotation marks' or 'its exact sources' and, consequently, as Martin argues, it 'infers great authority to moments of utterance unmitigated by an ex post facto mode of maturing memory' (Martin, 2006: 14). For Martin, then, any sense of authenticity within verbatim and documentary theatre derives not from the truth claims that are asserted by the play itself, but rather from its reliance on 'moments of utterance' and the reminiscences of unreliable witnesses. Arguably, however, this perspective overlooks what exactly constitutes authenticity in verbatim theatre and reveals something of the much-debated, fluid and somewhat slippery discourses of truthfulness, authority and replication that are adopted to define, understand and interrogate this form of theatre.

Verbatim theatre's promise of authenticity

The term 'authenticity' is often adopted, not only as a qualitative descriptor of verbatim theatre, but also as a distinguishing element of it. Often used to describe the facticity and truthfulness of this kind of work, authenticity in this context tends to be used to denote the use of real stories, real events and real personal narratives in the dramaturgy of verbatim theatre. Deirdre Heddon, for example, argues that it is the claim of authenticity and the troubling connotations of truth associated with it that come to ultimately define verbatim theatre:

> The use of the term 'verbatim' serves to align it with some notion of the 'authentic' and 'truthful'. 'Verbatim' and indeed 'documentary,' or even 'autobiography,' operate as signifiers that propose a relationship of veracity to the supposed facts and it is this relationship to 'truth' that makes these performances so potentially powerful. (Heddon, 2009: 117)

Similarly, Hare, who tends to use the term 'factual' rather than 'verbatim' theatre, argues that the potency of this form of theatre is its capacity to 'offer authentic news of overlooked thought and feeling' by 'using real people' as a basis for a new and reinvigorated realism (Hare, 2005: 112–13). Writing from an Australian context, Michael Anderson and Linden Wilkinson make a similar point, positioning verbatim theatre as an approach that 'provides a platform for diverse, authentic voices, unheard in popular media' (Anderson and Wilkinson, 2007: 154). However, unlike Heddon, Anderson and Wilkinson do not view this authentic quality of verbatim theatre as an alignment with truth and fact; rather, they argue that the claims of 'authenticity rest now on the credibility of its stories rather than the verbatim recounting of interviews undertaken in a research process' (Anderson and Wilkinson, 2007: 155). Yet within these different accounts of the authenticity of verbatim theatre, there remains some ambiguity about what 'authenticity' denotes in this context. There are several reasons for this. Firstly, there are many different dramaturgical forms of verbatim theatre making and consequently terms such as 'truthfulness' and 'authenticity' come to mean quite different things in different plays. Secondly, the term 'authenticity' is itself a somewhat slippery term that is much debated, describing very different qualities and meanings in different contexts. Authenticity, both as a value and a concept, has received much critical attention in recent years and has been examined across a wide range of scholarly disciplines. Writing about authenticity in relation to contemporary theatre, Daniel Schulze (2017) describes the term as denoting a structure of feeling associated with a 'longing' for some lost sense of 'sincerity, truth [or] reality' (Schulze, 2017: 14). In the context of theatre making, Schulze suggests the search for the authentic is a desire for something 'real' and is symptomatic of a loss of faith in fiction and a yearning 'for something more genuine than the economy of make-believe' (Schulze, 2017: 1). Conceptually, then, authenticity references the ideas of truth, authorship, authority and verification, while also denoting an existential element of being-in-the-world, in the sense of 'being genuine' or being in some way 'true to oneself'.

An etymological account of 'authenticity' reveals the roots of some of these different connotations. Tracing the term back to Classical Greek brings us to the word *authentikos* from which we get the connotation of 'being true, real or genuine' (Schulze, 2017: 15). However, the later Latin term *authenticus* has a slightly different connotation because it was used to describe 'documents believed to be written by authorities themselves' (Schulze, 2017: 15). In her discussion of authenticity in relation to aesthetics, cultural theorist Susanne Knaller argues that the twentieth-century usage of the term emerges from the 'interplay between two developments': the first deriving from the 'philosophy and aesthetics of the 18th and 19th centuries (*sincerity, naïveté, truth*)' and the second 'from metaphors or abstractions originating in juridical, philological and theological discourses (authorized, in reference to an author, certified)' (Knaller, 2012: 25). In the context of aesthetics, authenticity has also been theorised as being something of an illusion and paradoxical, since while the term appears to promise something singular and irreproducible, the very art practices that are described as 'authentic' tend to conceal the mimetic, representational practices that also mark them out as art. This account of the authenticity of art posits the concept of authenticity as possessing some form of transcendent quality that ultimately relies on 'an abstract and conceptual notion of truth' (Knaller, 2012: 26). In her examination of what she describes as the paradox of authenticity, cultural theorist Julia Straub examines what she describes as 'the double bind of the authentic' (Straub, 2012: 10), drawing attention to the way that the term authenticity 'sends off signals both of immediacy and mediation, genuineness and performance, spontaneity and staging' (Straub, 2012: 10). It is arguably within the loci of this 'double bind' that verbatim theatre finds itself situated: for while verbatim is defined by its capacity to be authentic, its techniques also conceal the mimetic functions that reproduce the authentic material they represent.

The discourses of authenticity associated with verbatim theatre tend to circulate around two interconnecting 'promises' that disclose different kinds of truth claims. Firstly, as theatre critic Michael Billington argues, verbatim theatre promises to present audiences with 'a source of (relatively) uncontaminated truth' and 'the bracing stimulus of fact' (Billington, 2012); secondly, it is a form of theatre that represents 'real' people who are expected to be sincere and genuine in what they say and whose personal narratives are assumed to reveal the underlying truths of an event. Underpinning these different promises is an acknowledgment that a verbatim play is not a work of fiction and that the process of verbatim theatre writing is in some way a move away from the fictional devices of dramatic theatre. Indeed, some creators of verbatim drama, such as the journalist Richard Norton-Taylor, do not even describe themselves as playwrights, preferring instead the title of 'editors' – someone who is not writing a play as such, but is marshalling pre-existing researched text into a play-like form. Philip Ralph, who is credited as the writer rather than the 'editor' of the verbatim play *Deep Cut* (2008), argues that the verbatim theatre form was simply the most suitable and truthful means to write about the deaths at the Deepcut barracks in Surrey and its subsequent closure. While verbatim theatre 'is not "truth"', he argues it is 'certainly as close as we are going to get in the theatre to the "truth"' (Ralph, 2008: 23). For Ralph, it was the promise of an authentic and truthful engagement with the complex issues surrounding the deaths at

Deepcut that 'dictated the form in which it should be told' (Ralph, 2008:
23). In this sense, for Ralph, as for many other theatre practitioners,
verbatim theatre's promise of authenticity is validated by its capacity to
offer some form of unmediated access and insight into a situation. The
'authenticity' of verbatim theatre then points to its capacity not only to
be factual, but to excavate 'hidden truths' and reveal narratives that have
not been disseminated by the media. This brings into focus another
connotation associated with the concept of 'authenticity' – its capacity
to denote an existential truthfulness. Here the term 'authenticity' does
not simply denote a factual truth, it also addresses a normative ideal in
relation to selfhood; the possibility of exhibiting the qualities associated
with being genuine and sincere.

In his book *On Being Authentic* (2004), the philosopher Charles Guignon
argues 'the basic assumption built into the ideal of authenticity is that,
lying within each individual, there is a deep, "true self" – the "Real Me",
and it is this possibility of identifying and being true to a "real, inner
self" that [makes] the person a unique individual' (Guignon, 2004: 6).
However, the claim that it is possible to possess some form of a hidden
'real' self that can be discoverable in some way and that can exist independently or beyond the discourses by which we know ourselves and
the world around us is deeply problematic. For this reason, other philosophical positions have sought to define the existential element of
authenticity somewhat differently. The philosopher Martin Heidegger,
for example, rejects the idea of selfhood being constructed around the
concept of a realisable life narrative or as a concept of coherence and
unity and, as Taylor Carman suggests, dismisses 'any such ideal of total
self-realization, self-actualisation, or completion' (Carman, 2003: 266).
Rather, for Heidegger, the self is understood as 'an essentially social
phenomenon' (Carman, 2003: 267) that exists only in relation with others
and within a world structurally marked out as being-with others. As
such, it is impossible for Heidegger to conceive of a self that exists outside
of the sociality of the world. 'Authenticity', in Heideggerian thought, is
not about being true to an imagined, hidden or inner self; rather it is an
existential state of being that flourishes when we come to terms with the
finitude of our life and our 'thrownness' into the world.[4] In Heideggerian
terms, authenticity is viewed in distinction to being *inauthentic*, denoting
a mode of being that he describes as a 'forerunning resoluteness' towards
death (Carman, 2003: 276) – by which he refers to that *mode of being* in
which *Dasein*[5] is *'toward* its death' (Heidegger quoted in Carman, 2003:
268; original emphasis).

While in the context of verbatim theatre, the term 'authenticity' tends
to denote a form of truthfulness and verification, the more existential

meaning of the term 'authenticity' also has some traction here. While the dramaturgical structure of verbatim theatre promises various degrees of truthfulness and facticity, arguably it is the representation of real people whose lived experiences give meaningful insight into certain events that makes the promise of authenticity in this form of theatre so compelling. In the dramaturgical context of the verbatim play, the 'authentic' verbatim witness then comes to be dramaturgically constructed somewhat differently from other more emblematic characters, such as representatives of the state or bureaucratic officials. Rather than using their words simply as factual evidence to verify a particular version of an event, the presence of these 'authentic' verbatim characters tends to be constructed around personal testimony, personal recollection and other personal responses to the event the play is examining. I am thinking here, by way of an example, of the characters Des and Doreen James in Ralph's play *Deep Cut*, who are the parents of Cheryl James who was shot and killed at Deepcut barracks. Des and Doreen, as they are known in the play, are constructed differently and with greater psychological and narrative detail than the other more emblematic characters, such as the journalist Brian Cathcart or Nicholas Blake QC, who authored the Deepcut Review. Both Cathcart and Blake emerge as characters who lead the action of the play through the more procedural elements of the story, with Blake representing the state's somewhat flawed response to the deaths at the Deepcut barracks and Cathcart exposing the elements of the case that were badly handled or covered up by the army and the police. Similarly, in Blank and Jensen's *The Exonerated* (2002), the characters of Delbert, Sunny, Robert, Gary, Kerry and David – the six 'exonerated' individuals we meet in the play – are also constructed very differently and with closer, personal detail and psychological cohesion than the more emblematic characters: White Guard, Robert's Judge or Kerry's Prosecutor. The 'authentic' witnesses whose stories penetrate the lived experience of the issues examined in the course of the play are therefore often dramaturgically constructed to be more immediately empathic characters, whose personal narratives are written and performed in such a way that it generates a point of direct and emotional connection with the audience.

The claim of authenticity in relation to verbatim theatre, then, does not only refer to the content of the play and the means by which an account of an event is verified and authorised. It also denotes how verbatim characters are constructed and how certain modes of address are adopted to perform a certain mode of authentic address. By this I mean that when an audience encounters a verbatim character who has lived through a critical event, their reiterated text tends not to be presented as a reiteration of facts that 'test out' or 'verify' what happened, instead, their personal testimony is used to generate a form of witnessing that establishes a direct and empathic engagement with the audience. As such, the dialogue of these witnesses is often framed not as a factual account of a past event but as intimate narrative of a lived experience. Often staged within domestic contexts, this kind of verbatim personal testimony lends the narrative an intimate and very personal quality. We see this in Ralph's play in a scene when Doreen recounts the moment when she first learned of her daughter's death:

> DOREEN: I was doing some flower arrangements and the doorbell rang and there was an Army officer and a policeman and I didn't know what it was, you just – you think – nothing had registered – anyway, I said come in. 'Mrs James?' What's the problem? 'I'm afraid we can't tell you,' he said. 'Where's your husband?' I said he's in work. What is it? Is it Cheryl? 'I'm sorry, we can't say anything. We have to inform your husband'. It's Cheryl isn't it? Something's happened to Cheryl … (Ralph, 2008: 52)

In this context, the act of bearing witness becomes a speech act that is self-authenticating, not because it tests out or verifies what others have reported or seen, but because it addresses what has been lived through and because it is structured to convey an intimate sense of empathic connection with a real person. Of course, this is not to suggest that every verbatim character who provides a personal, narrative of the past is necessarily positioned as this kind of 'authentic' witness. What I am arguing here is that it is the promise of an engagement with this kind of witnessing and this form of performance that informs the discourses of authenticity associated with verbatim theatre. The promise of authenticity that verbatim theatre seems to offer its audiences then is premised on the possibility of a direct empathic encounter with a witness. This arguably emerges from a longing for a more direct and emotionally driven engagement with a character who appears, in some vital way, to be real, free from artifice and, crucially, performed without evidence of the actor's use of the fictive, representational devices of characterisation.

Performing authenticity through the use of direct address

One of the ways this promise of authenticity is enacted in verbatim theatre is through the use of direct address; a mode of performance where the verbatim actor adopts a character and speaks directly the

audience. Direct address, which has become something of a distinguishing element of verbatim theatre, has a long history in theatre making
with its origins tracing back to the use of soliloquy in Medieval and
Shakespearean theatre (see Hirsch, 2003).[6] Its centrality in contemporary
verbatim theatre, however, is arguably traceable not to the soliloquies of
fictional theatre, but to forms of direct address adopted in the didactic
and agit prop theatre that developed in the early years of the twentieth
century by companies such as the Blue Blouse, or the Living Newspaper
projects, developed in Russia and then later by America's Federal Theatre
Project (FTP). In these forms of political theatre, direct address was
adopted largely to enact a mode of objectivity by allowing an actor to
comment on the action and to draw attention to the socio-political context
that framed the events explored in the play. Direct address was also a
means of working against the various tropes of naturalism that sought to
transform the actor into the character being performed and to structurally render invisible the representational process of acting itself. Rather
than constructing psychologically coherent characters, direct address
was a means of generating what Derek Paget aptly describes as, 'instant
characterisation where a character was signified at a "kind of emblematic
level"' (Paget, 1990: 64). As explored above in my discussion of *Waiting
Room Germany*, this emblematic form of characterisation continues
to be adopted at various point in many contemporary verbatim and
documentary dramas, particularly where actors take on several different
characters and move seamlessly from one role to the next. It is most
often employed when a character is introduced to represent a particular
perspective or viewpoint but whose spoken text does not comprise personal
life-narrative material. However, as discussed above, while many forms of
documentary and verbatim plays incorporate direct address in this way, in
some forms of verbatim and in testimonial and autobiographical theatre,
direct address is used to generate psychologically coherent characters.
In this sense, while direct address can be adopted to suggest a degree
of objectivity, it is also used (and often within the same play) for the
opposite effect, to generate a form of direct, empathic engagement with an
audience.

As discussed in Chapter 1, some of the earliest examples of the use of
direct address to create emblematic characters is evident in the early
political theatre of Erwin Piscator. Like the agit prop theatre that preceded
this, Piscator's theatre tended to make use of direct address to convey a
sense of objectivity and facticity in relation to the material the play
addressed. Regarding this as a means of making theatre 'dedicated to a
scientific objectivity' (Innes, 1972: 75), Piscator used placards, film and
other stage techniques to re-enact contemporary and historical events

while often employing direct address to provide a commentary on these events through the use of a narrator, resonant of the 'figure of the storyteller, the compère' (Innes, 1972: 105). The use of simultaneous acting spaces in his productions also enabled Piscator to move the action between the re-enactment of key historical events, the depiction of the everyday lives of working people and an on-going commentary on the connections between these issues and events by way of a narration. In his production of *War and Peace* (1955), for example, the character of Pierre re-enacted 'battles' by demonstrating 'tactics with toy soldiers' while also stepping out of the action to address the audience and comment on these battles, acting more '"as a lecturer"' than a dramatic character (Innes, 1972: 105). For Piscator, then, direct address was a means of creating more objective characters and signalled a move away from the construction of character determined by individual psychology.

Similar political and dramaturgical intentions were expressed by Bertolt Brecht who often employed direct address in his plays and wrote about this in his accounts of his version of epic theatre and its use of *verfremdungseffekt*.[7] However, for Brecht, the use of direct address appears to have been less about framing the objectivity and facticity of the material being presented and more to do with the process of generating a style of acting that could elicit a critical, as opposed to an empathic, response from audiences. Turning away from acting approaches adopted in forms of naturalism that encouraged actors to be 'transformed' in some way into the character being enacted, Brecht advocated the establishment of a critical distance between the actor and the character being enacted that would work against the production of empathy in the audience. He argued that an actor should 'not allow himself to become completely transformed on the stage into the character he is portraying. He is not Lear, Harpagon, Schweik; he shows them […] but he never tries to persuade himself (and thereby others) that this amounts to a complete transformation' (Brecht, [1940] 1964: 137). The employment of direct address allowed Brecht to establish a critical rather than empathic engagement within his audiences and reminded them that they were being addressed by actors who may or may not share the political views of the characters being represented. In a discussion of his play *Threepenny Opera*, for example, Brecht suggests that 'the spectator should not be set off down the path of empathy' (Brecht, 2015a: 75). Instead, he proposes 'a sort of communication' between the spectator and the actors that maintains a 'sense of distance and otherness', enabling the actors to 'address themselves to the spectator' (Brecht, 2015a: 75). By adopting direct address in this way the actors, Brecht argues, should also aim to 'tell the spectator more about the characters they are playing than "what it says in their part"' (Brecht, 2015a: 75).

However, as I have examined above, in many examples of contemporary verbatim theatre, direct address is also adopted not to establish a critical distance between audience and character, but to operate as a form of realism and to generate an almost hyper-real representation of a real person. There is some historical precedence here, for as Duška Radosavljević argues, there is an element of the verbatim theatre tradition that can be traced back to Stanislavski's use of 'ethnographic research' (Radosavljević, 2013: 132) and his desire to represent real people as truthfully as possible. Radosavljević draws attention to Stanislavski's approach to the direction of Gorky's play *The Lower Depths* (1902), in which he also starred, where Stanislavski encouraged members of the Moscow Arts Theatre to '[interview] Moscow's homeless people' as part of the rehearsal process (Radosavljević, 2013: 131). Gorky's play was not documentary of course, nor did it use direct address. However, this use of ethnographic research is certainly resonant of the way many contemporary verbatim processes draw on the genre of realism in performance, and Gorky's *The Lower Depths* in 1902 was a key reference point within Russian social realism that developed in the early part of the twentieth century (Worrall, 1996).[8]

The use of direct address in contemporary verbatim theatre, then, draws from two different genres of theatre making: epic forms of theatre making influenced by Brecht and Piscator and forms of social realism that draw on more psychologically coherent approaches to acting, such as those developed by Stanislavski. The employment of direct address as a means of conferring a sense of realism on a play has today become an element of verbatim theatre that further distinguishes it from documentary theatre traditions. As Derek Paget argues, in documentary theatre there is 'a historical tendency towards the non-naturalist' and these plays tend to '[favour] a two-dimensional presentation that habitually seeks breadth of content rather than depth of character psychology' (Paget, 2010: 181). The characterisation that tends to be used in tribunal theatre is a good example of this. Tribunal characters often lack psychological depth and nuance, not least because the dialogue tends to have been shaped almost entirely by the language and lexicon of a legalistic, tribunal process. However, in verbatim theatre, where the material being presented has been gathered not from documents but from interviews that were commissioned specifically for the theatre-making process itself, direct address is often adopted to create rounded, three-dimensional characters who speak to the audience directly. This hyper-real style of performance is evident in the pioneering verbatim theatre performances of the American actress and playwright Anna Deavere Smith who, in her solo verbatim performances, draws on interviews and other empirical research to recreate numerous real individuals from different backgrounds, cultures and ethnicities in order to explore key political issues and events of the time. It is arguably through her very careful replication of the gestures and speech patterns of everyday, real people that Smith is able to move seamlessly from one character to the next within each of her plays, producing a style of performance that has been very influential to the development of characterisation in many forms of contemporary verbatim theatre. I return to a more extended discussion of Smith's performance work and her production of *Notes from the Field* (2016) in Chapter 4, but move on now to consider a mode of verbatim performance that has been directly developed in response to Smith's influence in this area.

Direct address and headphone theatre

This use of direct address to create hyper-real characterisation has become an essential element of a form of verbatim theatre that in Australia, following the work of Rosyln Oades, tends to be known as 'headphone verbatim theatre' and in the UK, through the work of Alecky Blythe, is better known as 'recorded delivery'. Both these writers create a form of verbatim theatre in which actors wear headphones or some other audio feed 'throughout the performance, via which they are fed a carefully edited audio-script constructed from recorded interviews' (Oades, 2010: 84). Director Mark Wing Davey is credited as initially learning this technique from Anna Deavere Smith 'whose first ensemble show, *House Arrest*, he directed in 1998' (Blythe, 2008: 80). Later dubbed 'recorded delivery' by Blythe, it was an approach that Wing Davey explored at a workshop he called 'Drama Without Paper', which was attended by Blythe and Roslyn Oades in the early 2000s and which seeded an approach these two practitioners both went on to develop in new forms of verbatim theatre making. Blythe's first recorded delivery production was *Come Out Eli* (Arcola, 2003), a play that drew on interview material gathered from Blythe's local community in Hackney in East London where, in 2002/2003, Eli Hall blockaded himself into his bedsit precipitating a fifteen-day siege with the police. Following the success of this play, Blythe went on to set up her theatre company Recorded Delivery, which has subsequently created numerous headphone-based plays, including *London Road* (2011), a musical that used verbatim material as a libretto and which explored the murder of six sex workers by a serial killer in Ipswich in 2006. Having also attended Wing Davey's workshop in 2001, Roslyn Oades, continued working with 'Wing-Davey's company

Non-Fiction Theatre for another two years' (Wake, 2014: viii), before moving back to Australia and writing several headphone theatre verbatim plays including: *Fast Cars and Tractor Engines* (2005), *Stories of Love and Hate* (2008) and *I'm Your Man* (2012). Her first headphone play *Fast Cars and Tractor Engines* made use of oral history approaches and was initially developed as 'part of the Bankstown Youth Development Services' Oral History Project' (Wake, 2014: viii), a youth project based in an area of Sydney that houses a number of immigrant communities. *Fast Cars and Tractor Engines* explores the themes of migrancy, personal courage and survival by exploring the stories of those living in the Bankside area of Sydney.

In an insightful article about the evolution of headphone theatre, Caroline Wake examines the work of Blythe and Oades, drawing attention to how headphone performance changes depending on the material the play is examining and the style of performance the dramaturgy of the play demands. While the use of headphones or other audio input creates the sensation of a form of distance or alienation, in some instances, as Wake argues, the close reiteration of the vocal patterns and tics of the original verbatim subjects and the use of direct address lends the performance a potent form of authenticity. In this sense, headphone verbatim theatre makes use of both epic and naturalistic modes of performance and, as Wake argues, 'when in the *epic* mode, headphone verbatim aims for verbal authenticity and visual alienation' and 'when in the *naturalistic* mode, it aims for both verbal and visual authenticity' (Wake, 2013a: 327). What this useful analysis of headphone verbatim theatre highlights is how the somewhat fluid and changeable claims of authenticity associated with verbatim theatre largely depend on the dramaturgical structure of the play and the way characterisation is structured. I would argue that all verbatim theatre tends to appear in some way as authentic and real when an accurate rendition of another person's narrative is represented with a great deal of attention paid to the detail of the vocal tics and inconsistencies of everyday speech. However, the performance of authenticity is also determined by the dramaturgy that is adopted in the writing of the play and how, therefore, the use of direct address is constructed and delivered. As Wake's analysis of headphone theatre illustrates, for most contemporary audiences, a more naturalistically written script is more likely to generate a sensation of authenticity than a script generated around the structural principles of epic theatre. This suggests that playwrights can ultimately make certain characters appear more or less 'authentic' simply by the way they are written and as a result of the kinds of details included in the dialogue. Furthermore, many verbatim plays adopt what Wake describes as 'mixed modes' (Wake, 2013a: 329) of performance, making use of techniques developed in epic theatre and drawing these together alongside characterisation structured and performed around forms of naturalism and social realism. As a consequence, it is the authorial perspective of the playwright that possesses the capacity to confer a form of authenticity on the narratives performed within verbatim theatre, since it is the playwright who determines what stories and what voices are represented and how these characters are depicted. Of course, these different modes of performance also generate very different forms of spectatorship. While audiences might adopt a somewhat critically distanced stance in relation to a more emblematic, two-dimensional character, they are likely to be drawn, or manipulated even, towards an empathic response when engaging with a more psychologically coherently structured character who is sharing a poignant personal story.

By moving beyond epic theatre's use of direct address to generate objective and emblematic characters, contemporary verbatim theatre makers use direct address to generate characters that audiences feel empathically connected to. While Brecht encouraged his actors to establish a 'sense of distance and otherness' (Brecht, 2015a: 75) when directly addressing their audience, contemporary directors of verbatim theatre are more likely to encourage their actors to imagine addressing particular others when speaking directly to the audience. Consequently, verbatim theatre audiences can find themselves nominally being 'cast' as a character in the drama by the actor addressing them. Largely determined by the structure, content and style of the play, this process of 'casting' the audience also aligns the spectator with the authorial perspective of the writer or director who also constructs the dramaturgy of play text itself. In this sense, the use of direct address becomes an effective way of predetermining an audience's response to a play and predetermining the mode of spectatorship generated in its performance. Direct address can therefore be used to elicit a sense of commitment or responsibility from audiences who are appealed to emotionally by psychologically real characters that address them directly. In this way, direct address becomes a means of directing the audience's sympathy not only through the selection and editing of the play's text, but by the way character is created and how character narratives are emotionally framed and performed. It is the exploitative potential of this form of direct address, I suggest, that has largely contributed to the criticisms of verbatim theatre being 'duplicitous' (Martin, 2006: 14) or 'doubly illusory' (Bottoms, 2006: 59). For while some documentary and verbatim theatre makers do 'foreground their own processes of representation' and in so doing 'encourage audiences to adopt an actively critical perspective on the events depicted' (Bottoms, 2006: 61), the process of instilling this 'model of reflexivity' (Bottoms, 2006: 61) into the dramaturgy of a play does not necessarily determine how characters are enacted nor how direct address is employed and delivered. In order to think further about how direct address can be used to predetermine audience responses, I want to consider its use in the play *My Name Is Rachel Corrie* (Rickman and Viner, 2005). Not only does this play carefully structure the audience's emotional engagement with the material it examines, in so doing the dramaturgy of the play also delimits and potentially closes down critical responses to the political situation it addresses.

My Name Is Rachel Corrie: A contested and problematic dramaturgy

Commissioned by the Royal Court theatre and compiled by Alan Rickman and Katharine Viner, *My Name Is Rachel Corrie* (2005) tells the story of Rachel Corrie, a young American peace activist, killed by an Israeli Defence Force bulldozer in Gaza in 2003 while involved in a protest to protect a Palestine home from being destroyed. Sitting somewhere in between verbatim and documentary theatre, the play was written after Corrie's death, created from material drawn from Corrie's 'journals and emails' (Rickman and Viner, 2005) and is performed using direct address. As a consequence, the use of documentary and testimonial strategies become somewhat entangled and audiences are unlikely to know what material has been drawn from emails and what has been taken from Corrie's journals and private writing. Directed by Alan Rickman and written as a one-woman solo play, the central character, Rachel, was played by Megan Dodds when it opened in 2005. Addressing the Israeli-Palestinian conflict while depicting an American citizen actively campaigning for the Palestinian cause meant that the play inevitably courted some political controversy, which subsequently placed a lot of pressure on Dodds as its only actor. This escalated significantly when the planned transfer of the play to the New York Theatre Workshop (NYTW) in March 2006 was unexpectedly cancelled,[9] a decision that, in Carol Martin's terms, 'generated outrage' and led to accusations of censorship with the NYTW artistic director, James Nicola, being 'accused of yielding to pressure from pro-Israeli Jewish individuals and groups' (Martin, 2013: 143). This 'worldwide storm of protest' (Martin, 2013: 143) precipitated by the cancellation of the play was, of course, mainly a result of the issues the play addresses and its criticisms of the Israeli government. However, I would suggest that the dramaturgical structure of the play and the way it used direct address also contributed to the strong but mixed responses the play elicited and the disputes that surrounded it.

The play's dramatic action is framed around the personal and political journey of its protagonist, Rachel, who travels to Gaza propelled by a personal response to the injustices suffered by the Palestinians. As the different material used in the play, which was gathered posthumously, moves fluidly between Rachel's political response to the situation in Gaza and other more personal reflections from her journal, the dramaturgy fuses the political situation in Palestine with the life, aspirations and tragic death of this bright young American woman. Direct address is used here then not to establish any objectivity about the political issues the play examines, but is adopted to generate an empathic and direct connection with Rachel herself, who is dramaturgically constructed as a carefully drawn, psychologically coherent and fully rounded character. As such, it is Rachel's personal decision and motivations that frame the political focus of the play and its inexorable journey to the tragic conclusion. The direct and empathic connection forged between Rachel and the audience, through the use of direct address, operates so that the play in effect comes to be more about Rachel's life and death than about the situation she was protesting about. As Michael Billington points out in his review of the play, when it opened at the Royal Court in 2005, audiences felt that they '[had] not just had a night at the theatre: [they had] encountered an extraordinary woman' (Billington, 2005a). As a result, the play leaves little room for any critical engagement with the issues it examines and somewhat subsumes the suffering of the Palestinian people within a more direct and potent narrative of Rachel's death and the tragedy of her lost potential. As such, in many ways, the play ends up exploring the loss of this 'extraordinary' woman whose life was taken by an Israeli bulldozer, rather than the tragedy of the Palestinian people. As a consequence the play sits somewhat uncomfortably in between a political examination of the Israeli-Palestinian situation and an exploration of the life of a young and talented idealistic activist who decides to take a personal stand on an injustice. Given the play's entanglement within personal and political narratives and the emotional context of Rachel's death, made all the more potent through the use of direct address, it is perhaps no surprise that the play posed such a risk to theatre programmers and courted such political controversy.

The challenges and risks of performing direct address in this politically contentious play is discussed at length by Cantrell (2013). Drawing on interview material with Dodds, Cantrell examines how the actress responded to the challenge of the 'exclusive use of direct address' (Cantrell,

2013: 80) by developing 'new working processes in the play' (Cantrell, 2013: 83). Viewing Dodds's performance as 'a powerful act of surrogacy' (2013: 81), Cantrell considers the challenges of 'playing a person who had died' (2013: 81), while negotiating the 'ever-present' threat of an interruption of political protest aimed at the surrogate Rachel from a member of the audience (Watt-Smith quoted in Cantrell, 2013: 80). While the Royal Court's stage management team found ways of ensuring the wellbeing of Dodds during the performance by making sure she could arrive and leave the theatre safely, Dodds also decided that one response to these challenges was to mentally allocate the audience a role in the retelling of Rachel's stories. This led her to cast the audience, at least in her own mind, in the role of Rachel's friends and family. This, of course, automatically positioned the audience as allies of Rachel and critically gave Dodds some sense of security and a response to the potential threat of interruption that was feared. It also allowed Dodds to generate a more direct form of engagement with her audience, opening up more possibilities for interaction during her solo performance.

However, while this decision clearly helped Dodds to develop her performance, it also predetermined the kinds of responses the play would elicit from audiences, effectively minimising any opportunity for a critical response to any of the political issues being examined. Describing the play as a form of 'political theatre', *The Guardian* newspaper theatre critic Michael Billington praised its capacity for celebrating humanity and passionate self-sacrifice, arguing that while '[t]heatre can't change the world', *My Name Is Rachel Corrie* effectively communicates Rachel's 'passionate concern' for the issues she was protesting against (Billington, 2005a). However, this focus on humanity and the absence of politics within this play is also a source of criticism. Carol Martin, for example, suggests that *My Name Is Rachel Corrie* is a play that abdicates its political responsibility by doing little to interrogate the complexity of the Israeli-Palestine conflict, which leads Martin to argue that in their editorial role, Rickman and Viner use 'Corrie's personal narrative' as a 'diversion from the complexities of history in favour of championing one point of view' (Martin, 2013: 132). While the argument that documentary or verbatim theatre should avoid advocating one perspective over another is somewhat antithetical to the very nature of political theatre, Martin's point about the manipulation of personal narrative and the use of direct address to manipulate audience responses is important. Indeed, while direct address and Dodds's casting of the audience establishes a direct form of engagement with the audience, it is an approach that aligns spectators with the authorial perspective the play pursues and, in so doing, ultimately predetermines how audiences should respond.

What *My Name Is Rachel Corrie* usefully reveals, then, is how the use of pathos and empathic engagement can become structurally imprinted on a play, shaping its dramaturgical structure. As a consequence, I suggest, certain forms of characterisation are employed that are more empathic and directly encountered by the audience than others, and this ultimately serves to direct attention to certain perspectives and points of view over others. In the case of *My Name Is Rachel Corrie*, the issue of the Israeli-Palestinian situation becomes tied to the more personal narrative of heroism and loss personified through the play's central protagonist. As a consequence, in this play, the political issues confronted by the Palestinian people become overtaken by an emotionally charged story of an American woman's call to conscience and her tragic death. The decision to make use of this kind of approach derives from the specific methodological approach adopted when putting the play together. It is, of course, unsurprising that the play should become framed in this way, after all the material was gathered from Rachel's personal correspondence to her family and friends, comprising of 'journals, diaries, emails and letters' (Cantrell, 2013: 58). As consequence the play is intrinsically tied to the grief at Rachel's death and the story that is told enacts a testament to a daughter and sister who sacrificed her life for her beliefs. Yet, this narrative of loss and grief sits uneasily within the wider political context of the play, and as such there remains within the dramaturgical structure an uneasy alliance between the play's political engagement with the Israeli-Palestinian conflict and the story of Rachel herself.

Returning to the discussion of authenticity introduced above, I would also suggest that the use of direct address in *My Name Is Rachel Corrie* usefully reveals some of the contradictions in the way authenticity is enacted within verbatim-type plays. As I have already discussed, when the concept of authenticity is applied to verbatim theatre, it tends to denote both the claims of truthfulness and veracity of the script, and the way that certain characters in the play possess an existential grasp of the situations being examined. In *My Name Is Rachel Corrie*, the authenticity of Rachel arises both as a result of the kind of material that is edited together to form a play script and because of who she was and how this connects to what the play examines. However, what is also clear is that the authenticity of Rachel emerges in the play both because of her relationship with the events in Gaza and because of the way the character of Rachel is constructed and enacted. Of course, whether the material that has been edited together authenticates the play's truths or not is a question that must remain unanswered, because we have no access to the testimony Rachel would choose to perform had she lived. However, the integrity of Rachel's character and the significance of her insights into the situations she encountered in Gaza are signalled in the play both by the use of her personal correspondence and journal reflections and because of the way Rachel's character is written and performed. When applied to the integrity and existential quality of another person, the concept of authenticity denotes both a mode of being true to oneself and open to both the finitude of life and the inevitability of death, what, in Heideggerian terms, might be described as *being towards death*. Arguably, this mode of authentic being-in-the-world seems to be evident in the way the character of Rachel is represented in the play and how she seems resolute in the face of her own finitude and consequential death. We see evidence of this in her reflections on her own life and death, presented about three quarters of the way through the play when Rachel describes her experience of living in Rafah:

> I knew a few years ago what the unbearable lightness was, before I read the book. The lightness – between life and death, there are no dimensions at all. There are no rulers of mile-markers. It's just a shrug – the difference between Hitler and my mother, the difference between Whitney Houston and a Russian mother watching her son fall through the sidewalk and boil to death [...] And with that enormous shrug there, the shrug between being and not being – how could I be a poet? How could I believe in truth?
>
> And I knew, back then, that the shrug would happen at the end of my life – I knew. And I thought, so who cares? If my whole life is going to amount to one shrug and a shake of the head, who cares if it comes in eighty years or at 8pm? Who cares?
>
> Now, I know who cares. I know if I die at 11.15pm or at 96 years – I know. And I know it's me. That's my job. (Rickman and Viner, 2005: 35)

These comments on life and death poignantly depict Rachel reflecting on her own sense of purpose and being-in-the-world. They are made all the more haunting in the play because, as audiences, we know what the tragic ending of this story will be. Yet of course, these reflections have been carefully chosen by Rickman and Viner when constructing the play. In this sense, Rachel's authentic existence appears not simply as a result of the insights of the 'real' Rachel, but because of the dramaturgical choices of the writers and the structure of the play itself. In this sense, authenticity can be understood to be performed both through the way the character of Rachel is constructed and enacted and as a result of the choices made by the writers when editing and assembling the play's material.

Rachel's status within the play ultimately remains somewhat ambivalent. On the one hand, she is presented as a witness who lived, first-hand, the brutality of the Israeli Defence Force, and, on the other, she is also marked by a radical absence, where the play attests not to her presence but to the grief of those who mourned her loss. While the play seems to promise to speak on behalf of Rachel, it can do so only in a deferred sense and as such, the character of Rachel, reconstructed within the play, sits uneasily between the figure of the witness and as someone who is being reconstructed by others. While many forms of verbatim theatre bear witness to past events, the transformation of real people into characters, who are enacted by others, is a process that must always engage with levels of ambivalence and is a tricky negotiation of the real and the fictive. For while the enactment of interview material or personal email correspondence might usefully illuminate a situation that was experienced by another person, the replication of this text does not in itself become an act of attestation or witnessing.

In the second part of this book, I move on to consider the performance of testimony and witnessing more closely. Through an examination of different modes of testimonial performance, I consider the role of the witness both within the creative process of writing a play and in the dramaturgical structure of the play text itself. Drawing on different accounts of witnessing, I consider how a play's dramaturgical structure can foreground the presence and agency of the witness and how we might conceive of an ethical structure that enhances an understanding of the relationship between the theatre maker, the witness and the dramaturgical structure that tells the witness's story.

Notes

1 By which I mean a style of acting where 'the actor does not allow himself to become completely transformed on the stage into the character he is portraying' (Brecht, [1940] 1964: 137).

2 A posthumous collection of David Tinker's letters and poems was compiled by his father a year after his death in 1983, see Tinker, H. (ed.) (1983) *A Message From the Falklands: The Life and Gallant Death of David Tinker Lieut., R.N. From His Letters and Poems*. London: Penguin.

3 These included: *Half the Picture* (Norton-Taylor), *Nuremberg* (Norton-Taylor), *Srebrenica* (Kent), *The Colour of Justice* (Norton-Taylor), *Justifying War* (Norton-Taylor), *Guantanamo* (Slovo and Brittain), *Bloody Sunday* (Norton-Taylor), *Called to Account* (Norton-Taylor and Kent), *Tactical Questioning* (Norton-Taylor) and *The Riots* (Slovo).

4 Heidegger theorises existence as a form of 'thrownness', a term he adopts to describe the necessary and contingent nature of our existence in the world, both in terms of the social and historical context of the world we happen to be born into but did not choose, and the specific way we are compelled to be-with others. As thrown, any individual human existence takes its cue from

how 'everyone' else does things – what Heidegger terms 'das Man', translated as 'The One' (as in the expression 'one does this or that'). This conceptualisation of existence stands in stark contrast to accounts of selfhood as something that is already intrinsically individuated by a capacity for a unique self-narrative that can be completed and made whole under conditions of authenticity, but which lies hidden or buried within an individual. Although there are disputes about the nature of authenticity in Heidegger's work, it is unlikely that Heidegger viewed authentic being in the world in these narrative terms.

5 Heidegger uses the term *Dasein* (in the German 'Da-sein', literally meaning 'being there') to denote human existence, arguing that we become ourselves through our encounters with others.

6 Writing about the history of the Shakespearean soliloquy, James Hirsch argues that Western theatre makes use of three different forms of soliloquy, which he lists as: '*Audience-addressed speech*: The character (not just the actor) is aware of and speaks to the play goers. *Self-addressed speech*: The character us unaware of playgoers and speaks only to himself. *Interior monologue*: The words spoken by the actor do not represent words spoken by the character by words merely passing through the minds of the character' (Hirsch, 2003: 13). This analysis provides an interesting context for the analysis of soliloquy. However, it does not easily extend to the uses of direct address in documentary and verbatim theatre or to other forms of solo work such as autobiographical performance.

7 The term *verfremdungseffekt* was developed by Brecht in his account of his version of epic theatre. John Willet translates it as the *Alienation Effect* (see Brecht, [1940] 1964). It is a term that describes an approach to theatre making that aims 'to make the spectator adopt an attitude of inquiry and criticism' in response to the incidents a play explores (Brecht, [1940] 1964: 136).

8 For a discussion of the development of new forms of documentary and verbatim theatre in Russia from the 1990s onwards and the development of 'documentarism' that sought to work against the forms of socialist realism of the nineteenth century, see Lipovetsky and Beumers, 2008.

9 There appears to be some ambivalence about whether this was a postponement or a cancellation by the New York Theatre Workshop. As Carol Martin indicates, at the time, James Nicola, the theatre's artistic director, and Lynn Moffat, the managing director of the theatre, described it as a 'postponement' in response to current events taking place in Israel and within the United States at the time (Martin, 2013: 143). However, others viewed this postponement as a form of censorship and as evidence of a decision not to go ahead with the planned transfer.

Part II

Towards testimonial theatre

3

Theatre of witnessing: towards the decolonisation of testimonial theatre

To me 'testimonial theatre' is a genre wrought from people bearing witness to their own stories through remembrance and words. Material culled from memory is crafted into a compelling yet true narrative, which is then brought to life through text, performance and the visual devices of theatre. The essential component of this genre lies in its capacity for healing through speaking, hearing and being heard. (Farber, 2008b: 19)

In 2007, I interviewed the South African playwright and director Yaël Farber about her approach to making testimonial theatre. The interview, which appears in the publication of her trilogy of plays, *Theatre as Witness* (2008a), took place at a time when I was in the process of writing *From the Mouths of Mothers*, a verbatim play that tells the story of child sexual abuse through personal narratives told by seven mothers (Stuart Fisher, 2013). In the interview, we explored Farber's approach to testimonial work and the importance of the relationship she forges with the testimonial subjects who both act and tell their stories in her plays. It was an interesting and illuminating discussion in which I was struck by some of the key differences between the methodologies of verbatim and testimonial theatre making.

In my approach to writing *From the Mouths of Mothers* I followed a fairly typical verbatim theatre approach, drawing on interviews undertaken with seven mothers whom I had got to know through my engagement with Mosac, a charity that supports non-abusing parents and carers of sexually abused children.[1] In the process of writing the play, I edited together extracts from transcripts of the interviews with the mothers, ensuring that my final text drew only on the women's words and made use of the precise transcriptions of the interview recordings. One element of the play that was proving particularly difficult to write at the time was the moment when the mothers addressed the impact of their child's disclosure of sexual abuse. Each of the interviews had been marked by the shock of this revelation, the mothers' inability to make sense of what they were being told and their struggle to process the horror of what their child had revealed to them. For many of the mothers, this disclosure precipitated an encounter with the traumatic, with several of the interviewees receiving a diagnosis of post-traumatic stress disorder (PTSD) from their doctors. The profound impact of these disclosures radically disrupted the women's own biographical understanding of their lives, immediately forcing them to revise everything they thought they knew and understood about their family's circumstances and histories. As I tried to capture these traumatic experiences in the play, I found myself struggling to find a way of addressing what was felt by the mothers to be somehow unsayable and what therefore had not been spoken of directly in the interviews themselves. The verbatim theatre methodology I had committed to soon began to feel like a straitjacket. The decision to focus only on transcribed interview material predetermined the dramaturgical strategies available to me, and these were ones that seemed to refuse to allow space for the unsayable and the inexplicable.

As my discussions with Farber developed, a wholly different methodological approach began to emerge. Instead of having to rely on material that had been gathered during a single interview, in her testimonial theatre-making practice Farber had worked over a sustained period with the actors whose life-stories her plays examined. This had allowed her to form meaningful relationships with the testimonial subjects with whom she was working, enabling her to develop a far more integrated and collaborative working methodology than is usually available to verbatim theatre makers. In our interview, Farber described her creative process, as being 'entirely organic' (Farber, 2008b: 20), and this allowed her to engage with each testimonial subject differently. As a result, Farber was able to gain insight not only into the facts of each story being told, but also into the emotional responses each subject had in relation to their testimony and the past events they described, allowing her to explore what lay beneath the surface of what was and was not sayable. As Farber explained in her interview, the gathering of testimonial material for the play developed from this extended engagement with the cast, where the actors spent 'this period of creation in intensive interviews with [Farber]; singing childhood songs; writing letters to family members to say the unspoken; telling [her] their dreams in the mornings' (Farber, 2008b: 20). By structuring the creative process as a dialogue and as a collaborative exploration of the past, Farber, unlike a verbatim playwright, was able to unearth and forge new memories, drawing out elements of testimony that were emerging afresh, as a result of an engagement in the theatre-making process itself. With its focus on the re-enactment of only reiterated interview material, verbatim theatre tends to be stuck in a renarration of pre-formed memories of past events. In contrast to this, Farber's testimonial approach enabled her to generate a testimonial process that wove the past into the present. Her dialogical and collaborative approach enabled her to work creatively with the actors, revisiting the past in order to explore the potency of specific memories, drawing on symbolism to make connections with a wider historical narrative and with the broader politics of apartheid. While both my verbatim play and the three testimonial plays Farber created enact the witnessing of past events, their contrasting dramaturgical approaches ultimately produced very different types of testimonial practices, and it is to more fully understand what is at stake in this difference that I will now turn. While the first part of this book engaged with the new forms of verbatim theatre that emerged in the 1990s, in this chapter, which inaugurates the second part of this book, I turn my attention to an examination of different forms of testimonial theatre that have emerged in the first two decades of the twenty-first century.

   While verbatim plays often draw on testimonial accounts of past events, the witness's testimony in this form of theatre tends to be positioned alongside other forms of evidence, such as juridical proceedings, published reports and other transcribed iterative speech. Testimony in this context becomes a means of authenticating or verifying a predetermined narrative that also directs the editorial process and dramaturgy of the play as a whole. The term 'verbatim' of course describes *how* material is collected and reiterated in the course of the play, not the truth claims that are attached to it. This stands in contrast with 'testimony', a term that denotes a certain form of truth telling in relation to past events. 'Testimonial theatre', then, could be understood as describing a set of dramaturgical practices that foreground the act of witnessing itself, placing the experience of the witness at the heart of the dramaturgical process. Rather than testimony being incorporated as a means of evidencing predetermined narratives, in testimonial theatre making the truth processes that emerge from the act of attestation itself drive the dramaturgical development of the play. In this sense, in testimonial theatre practices, it is the *presence* of the witness and the act of witnessing itself that determines the play's dramaturgy. Testimonial performance does not simply narrate the past, it foregrounds the witness as an ethical presence. As such, the play-making process itself is opened up to the possibility of ethical experience and the ethical imperatives that this places upon theatre makers and their audiences.

To distinguish testimonial theatre from verbatim theatre practices, then, is to acquire a more developed understanding of what it means to 'bear witness' and how different forms of witnessing operate. For, as I shall go on to argue, not all acts of witnessing are structured around the narrative retrieval of a past event. To understand testimonial theatre practice, it is important to look beyond witnessing as a retrieval of a past event and to critique the discourses that tie the testimonial act to event-based trauma. In this sense, my engagement with contemporary testimonial theatre is also an attempt to decolonise the discourses of testimony and witnessing, which have become dominated by Euro-American perspectives and an engagement with the trauma of the Holocaust. A decolonising of testimony requires moving beyond what Michael Rothberg describes as the 'Euro-American conceptual and historical frameworks' of trauma (Rothberg, 2008: 225) that originated in trauma studies and which have underpinned discourse in the humanities, literary studies and in drama, theatre and performance. By moving testimonial theatre beyond psycho-analytical accounts of trauma and witnessing, I argue, it becomes possible to rethink and better understand the political and ethical demands of testimonial practices and the multiple modes of witnessing that shape contemporary approaches to testimonial theatre making.

The 'era of testimony': The rise of the psychoanalytic witness

In *Testimony: Crises of Witnessing in Literature, Psychoanalysis, and History* (Felman and Laub, 1992), literary theorist Shoshana Felman describes living in an era that is one 'precisely defined as the age of testimony' (Felman, 1992: 5). Published just one year before the first tribunal plays opened at the Tricycle Theatre in 1993, the influence of Felman's interventions within current approaches to thinking around witnessing and acts of attestation has been immense. Since its publication, *Testimony* has become a much-cited text both by scholars in trauma, literary and memory studies (see Caruth, 1996; Hartman, 1996; Leys, 2000) but also by a range of scholars interested in theatre's relationship with testimonial theatre practices (Martin, 2013; Wake, 2013b). The concept of witnessing that is developed in *Testimony* emerges as a result of Felman and Laub's engagement with Holocaust testimony. Conceptualising testimony as a *'speech act'* (Felman, 1992: 5; original emphasis) that is inherently performative, Felman argues that bearing witness is not simply the communication of evidence or facts, but is an action in which the witness puts themselves forward and promises, by way of an oath or pledge, to speak truthfully about what has been witnessed. Testimony, then, is distinct from documentary evidence and, as Felman argues, should not be understood as providing 'a completed statement, a totalizable account' of the event (Felman, 1992: 5). Rather, it should be understood as a 'discursive *practice'* (Felman, 1992: 5; original emphasis) constitutively tied to the subjectivity of the witness and the transmission of memory as opposed to objective facticity. In Felman's terms, testimony is 'composed of bits and pieces of a memory that has been overwhelmed by occurrences that have not settled into understanding of remembrance, acts that cannot be constructed as knowledge nor assimilated into full cognition, events in excess of our frames of reference' (Felman, 1992: 5).

Felman and Laub both conceptualise testimony as communicable, individual, singular and lived experience. Referencing the poet Paul Celan, Felman conceptualises the act of witnessing as a 'radically unique, noninterchangable and solitary burden' (Felman, 1992: 3) that is encountered as an individuated responsibility and which can be undertaken only by the witness him or herself. Similarly, Laub, whose exploration of witnessing is structured around his personal experience both as a Holocaust survivor and a psychiatrist, associates the act of bearing witness with the psychoanalytic dyadic relationship between patient and analyst: an encounter centred around individual experiences and personal narratives. The characterisation of the second half of the twentieth century as an 'era of testimony' arguably references the 'turn to ethics', which occurred in the humanities, arts and politics at this time (Goodman and Severson, 2016). Certainly, the growing interest in testimony and witnessing reflects a contemporary ethical revaluation about how we know and remember the past and whose voices are included as part of this historiographical process. If Felman is right in her appraisal of this being an 'era of testimony', it would be correct to also suggest that the proliferation of testimonial texts, personal memoirs and other autobiographical texts and performances that appeared in the second half of the twentieth century are symptomatic of the prominence of trauma and memory studies emerging at this time. For testimony – certainly as it is theorised in trauma and memory studies – is inextricably connected to accounts of the traumatic and to the cultural trauma of the Holocaust specifically. As I discuss in Chapter 1, Felman associates this turn towards testimony with a cultural 'crisis of truth' (Felman, 1992: 6) and the failure of historical accounts of the past to adequately transmit the catastrophe of the Holocaust. Testimony, she argues, is always called upon 'when historical accuracy is in doubt and when both the truth and its supporting elements of evidence are called into question' (Felman, 1992: 6).

These inextricable interconnections between trauma, witnessing and the Holocaust have tended to underpin scholarly engagements with testimonial practice within the context of trauma studies and across other areas, certainly in Europe, the United States and Australia from the 1980s onwards. Rooted in the psychoanalytic theory of Freud and Lacan, the concept of trauma, as it is explored in trauma studies, is understood as a psychic response to an external event that exceeds the realm of cognition and which therefore remains outside of the symbolic framework of language, experienced indirectly, through a form of 'belatedness' and a deferred encounter with the 'real' (Caruth, 1996). In her genealogical account of trauma, Ruth Leys traces this model of trauma back to the 1980s, when the impact of the Vietnam war on the returning veterans was finally acknowledged and post-traumatic stress disorder was 'first officially recognised by the American Psychiatric Association in 1980' (Leys, 2000: 2). In this sense, contemporary accounts of trauma were founded on a conceptual structure that positioned the traumatic as a psychic loss of self that could be healed through forms of self-narration and a process of bearing witness, where past trauma is transformed into a form of remembering. The model of 'remembering, repeating and working through' as a means of coming to terms with trauma, first emerges in Freud and is explored in his essay, 'Remembering, Repeating and Working Through' ([1914] 2006). It has also been widely adopted by scholars of trauma working in literary and other cultural contexts, most notably in the work of the historian Dominick LaCapra who has argued that the act of writing about the past can be determined by an over-identification with historical trauma, leading to an inadvertent 'acting out' of past trauma and an appropriation of other historical trauma as one's own (LaCapra, 2001).

This framing of trauma as a psychoanalytical and, essentially, unconscious phenomenon has become the subject of much debate in recent years however. Scholars engaging in post-colonial theory and other disciplinary contexts have criticised the way trauma theory has tended to foreground a Western experience of trauma. Most critically, this model of trauma theory has been accused of being constructed solely to account for Euro-American experience and has 'failed to recognise the suffering of non-Western others' (Andermahr, 2016b: 1). While Cathy Caruth, one of the founding theorists in trauma studies, argued that greater understanding of trauma theory might 'provide the very link between cultures', opening up an engagement with 'what we don't yet know of our own traumatic pasts' (Caruth, 1995: 11), there has been little evidence that trauma studies-based scholarship has sought to seriously address non-Western suffering. Consequently, while Euro-American, psychoanalytic engagements with trauma dominated the accounts of witnessing that emerged in the second part of the twentieth century, the first decades of the 2000s saw the emergence of a call for a 'decolonising' of trauma studies and theories of witnessing. Theorists such as Jill Bennett and Rosanne Kennedy (2003), Michael Rothberg (2008), Stef Craps (2015) and Sonya Andermahr (2016a), in different ways, have sought to intervene in the way we think about trauma and witnessing and have shifted the discourse away from the cultural trauma of the Holocaust and accounts that have addressed experience of the 11 September attacks in America in 2001. These theorists, along with many others, have begun to critique traditional approaches to thinking about trauma, opening up new ways of conceptualising the relationship between trauma, witnessing and testimony. A central premise of trauma theory that has been reinterrogated is the persistent foregrounding of event-based trauma, which, as literary theorist Michael Rothberg points out, overlooks 'everyday forms of traumatizing violence' such as racism and other forms of discrimination (Rothberg, 2008: 226). The breadth of criticisms levelled against trauma theory by those calling for a 'decolonisation' of the field are summed up particularly clearly by Stef Craps, whose book *Postcolonial Witnessing: Trauma Out of Bounds* (2015), has been highly influential in this area. Craps views the failure of trauma studies to engage with forms of 'cross-cultural ethical engagement' as falling into four areas:

> They marginalize or ignore traumatic experiences of non-Western or minority cultures, they tend to take for granted the universal validity of definitions of trauma and recovery that have developed out of the history of Western modernity, they often favour or even prescribe a modernist aesthetic of fragmentation and aporia as uniquely suited to the task of bearing witness to trauma, and they generally disregard the connections between metropolitan and non-Western or minority traumas. (Craps, 2015: 2)

In his book, Craps is particularly critical of the way dominant discourses of trauma tend to focus on individualised encounters with the traumatic and not the social situations that produce them. Drawing on Franz Fanon's pioneering work around the 'psychopathology of racism and colonialism', Craps draws attention to the 'insidious trauma' wrought by 'systematic oppression and discrimination' (Craps, 2015: 28–30), usefully drawing attention to how individual encounters of trauma are embedded within the social and political contexts in which acts of violent oppression are produced and sustained.[2]

The limitations of the psychoanalytical framing of witnessing and the implications of this on the way testimony is understood and conceptualised are clearly explored by Rosanne Kennedy and Tikka Jan Wilson in an essay analysing the testimonial narratives presented in *Bringing Them Home* (1997), a report by the Australian Human Rights and Equal Opportunities Commission on the forced removal of Aboriginal and Torres Strait Islander children from their families. In their reading of the testimonies by indigenous subjects presented within the report, Kennedy and Wilson problematise the psychoanalytic model as a means of engaging with the testimonies of non-Western witnesses. Arguing that Felman and Laub's account of witnessing precludes certain forms of testimonial practice and pre-empts what kind of address testimony can generate, Kennedy and Wilson argue for a reappraisal of the relationship between witnessing, testimonial practices and the way knowledge of the past is transmitted. By structuring the act of bearing witness through a framework constructed around the catastrophe of the Holocaust and the role of the unconscious in the traumatic memory of this, Felman, they argue, develops an account of witnessing that refuses 'the writer's (and reader's) assumption of a direct, transparent relationship between language and traumatic event' (Kennedy and Wilson, 2003: 122). Yet such accounts of witnessing fail to 'conform to the requirements of a realist narrative, with its humanist notions of character, plot and event' (Kennedy and Wilson, 2003: 122–3). The implication of this is that in psychoanalytic accounts of witnessing, testimony is only conceptualised as such when it addresses unconscious truths and is determined by an essentially modernist aesthetic that adopts forms of innovation that resist any transparent, self-evident narrative form. However, this foregrounding of a 'testimony of the unconscious' has implications for those who wish to use testimonial practices 'to make political and social claims' (Kennedy and Wilson, 2003: 123), for it understands suffering of the past as an uncommunicable trauma that is therefore unsayable and ultimately unknowable. For in psychoanalytical conceptualisations of the traumatic, the event of trauma is understood as being beyond language and therefore experience. It cannot consequently be directly acknowledged within the psychoanalytical encounter. Furthermore, by determining testimonial practice through psychoanalytic discourses of trauma, the act of witnessing must then be relegated to an *individual* act that is encountered as a 'solitary burden' by the witness (Felman, 1992: 3) and as such it cannot be a shared experience nor can it have a communal, collective quality to it. As such, witnessing loses its capacity to be activated as a mode of solidarity or advocacy with others, who also share traumatic histories. As Kennedy and Wilson argue, 'psychoanalysis favours testimony that is inaccessible to cognition and to being spoken. It therefore neglects, and calls into question the value and validity of acts of testimony in which the narrator claims to speak as an 'expert' about her own condition or experience' (Kennedy and Wilson, 2003: 123).

The individuated and event-based account of witnessing also produces a certain mode of dyadic address that positions the listener or addressee of testimony as being radically outside of the testimonial context. The importing of the psychoanalytic model of analysand and analyst into the act of witnessing therefore 'imagines the reader as a critic/analyst, rather than as a non-specialist member of a community being addressed' (Kennedy and Wilson, 2003: 126). Consequently, the addressee of testimony is positioned not as a potential political advocate or ally, but as a vicarious victim of trauma who subsumes or appropriates the suffering of the testifying other. While a psychoanalytic account of trauma and testimony continues to determine many scholarly engagements with witnessing, many contemporary testimonial theatre makers have developed dramaturgical strategies that, I suggest, move beyond this delimiting structure. Through an examination of how contemporary testimonial plays reperform modes of witnessing, it becomes possible to conceptualise a decolonised form of testimonial theatre that relocates testimony beyond a Euro-American articulation of the subject, opening up new ways of understanding witnessing and how the performance of testimony might be encountered by audiences.

Rethinking testimony in theatre: Stepping beyond the psychoanalytic frame

In order to begin to think about how decolonised forms of testimonial dramaturgy might be constructed, I want first to consider some of the ways the psychoanalytic model of witnessing has been adopted within theatre and performance scholarship and how this has influenced approaches to spectatorship. As indicated above, one of the key problematics of viewing witnessing as an extension of the psychoanalytical encounter is that it becomes symptomatic of trauma and is not therefore conceptualised as a voluntary and decisive action. Notwithstanding this, however, the concept of witnessing has held much appeal for practitioners and scholars who have sought to conceptualise forms of audienceship that moves beyond an account of passive spectatorship. As such, psychoanalytic conceptualisations of witnessing have been adopted by many scholars addressing themselves to performance and its audience. Diana Taylor (1997), Tim Etchells (1999) and Peggy Phelan (1993, 1999), for example, have all referenced the theorisation of witnessing developed in memory and trauma studies, using this to address audience spectatorship and have argued that the role of the audience can, in some instances, be understood as a form of witnessing. As Caroline Wake points out, these engagements with the 'spectator-witness' are established around the proposition that 'witnessing is a mode of "active" and "ethical"' spectatorship (Wake, 2013b: 35) that is therefore more engaged and more ethically attuned than other modes of engagement with performance.

The artistic director of Forced Entertainment, Tim Etchells, is a key proponent of this idea and argues that witnessing a performance event signals a more profound, meaningful form of engagement: 'to witness an event is to be present at it in some fundamental ethical way, to feel the weight of things and one's own place in them, even if that place is simply, for the moment, as an onlooker' (Etchells, 1999: 18). Similarly, pointing out that 'theatre has borrowed the understanding of witnessing from psychoanalysis and political ethics', performance theorist Phelan develops Etchells's argument further by connecting the spectator-witness with the concept of trauma, arguing that the spectatorship of performance should be understood as a belated or deferred experience, exceeding the 'spatial and temporal boundaries' of the performance itself (Phelan, 1999: 13).

Wake (2013b) usefully analyses these engagements with the spectator as witness and, drawing on psychoanalytic accounts of the witness developed in trauma studies, seeks to develop some clearer definitions of primary, secondary and tertiary forms of witnessing. As Wake points out, the theorisation of witnessing in relation to the spectatorship of theatre is somewhat underdeveloped and at times problematic, not least because 'there are many modes of activity – self-conscious seeing, unconscious seeing, listening, identifying, imagining – currently being classified under the practice of witnessing' (Wake, 2013b: 52). This leads her to suggest that there is an 'insufficiency' in 'our current definition of the witness as an "active spectator"', which evidences a 'lack of interaction between theories of witnessing and spectatorship more generally' (Wake, 2013b: 52). The performance theorist Diana Taylor seems to draw a similar conclusion when, in her theorisation of national identity and spectator-ship in Argentina's 'Dirty War' during the dictatorship of 1974–83, she addresses the problematic usage of the term 'witnessing' in relation to spectatorship (Taylor, 1997). Looking for a way to describe a mode of spectatorship that is 'involved, informed, caring, yet critical' (Taylor, 1997: 25), Taylor argues that she has adopted the concept of 'witnessing' as it emerges through the theorisation of Felman and Laub (1992) 'for lack of a better term' (Taylor, 1997: 25).

While the possibility of producing an active and ethical form of spectatorship is a desire shared by many practitioners, the term 'witnessing' continues to sit somewhat uneasily within theories of spectatorship and, I argue, becomes problematic when used to describe an audience for testimonial theatre. My questioning of the spectator-as-witness model arises from four main concerns. Firstly, I suggest, there is no intrinsic quality within the act of bearing witness that automatically makes it a more 'ethical' form of spectatorship than others. While I agree that acts of witnessing often emerge from complex ethical and political situations, to suggest that it is the act of witnessing rather than the situation itself which reveals ethical experience seems misguided. Secondly, the delineation of which performances produce 'witnesses' as opposed to 'spectators' seems to be determined by a somewhat arbitrary process. While certain performances, such as Chris Burden's *Shoot* (1971),[3] are often cited as exemplary performances in which the audience members become witnesses instead of spectators, what remains unclear is how such an 'active' form of spectatorship is to be measured and evidenced. It would be stretching the point, for example, to suggest that an audience member watching *Hamlet* should be viewed as a witness as opposed to a spectator; in the case of Burden's performance, the idea of the witness seems to be predicated on the simple fact that the audience was present when Burden was shot – the key distinction being then that one event is merely 'theatrical', the other is 'real'. But here the concept of the witness is effectively limited to that of the idea of a bystander (which is also a synonym for spectator); and so why and how a witness is produced, remains underdetermined. Furthermore, distinguishing the act of witnessing from spectatorship simply by determining whether the event being observed is real or fictive, seems to side-step any engagement with the problematics of what it means to be called upon to bear witness to an event. Consequently, this conceptualisation of witnessing does little to reveal the ethical problematics of bearing witness and the responsibility incurred when the witness feels compelled to speak out about what has been observed or experienced. Thirdly, there seems to be no guarantee that the call to come forward as a witness rather than a spectator, who happens to have been present at an event, applies to every member of the audience. It is, for example, difficult to imagine the circumstances by which every member of the audience at the performance of Burden's *Shoot* would think of themselves as 'witnesses' and not simply as someone observing the performance as a spectator. Finally, by delineating primary and secondary witnesses, the spectator-witness is ultimately constituted around an event-based model of trauma, where some witnesses are more directly affected by the event than others. As discussed above, this event-based model has little traction when applied to ongoing traumatic situations such as persecutions or injustices that result from systemic forms of oppression. While the conceptualisation of audience spectatorship as a form of witnessing is somewhat problematic, conceptualising testimonial theatre as a mode of performed witnessing can establish a productive way of understanding the ethico-political process by which personal narratives are used as a basis for theatre making.

However, in order to understand the potential of such acts of performed witnessing, testimonial theatre, I suggest, must move beyond psychoanalytic formations of witnessing. To understand how testimony can be 'decolonised' and liberated from the grip of psychoanalytic discourse, the act of witnessing itself must be re-examined and reconceptualised. While the psychoanalytic account of witnessing, as developed by Felman and Laub, tends to dominate much of the discourse in this area, etymologically the term 'witness' has boarder connotations. As Giorgio Agamben usefully points out in his book *Remnants of Auschwitz: The Witness and the Archive* (1999), the term 'witness' has two meanings: one that is rooted in a juridical, legalistic context and the other denoting the broader context of survival and living through an event. Drawing on the Latin derivation of the term, Agamben writes that:

> In Latin there are two words for 'witness'. The first word, *testis*; from which our word 'testimony' derives, etymologically signifies the person who, in a trial or lawsuit between two rival parties, is in the position of a third party. The second word, *superstes*, designates a person who has lived through something, who has experienced an event from beginning to end and can therefore bear witness to it. (Agamben, 1999: 17)

The witness as third (*testis*) would seem, then, to align with the connotations of a bystander, an 'eye witness' or even a 'spectator', denoting the one who takes on the role of an arbitrator between two opposing perspectives. This contrasts with the witness as first (*superstes*), who has none of this impartiality and therefore 'his [or her] testimony has nothing to do with the acquisition of facts for a trial' (Agamben, 1999: 17). While the term 'witness' has a legalistic etymology, the meaning of the term exceeds this, denoting acts of attestation undertaken not as a means of attributing culpability or guilt, but as a process of remembering and attesting to the past. In this sense, 'witnessing' itself is constitutively marked by an ambivalence. While it is a term that implies the impartial observation of an event, it also denotes the opposite, a form of active engagement with something that has been lived through, experienced and is personally remembered and recalled.

In Derrida's etymology of witnessing in his essay, 'Poetics and Politics of Witnessing' (2005), he draws similar distinctions to Agamben, but points out that 'Latin semantics (*testis, terstis, superstes*) denotes only one etymological-institutional configuration amongst others' (Derrida, 2005: 74). By way of contrast, Derrida draws attention to the German family of terms '*Zeugen, bezeugen, Bezeugung, Zeugnis*', that translate as '"witness," "to bear witness," "testimony," "attestation"' but which draw from 'a completely different semantic network' and have connotations with '"tool, procreation, engendering,"' and, precisely, "generation" – at the same time biological and familial' (Derrida, 2005: 74). In the German then, 'witnessing' loses its denotation of the 'witness as third' (*testis*) and, indeed, does not reference presence, but rather points towards witnessing as possessing a generative quality. Developing this further, Derrida considers the Greek etymology of 'witnessing', where there is 'no explicit reference to the third, to surviving, to presence, or to generation', and which instead draws on the Greek root '*martus, marturos*, the witness, who becomes the martyr, the witness of faith' (Derrida, 2005: 75). Deriving from the Greek term *marturion*, the witness 'as martyr', as Derrida indicates, also 'means, following the institutional usage, "bearing witness", but also "proof"' (Derrida, 2005: 75) in which the material presence of the witness him or herself becomes a form of evidence.

This account of witnessing is a particularly productive way of understanding strongly performative acts of attestation that do not seek to narrate a historical account of the past, but instead enact a moment of proof and presence through performance itself. The Mothers of the Plaza de Mayo in Argentina provide a useful illustrative example here. Since April 1977, every Thursday afternoon, a group of mothers have processed around the Plaza de Mayo square in Buenos Aires protesting against the injustice wrought against their children by the last Argentinian dictatorship (1976–83). As Diana Taylor indicates, they march '[a]rm in arm, wearing their white head scarves' and 'demand justice for the human rights violations committed by the brutal military dictatorship that abducted, tortured, and permanently "disappeared" thirty thousand of their children' (Taylor, 1997: 183–4). Described as 'one of the most visible political discourses of resistance to terror in recent Latin American history' (Suárez-Orozco quoted in Taylor 1997: 191), the Mothers of the Plaza de Mayo continue to march today, punctuating their procession with rallying calls 'for the *aparición con vida* (alive appearance) of their children' (Sosa, 2014: 15). This ritualised processing, which at the time of writing has continued for forty-two years, is both a political protest, but also a collective form of remembrance and witnessing, attesting both to the loss of the many children who were 'disappeared' during this time and the continued suffering and rage this and other injustices have precipitated. However, interestingly, this procession of witnesses does not centre on a narration of the past. Through their ritualised presence, and the embodied gesture of the procession, the Mothers of the Plaza de Mayo hold the past open and bear witness to it through their very presence. In this sense, the mothers' presence and the procession itself become evidence of an injustice in and of itself, rather than providing a narration of an event that has been lived through or observed.

Acts of witnessing, then, should not be conceptualised through a universal and static definition but understood instead as embodied engagements with the past that become framed differently within different cultural contexts and through the assertion of different types of testimonial truths. Underpinning these different modes of witnessing is a fidelity to an act of truth telling. In the act of witnessing, the witnesses offer themselves and their own integrity in what Derrida describes as an 'appeal' to the faith of another. For 'whether or not he is explicitly under oath', Derrida writes, 'without being able or obligated to prove anything', the witness 'appeals to the faith of the other by engaging himself to tell the truth' (Derrida, 2000: 29). In this sense, as Derrida indicates, witnessing is more than simply an affirmation of a particular account of an event; rather it is an act in which the witnesses offer themselves up through the process of a promise or an oath. It is the existential quality of witnessing and the engagement of the self in this truth-telling process that reveals the ethico-political dimensions of theatre making that engages with witnessing through the process of testimony. For in this sense, the performing of other people's suffering is a political and ethical act. While the performance of testimony can potentially galvanise a community of listeners that emerge as critical addressees to a testimonial address, the performance of narratives of suffering can also elicit an audience response embedded in what Luc Boltanski describes as a 'politics of pity' (Boltanski, 2004) which reduces the other to a form of victimhood, limiting the possibility for critical forms of engagement with testimonial performance. Consequently, one of the tensions inherent in testimonial theatre making is how to establish a critical engagement with others without falling into a mode of performance that simply reproduces a form of spectatorship that is predetermined by, and reaffirming of, the social norms and the hegemonic values of its audience.

Lilie Chouliaraki's research on the spectatorship of suffering is useful here. In her examination of how popular media produces and upholds a binary between the 'distant sufferer', who appears on our television screens, and 'us', the Western spectator, Chouliaraki (2006) examines how popular media mediates other people's suffering not only to determine what 'we', in the West, know about the suffering of 'distant others', but crucially how we feel we *ought* to respond to this suffering. As she goes on to argue, 'television uses image and language so as to render the spectacle of suffering not only comprehensible but also ethically acceptable for the spectator' (Chouliaraki, 2006: 3). In so doing, forms of spectatorship are created that reaffirm, as opposed to challenge, what we (the West) understand about the images and stories we are presented with. Importing these ideas into my examination of testimonial theatre problematises the way that testimonial dramaturgy negotiates testimonial truths and how this process might ultimately predetermine and manipulate the ethical stance of the audience. After all, while the reperformance of witnessing in testimonial theatre has the potential to break down a perception of 'distance' between the testimonial subject and the audience member, by using dramaturgical conventions to activate empathy and other forms of identification, the re-enactment of narratives of suffering can also reproduce and solidify certain binaries that serve to separate witnesses from the audience. In this sense, personal narratives of suffering in testimonial theatre can be used to draw audiences and witnesses together or to establish an immoveable demarcation between the spectator and the spectated, reinscribing into the audience an ethical response to the performed testimony that is predetermined and 'acceptable for the spectator' (Chouliaraki, 2006: 3). The ethics of testimonial theatre making therefore are haunted by the possibility of reproducing a 'politics of pity' (Boltanski, 2004), where the play's dramaturgy produces not critical spectators, but establishes and sustains 'a distinction between those who suffer and those who do not' (Boltanski, 2004: 3). Such a form of spectatorship could be defined as an 'observation of the *unfortunate* by those who do not share their suffering, who do not experience it directly and who, as such, may be regarded as fortunate or *lucky* people' (Boltanski, 2004: 3; original emphasis). In other words, one of the key ethical challenges confronting the testimonial theatre maker is how to establish testimonial narratives within a dramaturgical structure that do not simply establish a binary separation between the enacted testifying subject (the 'victim') and the 'liberated' audience member. For this kind of dramaturgy of suffering arguably not only predetermines certain modes of spectating, but also simply reaffirms the hegemonic morality that is already familiar to audiences through its dissemination in popular forms of media.

Towards a decolonised testimonial theatre

Reflecting back on the process of writing my verbatim play *From the Mouths of Mothers*, I now recognise that while a verbatim theatre methodology signalled my commitment to certain processes of replication, this approach did little to convey the multi-dimensional elements of the testimonies I encountered. One of the problematics of the verbatim theatre form is that it relegates dramaturgical text to the everyday, communicable language of an interview. This means that the interview format imprints itself not only on the kind of material that is gathered, but how narratives are told. Any engagement with past events tends to be articulated through a somewhat literal process of iteration, where experience is always rendered directly transmissible and communicable because it has been conveyed as part of an interview. Certainly when I was writing the play and listening to the recorded interviews with the mothers, I became aware that the traumatising nature of child sexual abuse could ultimately render some events simply too overwhelming to be brought into the interview encounter and that, at times, it was clear that the verbatim subjects who were being interviewed were struggling to find words and a narrative with which to communicate the difficult elements of their story. Furthermore, in the process of editing the material and writing the play, I also became very conscious that the audience would be coming to see a play that they knew was about child sexual abuse. As such, the issue of abuse would be established in the minds of the audience before the play had even begun. Yet somehow, the dramaturgy had to convince audiences of a time in the mother's lives when they knew nothing about this. Without being able to stage this space of unknowingness, I would be unable to authentically explore the suspicions and concerns that emerged as the mothers began gradually to realise things were not quite right with their children. Alongside this was a concern about how to dramaturgically represent the visceral and, at times, unbearable suffering these mothers and their children endured, particularly as their worlds fell apart and they failed to receive the support they desperately needed. While I wanted also to show the strength and the resilience of these mothers, I felt it important that the play also bore witness to the psycho-social impact of sexual abuse and the trauma this precipitated across the family. In this sense, the challenges of writing *From the Mouths of Mothers* revealed the problematic of moving beyond the binary of the unlucky victim and liberated spectator as outlined by Boltanski in his discussion of the 'politics of pity' (2004). To conceptualise a theatre of testimony that can move beyond such a binary by establishing a more multi-dimensional and critical engagement with the transmission of testimony therefore requires a rethinking of the way witnessing operates in verbatim and testimonial theatre and the different testimonial truths such dramaturgies might produce. In the second section of this chapter, I endeavour to do this by exploring three different modes of witnessing that emerge in contemporary testimonial theatre making.

Like Rosanne Kennedy, Lynne Bell and Julia Emberley, I agree that the psychoanalytic structure of witnessing has been a useful approach with which to understand testimony that addresses 'an event as unprecedented and inassimilable to Western frames of cognition as the Holocaust'; where 'direct witnessing' is not possible (Kennedy, Bell and Emberley, 2009: 5). However, there are limitations to this approach, particularly when engaging with testimonial practices that do not address a limit-experience[4] or where plural testimonies operate together to produce a collective act of witnessing. As discussed above, Felman articulates her conception of testimony as a 'solitary' endeavour (Felman, 1992: 3), where the act of bearing witness is structured around a singular address of the past. However, in many testimonial plays, witnessing emerges through multi-perspectival processes, where different testimonies interact with one another dialogically. Often in such plays, these multiple testimonies do not address event-based trauma, but instead engage with ongoing oppression and sustained, systemic injustice. Furthermore, while some testimonial plays enact a form of witnessing in which a past event is narrated from beginning to end, activating a mode of witnessing described by Agamben as *superstes*, many testimonial plays represent acts of witnessing where it is the co-presence of the witness before us that evokes a past injustice, rather than the renarration of a past event. In this sense, the conception of testimony as an entirely individualised process is problematised by the collective acts of witnessing that are presented in many testimonial plays.

Of course, some testimonial plays address event-based trauma and are focused around a singular witness. Emily Mann's *Annulla: An Autobiography* ([1988] 1997) is such an example. In this play, Mann draws on word-for-word material gathered from interviews with Annulla Allen, whose testimony reveals the extraordinary story of Annulla's life as a young Jewish woman who eluded the Nazis in Germany during the Second World War by pretending 'to be an Aryan' (Mann, [1988] 1997: 10). The testimonial text of this one-woman play is framed with Mann's own account of her interview with Annulla, her own personal history and her visit to Ostroleka, a village in Poland where previous generations of her family had been murdered and deported by the Nazis. Presented in

the script simply as 'Voice', the interventions of Mann's story via the
disembodied voice arguably evoke the psychoanalytical encounter and
impose this on the act of witnessing. As such, the testimony that emerges
addresses a traumatic memory and, as Attilio Favorini argues, engages
with 'the hole or void surrounding the traumatic event' (Favorini, 2011:
152). In Mann's play the testimonial subject, then, is presented as returning
to the past in order to retrieve a traumatic truth and needs to do so, it
seems, in order to move on in some way from the past. This is illustrated
when Annulla says: 'It is like in psychoanalysis. You must know what
happened to you' (Mann, [1988] 1997: 10). This form of engagement
with Annulla's traumatic past works well in Mann's play, not least because
the trauma the play addresses is the event-based trauma of the Holocaust
and, of course, this is a one-woman play where the focus must remain
centred upon one individual: Annulla. However, in other forms of testimonial theatre that do not address singular, event-based traumas,
testimonial truth tends not to be constituted by the recovery of a singular
unconscious memory of the past but emerges through the process of
witnessing itself and the relational encounter between one witness and
another. In order to understand how testimonial theatre making moves
beyond forms of event-based trauma, in the discussions that follow, I
consider how testimonial truth telling shifts and adapts when framed
around collective experience.

     In my account of the three different modes of witnessing below, I
attempt to establish a more nuanced understanding of the relationship
between different forms of witnessing and the truths that are dramaturgically produced in testimonial theatre. In this sense, my intention here is
not to formulate a comprehensive account of testimonial theatre dramaturgy, nor is it to reconstruct its history or lineage. While such a historiographical undertaking might be possible, its scope would be extremely
broad and arguably so expansive as to not be of much use. One reason
for this is that testimonial theatre is not reducible to an easily reconstructed
set of codes or a 'genre' that could be invented or dramaturgically defined.
Rather, it refers to singular forms of theatre where new, responsive and
highly personal modes of truth telling are forefronted as demanded by
the collaboration of theatre maker and witness. Moreover, testimonial
theatre emerges through processes of witnessing that are interwoven
within the political and cultural heritages of the context in which they
are produced. The different modes of witnessing I explore below do not
establish a form of categorisation that can define each and every testimonial
play. Instead, these modes of witnessing could be best understood as
forming part of what the philosopher Ludwig Wittgenstein describes as
'family resemblances' (Wittgenstein, 2009: 37). By which I mean that

when taken together these modes of theatrical witnessing produce a 'complicated network of similarities overlapping and criss-crossing' (Wittgenstein, 2009: 36) one another that reveal some of the shared truth-telling processes that, in different ways, constitute the range of testimonial dramaturgies that are being developed today.

Three modes of witnessing: Truth-telling processes in contemporary testimonial theatre

The first mode of witnessing I want to develop is characterised by what I am calling a 'poetics of witnessing', a mode of witnessing where the past is pieced together through a text constructed through a poetics of memory and where testimony emerges from the use of figurative language, symbolic gestures and other poetic engagements with the past. This mode of witnessing therefore is not constructed upon a simple recounting of past events, but around an existential examination of the impact of past and ongoing suffering and how this has shaped the testimonial subject's present. To examine how this 'poetics of witnessing' operates within the dramaturgy of a testimonial play, I turn my attention to *A Woman in Waiting*, a testimonial play by the South African playwright and director Yaël Farber that was created in 1999, in collaboration with the acclaimed South African performer Thembi Mtshali-Jones, whose life story the play examines. Following this, I move on to examine a second mode of witnessing which, borrowing from Kennedy and Wilson's writing about aboriginal testimonies in Australia, I describe as a testimony produced by 'witness-narrators' (Kennedy and Wilson, 2003). Here, the act of witnessing becomes a shared endeavour where the witnesses, who emerge as experts of their own community, address the audience with a multiple-perspectival account of past injustice. Drawing on *Parramatta Girls* (2007), by the Australian playwright Alana Valentine, I consider how, in this play, personal testimonies establish an interwoven, shared narrative of collective and systemic injustice. Drawing on different dramaturgical strategies to address a shared history of the past, Valentine's play, I argue, seeks an active form of audienceship that encourages a critical as opposed to an emotional response to the narratives of suffering the play examines. The third and final mode I examine is one I describe as 'witnessing as resistance'. Here, singular testimony stands in for collective and community histories and the witness draws on personal testimony and significant life events not to reconstruct an individual life story, but to address a shared experience of an unjust social situation. To examine this mode of witnessing I discuss a play by the New York-based indigenous theatre collective, Spiderwoman Theater. Written by Lisa Mayo, Gloria Miguel and Muriel Miguel, core members of the company, *Persistence of Memory* (2002) draws on a series of short review-like scenes to present a testimony of the company's history and the ongoing struggle of indigenous American women to be free of the structures of oppression and stereotypical identities that are imposed upon them.

A poetics of witnessing: *A Woman in Waiting*

Laub conceptualises testimony as being underpinned by a 'commitment to truth', where the witness returns to the past in order 'to recapture the lost truth of that reality' (Laub, 1992: 91). However, the lived experience of non-event-based trauma means that past suffering and injustices are often enduring and cannot therefore be entirely relegated to the 'past'. In a testimonial theatre practice rooted in a poetics of witnessing, the search for a 'lost truth' is replaced with a poetic engagement with past injustice through the transmission of an affective response to the lived experience of a collective history. In this mode of witnessing, truth and fiction operate together in order to explore the existential rupture wrought by this history and its legacy upon the future. A key historical influence to this form of testimonial theatre is the South African anti-apartheid plays that emerged in the 1970s and 1980s and which, as Loren Kruger explains, were part of a 'theatre conventionally associated with the anti-apartheid movement […] with "protest" and "resistance" and with the names of Athol Fugard, John Kami, or Barney Simon' (Kruger, 1999: 12). While this form of theatre addressed the everyday reality of South Africa's oppressive apartheid system, it did so by drawing on both fictional and factual representations of the time, producing individual and collective acts of witnessing of the injustices of this period of South Africa's history. As Kruger explains, 'This theatre of testimony is distinguished by the dramatic interpretation of individual and collective narratives, and of politically provocative topics, such as the pass laws, prison conditions, workers' rights, and, to a lesser degree, the condition of women' (Kruger, 1999: 147).

The blurring of actuality and the fiction within these testimonial plays had two dimensions. Firstly, by adopting a dramaturgical structure that mixed elements of actuality with more theatrical inventions, the performers were able to evade the censorship of strict laws prohibiting particular political activities. Secondly, it established a mode of theatre making that was political and which endeavoured to both represent and *transform* the reality it depicted, generating what Kruger describes as a 'counter-publicity' – a 'virtual public sphere […] where South Africa could be depicted as it could have been and might yet be, as well as where actual conditions might be critically represented' (Kruger, 1999: 12). This sense of a fluid shifting between the actual and the fictive is characteristic of other forms of African theatre making. As Yvette Hutchison explains, in African story-telling cultures, the story that is being told takes on a central importance, becoming 'a mode through which we know ourselves and explore our history, identity and collective value systems' (Hutchison, 2011: 211). As such, these oral story-telling traditions are marked out by this sense of a fluidity between the fictional and the actual and, as Hutchison indicates, the story 'is no less true for being fictional or constructed' (Hutchison, 2011: 211). As a consequence the South African theatre of testimony drew on a wide range of theatre devices, making use of 'physical and verbatim comedy, impersonation of multiple roles with minimal props' while also using 'direct address to the audience by performers representing themselves and their own convictions as well as those of fictional characters' (Kruger, 1999: 154).

While the South African theatre of testimony was not established around the reiteration of a singular testimonial narrative, these plays enacted a form of witnessing by attesting both to the lived experience of apartheid and collectively imagining ways of transforming it. In this sense, while Pedzisai Maedza (2017) and Helena Enright (2011) both historicise the term 'theatre of testimony' as first being used by Athol Fugard in his account of watching Emily Mann's testimonial play *Still Life* with the South African director, Barney Simon (Fugard, 1997: x), I would suggest, following Kruger, that the practice of testimonial theatre predates this moment and can be applied to approaches adopted within some of the South African anti-apartheid plays of the 1970s and 1980s, even if this was not recognised in such terms at the time. The mode of witnessing adopted within this form of South African theatre drew on the hybridity of theatrical approaches and testimonial conventions and, as Kruger argues, can be called '*syncretizing*' because 'it marks an ongoing negotiation with forms and practices, variously and not always consistently identified as modern or traditional, imported or indigenous, European or African' (Kruger, 1999: 21; original emphasis). It is this hybrid approach, along with the fluid incorporation of the real and the poetic, that underpins what I am describing as a 'poetics of witnessing'. It is a mode of witnessing that addresses historical injustices not through the recuperation of a linear narrative of a historical event, but by activating and performing different modes of remembering and witnessing and the diversity of forms by which this is performed.

A *Woman in Waiting* adopts this approach, drawing on a poetics of witnessing to attest to the everyday, oppressive apartheid laws and the impact of this system on a young girl whose coming of age story is depicted in the course of the play. By interweaving personal testimony with accounts of the history of the apartheid system, *A Woman in Waiting* attests both to the lived experience of apartheid and to the social-political trauma this political system wrought on the lives of black South Africans who were so brutally subjugated by this regime. Drawing on poetry, song, testimony and the indigenous languages of South Africa, the play constructs a poetics of witnessing in which the past is not simply reconstructed through an account of what has gone before, but through a series of reflections on the existential impact of the apartheid system. In so doing, *A Woman in Waiting* examines not just the pastness of apartheid, but the passing of time itself. By speeding up and slowing down time, Farber's dramaturgy shifts Thembi's life story beyond a simple chronological narration of the past and instead explores the impact of South Africa's history and how it shaped Thembi's growing sense of self and the aspirations she held. While the violence and coercive structures of apartheid forge a traumatic history for Thembi, the play's testimony does not circulate around a pathological or 'traditional event-based model of trauma' (Craps, 2015: 4). Thembi's testimony bears witness to an 'insidious trauma due to systematic oppression and discrimination' (Craps, 2015: 29) attesting to forms of racial hatred 'established in a myriad of minute acts of indignity that were perpetuated by ordinary people' (Durrheim, Mtose and Brown, 2011: 7). The poetics of witnessing adopted in the play heightens this by framing the action and imagery of the play around an endless process of waiting. In the opening scenes, for example, we encounter the young Thembi, living with her grandparents and waiting a whole year to see her parents who can afford to return only at Christmas time. For the child Thembi, the years take ages to pass and time is experienced slowly, measured by how 'many more moons for your arm to grow long enough ... (*Reaching over her head to touch the opposite ear*) ... to touch your ear' (Farber, 2008c: 43). Correlatively, Thembi's parents struggle to keep up with the passing years that mark out the time in Thembi's childhood they have lost out on while working in the city. This sense of time being lost or stolen is symbolised in the play by the Christmas shoes Thembi's parents bring as gifts, shoes which never fit because, of course, Thembi's feet are growing and 'don't stay the same size as when they measured them with a *stling* [string] last *Chlismas*' (Farber, 2008c: 42; original emphasis).

As the play develops, the motif of separation and waiting is repeated when Thembi also becomes a mother and in turn must leave her child to work for a white family in the city. Thembi's testimony, then, not only addresses past sorrows, but what was irrevocably lost as a result of apartheid and the regulatory pass law system. This is reflected in the years of her daughter's life she was never able to experience because, like her parents, she was forced to work away from home in the city. In this sense, the poetics of witnessing in *A Woman in Waiting* addresses a present that is entangled within the losses precipitated by the passing of time and the impact of the history of apartheid on Thembi and her family. This is illustrated well in a moment when Thembi recounts how her time with her child was stolen away both by her white employers and the Blackjack Municipal Workers who were 'assigned to search people's houses in the township – hoping to catch those staying "illegally" in areas they do not have a permit for' (Farber, 2008c: 69). Through this account of the experience of living under the harsh racialised rules of apartheid, Thembi's testimony addresses both the injustice of this political system as well as the day-to-day lived experience of it, while drawing attention to what was irredeemably lost as a result. Near the end of the play, Thembi returns to this sense of lost time and what was taken from her and her daughter, Phumzile:

THEMBI (TO *PHUMZILE*)
Phumzile: There is time lost that I mourn. Time I can never reclaim. I would give up a list of things I have treasured most: loves, friends, productions, my worldly goods. I would give all this and more – if I could only travel backwards in time to your first years … To rewrite the hours I encouraged words from the mouth of someone else's child – while you said your first 'mama' and I was not there to celebrate it. (Farber, 2008c: 73)

The poetics of witnessing in *A Woman in Waiting*, then, shifts between the past, present and future of South Africa, exploring how the country's past is continually framing and troubling its present. This approach is arguably reflective of many post-colonial contexts, where the trauma of colonial violence does not remain bound to a set of past events but becomes inscribed into present-day lived experience, determining the futurity of the post-colonial subject and influencing how the past should be remembered. In their discussion of post-apartheid South Africa, Ewald Mengel and Michele Borzaga examine the collapsing and overlapping of time in this context, describing post-apartheid as an era where the past and the present co-exist, knitted together. As they point out, because of its colonial history, in South Africa 'past and present are also entangled in a complex way. They cannot now be distinguished as two clearly identifiable phases in a continuum of time but are superimposed on each other, interpenetrate one another, and in this way, form a "tangle" or knot in which their separation is suspended' (Mengel and Borzaga, 2012: viii). It is this entangled knot of the past, present and future that Thembi addresses at the end of the play when she turns to consider the public testimonies that were presented to the Truth and Reconciliation Commission (TRC), which were also broadcast on national television. Addressing the women giving their testimonies to the TRC, Thembi aligns herself with their experience of waiting and long-endured suffering, but also with their patience. She says:

> Bomama, you sat with your backs straight – your handbags on your laps and your handkerchiefs in your sleeves. You waited with a dignity and attention that shamed all those who have never had to wait for anything.
> You said nothing, but when you began to speak – you broke a lifetime of silence. (Farber, 2008c: 82)

Premiering only a year after the conclusion of the TRC process, *A Woman in Waiting* implicitly addresses itself, then, to the possibility of moving on from South Africa's past by bearing witness to the legacy of apartheid and the challenges this history presents South Africans today. Unlike the TRC, of course, the play has no juridical function and therefore it is freed from any agenda of an enforced closure on the past, which has been a criticism that has been levelled at the TRC. By representing the history of apartheid as an unfinished and ongoing issue, the dramaturgy of the play resists viewing the past through an event-based model of trauma, where the past is reduced to a singular, time-bound event. Instead, *A Woman in Waiting* establishes a testimonial approach that moves beyond a narrative of healing and forgiveness and presents the past as being in some way unfinished, or at least continually entwined within the present. In this sense, when Thembi describes the women in the TRC preparing to break 'a lifetime of silence' (Farber, 2008c: 82), she does not seem to suggest that, in so doing, the testimonial process will transform individual experience. In these final moments of the play, Thembi addresses an interweaving of her own personal history with the socio-political context of post-apartheid South Africa. As she reflects on what she describes as 'this museum in me' (Farber, 2008c: 84), she evokes a sense of collective mourning that does not seek to retrieve the past, but addresses what has been lost and what ultimately remains irrecoverable. If, as Farber states in the epigraph at the top of this chapter, testimonial theatre has the capacity to heal, I would argue that the process of healing called upon by a poetics of witnessing is not constituted by individual transformation or psychic recovery, as tends to be articulated in Euro-American accounts of witnessing. Rather, I argue, by employing a poetics of witnessing, a play such as *A Woman in Waiting* stages an act of witnessing to a shared injustice while addressing how this history continues to shape the present and the future. Instead of excavating what Laub describes as a 'lost truth' by retrieving the past (Laub, 1992: 91), the poetics of witnessing in Farber's play attests to the survival of the past and the need for black South Africans to continue to speak of what was endured as a form of collective remembrance and as a way of holding the past open, as opposed to imposing a sense of closure. This need to speak out and address the past is evoked Thembi's final lines of the play:

> And we *must* speak … or it will eat us inside.
> We must speak …
> Or our hearts will burst. (Farber, 2008c; original emphasis)

The possibility of testimony becoming a way of narrating the past and transgressing individual lived experience in order to address a collective experience of a shared history is a thematic that is developed in the second example of witnessing I now address.

The witness-narrator: *Parramatta Girls*

As I indicated above, my adoption of the term 'witness-narrator' is borrowed from Kennedy and Wilson's account of bearing witness to shared histories and what, elsewhere, Kennedy has referred to as 'decolonised testimony' (Kennedy, Bell and Emberley, 2009). Kennedy and Wilson (2003) use the term 'witness-narrator' in their reading of testimonial accounts of the past in which the witness is positioned, not as a victim of trauma who struggles to retrieve the truth of a past event, but as a 'narrator' who 'claims to speak as an "expert" about her own condition or experience' (Kennedy and Wilson, 2003: 123). The importation of this concept into my discussion of testimonial theatre enables me to the construct a mode of witnessing where the act of attestation is no longer conceived as an involuntary repeated gesture of a traumatised victim, but is instead relocated as a decisive, voluntary recounting of the past.

A testimonial theatre that draws on witness-narrators tends to focus on multiple narratives of the past where different testimonies are placed together in dialogue in order to construct a shared history of an event of injustice. In this testimonial practice, it is the plurality of voices and the criss-crossing of narratives that become a means of collective bearing witness to the past and which co-creates a shared history of it. As a consequence, many of these testimonies tend to be framed around the endurance of the past as well as the process of survival. It is a mode of witnessing that we encounter in Alana Valentine's *Parramatta Girls* (2007). While described by many theatre scholars in Australia as a 'verbatim play' (Oades, 2010; Peters, 2016), *Parramatta Girls* is, in my view, better understood as a play that is testimonial. For while Valentine drew on numerous verbatim and other sources while researching this play, in the final writing of it she ultimately adopts a mode of story telling that is enacted through the testimony of eight composite characters. These characters emerge in the play as testimonial subjects, who in the narration of their lived experience of Parramatta Girls Training School (GTS), construct a shared history of this now infamous site of incarceration and correction.

Roslyn Oades argues that it is the incorporation of 'historical fact, unflinchingly gruesome details and the distinctly familiar mannerisms of verbatim speech peppered with a good deal of gallows humour too odd to invent' that bestows 'a weighty sense of authenticity' upon the *Parramatta Girls* (Oades, 2010: 61). However, I would suggest that the play's authenticity is better understood as a promise of testimonial truth, constituted by the use of plural testimonial narratives, which provides an insight into the cruelty of the Parramatta GTS from the perspective of those who were incarcerated there. While the testimony that is presented in the play is not reiterated word-for-word from the interviews Valentine undertook when researching the play, it is the stories of these former 'Parramatta girls' and their personal memories of the Parramatta GTS that drive the play's dramaturgy. The play also makes use of direct address, not only to convey the testimonial quality of the stories that are narrated in the play, but also as a means of forging a direct form of communication with the audience who are invited to engage with these characters and their testimony of the past. Direct address also emerges in the play as an effective way of examining the process of remembering itself. In the moments when the play sets aside dialogue and uses direct address, the audience encounter characters who are not only addressing past events, but are exploring the difficult process of remembering and returning to this period of their lives. In these moments, it is the difficulties and risks associated with the act of witnessing that produce some of the most compelling moments in the play. An example of this is Lynette's speech in scene three, in which she describes her own fear of remembering her childhood and returning to Parramatta GTS:

> LYNETTE: Every time I smell something that reminds me, or see something that reminds me, it's like the devil's got hold of one arm and God's gotta hold of the other and they start to pull [...] And it's like I want them to pull harder, pull harder so that they tear my heart in half and tear out my throat and split my jaw and separate my eyes. And that's what every memory of being a child is like. There's no safe place to go back to. It's just the minute I start to remember, the tearing in half begins. And the minute I walked in that gate, that's when the tearing started up again. (Valentine, 2007: 28)

However, through the incorporation of testimony from multiple narrators, the scenes of dialogue and moments of direct address, Valentine is able to move her play beyond a simple examination of suffering and victimhood. Instead, by establishing a collective and dialogical exploration of the past, she draws on multiple testimonies to highlight the social and psychological damage wrought by the brutality of Parramatta GTS, placing this alongside references to the moral discourses around poverty, sexuality and family life that enabled such an institution to exist for so long. In this sense, the play in some way attests to the long and brutal history of the 'notorious Parramatta Girls Home' (Higson, 2007: 6) and the pervading traumatic legacy it left inscribed on those who found themselves confined within its walls. The long history of Parramatta is interwoven with its changing function as a correctional facility, prison and so-called care home. Established on the site of a former Roman Catholic Orphan School, that was once 'Australia's first purpose built establishment for convict women', Parramatta GTS was originally one of Australia's Industrial Schools for Girls where, between 1887 and 1983, approximately 20,000 young women passed through its doors (Parragirls, 2018). These industrial schools 'were not schools in the accepted meaning of the word' (Parragirls, 2018), rather they were the embodiment of how discourses of poverty and neglect were entangled within attitudes towards criminality and morality at the time. The industrial schools were 'intended for children who were neglected, abandoned, orphaned, destitute or had been convicted of a criminal offence' (Parragirls, 2018), and, as such, places such as Parramatta became regulatory institutions for those who, for one reason or another, did not fit into accepted social norms. As such, young people from a range of differing family situations and circumstances were incarcerated together in an institution that was more like a prison than a school, for 'children were committed by a court for a prescribed length of time, and were confined to the institution with very limited contact with the outside world' (Parragirls, 2018).

The Parramatta GTS is examined in a report commissioned by the Australian Senate called *Forgotten Australians: A Report on Australians Who Experienced Institutional or Out-of-home Care as Children* (2004), which addresses the experiences of some 500,000 children who were forced into institutional care. The narratives of the 'Forgotten Australians' share some commonality with many of the indigenous children who were forcibly removed from their families and whose testimonies in the *Bringing Them Home* report (1997) are examined by Kennedy and Wilson. Like these indigenous children, the 'Forgotten Australians' were 'overwhelmingly from poor backgrounds' (Higson, 2007: 5), and their lives were blighted by the brutal and cruel regulatory regimes of the institutions in which they were confined. Valentine 'attended hearings at Parramatta' as part of the Senate inquiry and heard first-hand about the harsh realities of Parramatta, which involved girls 'being addressed by their numbers rather than their names, horrible haircuts, being forced to scrub and perform other domestic duties, and, for many decades, missing out on education' (Higson, 2007: 6). In the dramaturgical development of her play, Valentine drew on this historic material, developing it further by undertaking interviews with 'over 35 women' who had experienced Parramatta GTS (Valentine quoted in Smith, 2014: 18). This was then distilled together to create the eight composite characters who appear in the play when they return to Parramatta GTS as part of a fictive reunion. In the list of characters at beginning of the play, Valentine stipulates that three of the eight women are indigenous, and the indigenous cultures and traditions of these women become interwoven into the action of the play as a whole, creating a shared account of the past that is narrated by both indigenous and non-indigenous women alike.

Describing her dramaturgical process as a form of 'massaged verbatim' (Valentine quoted in Oades, 2010: 59), as discussed above, Valentine's dramaturgy did not seek to replicate the women's 'exact' words, instead her approach focused on capturing 'the spirit, the soul, the way of being in the world that those women were' (Valentine quoted in Oades, 2010: 59). Initially, however, Valentine had started the play by using what she describes as 'pure' verbatim, drawing directly on interview material which she then 'cut up and arranged' (Valentine quoted in Oades, 2010: 60). However, as she got more familiar with the material she was dealing with, she began to see 'patterns' emerging in the women's testimony, both in relation to what the women told her and 'in the way they coped' with their past experiences (Valentine quoted in Oades, 2010: 60). It was this growing awareness of a *collective* experience that led her to make the decision to 'collapse the stories together' and adopt a dramaturgical approach rooted in a collective testimony that would incorporate Valentine's own fictive interventions (Valentine quoted in Oades, 2010: 60). Valentine describes this shift in her approach as being driven by a 'sense of ethical responsibility and the desire to tell a shared story as opposed to focussing on the potentially voyeuristic horror of individual trauma' (Oades, 2010: 61). As Oades suggests, it seems that, for Valentine, the move away from the tightly pre-defined protocols of a verbatim theatre opened up a wider range of dramaturgical approaches that ultimately enabled her to engage with the women's stories in a more nuanced and careful manner. This usefully draws attention to the differences between verbatim and testimonial theatre practices, suggesting that while verbatim theatre approaches can promise a certain commitment to the replication and re-enactment of factual material, this approach does not necessarily produce an ethical dramaturgical response that effectively honours the experience of another person.

By moving away from the word-for-word re-enactment of individual stories, Valentine was able to establish a more ethical practice where she established characters who emerged not as casualties or victims of the past, but as the narrators of it. In this sense, this change of direction in her approach, from verbatim theatre characters to the creation of witness-narrators, was a response to the ethical demand of the women's testimony. By setting aside a more traditional verbatim theatre approach, Valentine instead generated a testimonial form of theatre that established a relational engagement with these women's narratives, where dialogue and interaction between different and contested memories were enabled. An example of this collective and interactive process of witnessing emerges at the start of the play when Gayle and Judi discuss a memory of a dungeon at Parramatta GTS:

> GAYLE: My daughter said don't go down into the dungeons, it won't do you any good. But I want to go down and look at them. I want to see those dungeons. I want to see them again with my own eyes.
> JUDI: There weren't any dungeons. And there's no way guards could have assaulted anyone. They wouldn't have jeopardised their jobs. And they were always with another guard. There was no place down below, no dungeon. It's memory playing tricks on you.
> GAYLE: There were.
> JUDI: Well, I was in here for four years and I don't remember 'em.
> GAYLE: What would you know? (Valentine, 2007: 18)

The collective narration here and at other points in the play enables the women's contested memories to co-exist, sometimes, like in this scene, within an antagonistic manner, where memories conflict. Furthermore, the shared process of remembering also enables the play to bear witness to the importance of friendship and the strong sense of solidarity that emerges among these women both in the past, when incarcerated at Parramatta GTS, and when they revisit the memory of this time and bear witness to it. This enables Valentine to examine the impact of the systems of oppression, violence and degradation of the Parramatta regime on the women's lives, while simultaneously drawing attention to their resilience and their collective struggle to survive. It is an approach that also offers the women themselves some level of protection from the possible effects of retraumatisation that a close retelling of the past can precipitate. This leads me to suggest that the decision to adopt this kind of testimonial approach was rooted in both an ethics of practice and dramaturgical acumen, for it also allowed Valentine to represent characters as multi-dimensional, rather than victims of their past.

The decision to abandon a 'pure verbatim' approach permits the action of the play to move beyond the temporal frame of Valentine's interviews with the women, enabling her to develop a narrative that moves freely between present time and the women's remembered past. This approach also allows for the possibility of the character Maree, a non-indigenous young woman who committed suicide at Parramatta GTS and whose ghostly presence haunts the play and the women's memories throughout. In this sense, the testimonial approaches adopted by Valentine opens up the possibility for the creation of characters who are not bound by their history, but who become actively engaged in the process of remembering the past, not as traumatised subjects, but as witness-narrators who are experts on their own community and the histories that they share. The women we meet in the play return to the past not because psychologically they are in some way stuck there, but to confront this history and, in the words of one of the characters in the play, 'to shake hands with them ol' demons' (Valentine, 2007: 13).

This mode of witnessing, I suggest, moves beyond the psychoanalytical structure of the witness developed in Felman and Laub (1992). For as Kennedy and Wilson point out, in Felman's account of witnessing she 'imagines the reader as a critic/analyst rather than as a non-specialist member of a community' (Kennedy and Wilson, 2003: 126). The use of multiple witnesses in Valentine's play is not configured therefore to reproduce the kind of dyadic analyst/analysand-type relationship of the therapeutic encounter, nor does it seek to unearth a hitherto buried or unconscious truth. By activating multiple witness-narrators in the way that she does, Valentine's play pieces together a shared history that reveals how the moral and political values of the time generated certain structures of prejudice in which, it could be argued, many contemporary Australian institutions continue to be enmeshed. Instead of eliciting empathy or vicarious feelings of distress and trauma from the spectator, Valentine's play addresses the audience as a community, inviting a shared response to the social injustice that generated and sustained the Parramatta GTS. The significance of testimony that is formed as 'an address to a community' is examined by Kennedy and Wilson, who point out that it is a mode of testimonial practice that 'has been neglected by cultural critics in favour of an individualised psychoanalytic approach' (2003: 127). Rather than producing an individualistic, emotional response, testimony performed by witness-narrators can generate active and critical reactions in those whom it addresses, evoking 'feelings of guilt or uncertainty, or an awareness of one's own subject position as white and privileged' (Kennedy and Wilson, 2003: 120–1). This leads me to argue that Valentine's use of testimonial dramaturgy in *Parramatta Girls* not only has an ethical dimension, but a political one. Furthermore, by moving away from a Euro-American formation of testimony, the play also contributes to the wider project of a decolonisation of testimony. Certainly by incorporating indigenous and non-indigenous characters within her play, and by placing these different women alongside each other in friendship, Valentine ensures she does not focus on only one individual narrative of suffering. Through the activation of multiple perspectives and a collective narration of the past, the play generates a shared history that is determined not by a homogeneity of suffering, but by multiple, different experiences. By placing acts of resilience alongside narratives of suffering, the play establishes plural accounts of difference that are informed by moments of allyship, friendship and solidarity in the face of a shared oppressor.

The possibility for testimonial performance as a form of resistance to a shared experience of oppression underpins the third and final mode of witnessing I want to move on to discuss now. Here, I develop an account of what I am calling 'witnessing as resistance' in which the testimonial subject performs and in some way speaks on behalf of a community or for a people, and where the performance of testimony enacts a mode of resistance to hegemonic structures of oppression, historical silencing and genocidal erasure.

Witnessing as resistance: Spiderwoman Theater's *Persistence of Memory* (2002)

In testimonial theatre that enacts what I am describing as a 'witnessing as resistance', it tends to be the witness him or herself, rather than the narrative of a past event, that verifies and authenticates the act of attestation. In this sense, 'witnessing as resistance' refers to testimonial practices that can be best understood as reflecting the Greek etymological account of the *witness as martyr*. As described by Derrida in the discussion above, in formations of the witness as martyr there is no 'explicit reference to the third, to surviving, to presence, or to generation' (Derrida, 2005: 75), instead it is the witness him or herself who becomes 'proof' (Derrida, 2005: 75) and who appeals to the faith of others who in that moment are called upon to attend to and *approve* in some way this act of witnessing. This is not to suggest that the truths asserted within these acts of witnessing are of no relevance at all to the act of attestation being performed. Rather, what I am arguing here is that in this mode of performed witnessing, the dramaturgical positioning of testimony is different from accounts of bearing witness that are framed around the transmission of a narrative of the past. In this mode of witnessing, the promise to speak truthfully grounds the testimonial act which emerges not as a retrieval of the past, but as an act of fidelity to the process of witnessing itself. In this sense, modes of witnessing as resistance set out to trouble or unsettle certain known historical and political narratives, not simply by offering an alternative account of the past, but by insisting on a privileging of the act of witnessing itself both as a performative intervention in which the witness presents themselves as the locus of attestation and as embodied proof.

My conceptualisation of this mode of witnessing is influenced by forms of *testimonio* that have been developed in Latin American contexts. *Testimonio* is a term 'developed to describe a new literary form that emerged in Latin America in the 1960s' (Kennedy, 1997: 235), which was associated with the perspective of the subaltern and a process of speaking out against Western colonial discourses. As Georg Gugelberger and Richard Kearney explain:

> In contrast to conventional writing about the colonial situation, which is produced at the centers of global power and near the apices of class difference, testimonial literature is produced by subaltern peoples on the periphery or the margin of the colonial situation. Thus the margins of empire are now 'writing back' in an overdue attempt to correct the Western canon and its versions of 'truth'. (Gugelberger and Kearney, 1991: 4)

The concept of *testimonio* points towards a form of witnessing that is formed around acts of resistance and the struggle for certain identities and perspectives to be recognised and attended to. *Testimonio* practices are constructed around an insistent challenge to social and historical hegemonic narratives by presenting not only an alternative account of the past, but by foregrounding alternative voices, subject positions and perspectives that have been systematically subjected to processes of erasure and oppression due to historical oppression or genocide. Traditionally rooted in oral presentations, as opposed to written narratives, *testimonio* is a performative act that addresses itself not to individual experience but to collective suffering and social contexts of systemic injustice. It is this shift away from an individual story and its central focus on political resistance that distinguishes forms of *testimonio* from oral history and autobiographical practices. While autobiography, it can be argued, is a 'Western construct' in which cultural and historical narratives are embodied by an individual narrator (Taylor, 1997: 165), *testimonio* counters this approach and 'reflects an antihegemonic and minority practice committed to representing "the people as agents of their own history"' (Sommer quoted in Taylor, 1997: 165). Unlike Euro-American conceptualisations of testimony, which are constitutively determined by individuated witnessing of singular events, the narrator in acts of *testimonio* becomes a representative and tends to speak on behalf of others, for a community or for a people, an approach that is summed up clearly by John Beverley who argues that 'the situation of the narrator in *testimonio* is one that must be representative of a social class or group' (Beverley, 1996: 27). As a consequence he argues, 'the narrator in *testimonio* [...] speaks for or in the name of, a community or group, approximating in this way the symbolic function of the epic hero, without at the same time assuming his hierarchical and patriarchal status' (Beverley, 1996: 27). The witness who narrates *testimonio*, then, is conceptualised very differently from the psychoanalytic subject who seeks to reconstruct the past in order to retrieve remembered events or to in some way process or come to terms with psychic trauma. While the psychoanalytic witness that emerges in Euro-American accounts of witnessing tends to focus on a past event of trauma, the witness in practices of *testimonio* addresses current contexts of trauma and oppression, engaging with the ongoing and long enduring effects oppression and colonisation.

   While Latin American forms of *testimonio* have grown out of the very specific socio-political history of Latin America, the structure of this form of witnessing has been influential in the development of certain forms of testimonial theatre where witnesses emerge to address collective and ongoing situations of oppression. In testimonial plays where this mode of witnessing is used, truth telling is driven not by individual or biographical veracity, but by collective truth-telling processes. To further develop an understanding of how this mode of witnessing operates in practice, I turn now to a play called *Persistence of Memory*, by Spiderwoman Theater.

Founded in New York in 1975, as Ann Haugo explains, Spiderwoman Theater emerged out of the 'feminist theatre movement' that was prevalent at the time (Haugo, 2013: 46) and as such placed women and women's experiences at its heart. The development of the company was initiated by the experimental artist Muriel Miguel, who brought 'women together to perform their own stories' (Haugo, 2013: 47), and, as a consequence, the company's work has tended to foreground personal narrative and the incorporation of actual lived experience into the dramaturgy of its productions. At the point of Spiderwoman Theater's formation, Miguel had been working as a 'modern dancer and choreographer' with Joseph Chaikin and Peter Feldman's Open Theater. She initially formed Spiderwoman Theater by bringing together her two sisters Lisa Mayo and Gloria Miguel, who would later become core members of the company along with Lois Weaver[5] and Brandy Penn (Haugo, 2013: 46). Miguel had grown up 'in a Native family in New York City' with a mother who 'was Rappahannock (American Indian)' and a father who 'was Kuna, an indigenous tribe from the San Blas Islands off the coast of Panama' (Haugo, 2013: 46). As a consequence, Spiderwoman Theater went on to place native American culture and community at its centre, a decision that became formative to its development. While the company often finds itself described as *a Native American* theatre group, since its foundation, its theatre-making approaches have also addressed wider intersectional issues, such as gender, race, class and sexuality. As Miguel indicates in an interview about the foundation of the company:

> We started to define ourselves. We were not White people. We were women of color. We were women. And that is the reason why it eventually turned into a Native theatre, because we had all these things happening to us. [...] We were all sizes, we were all colors, we were all ages, we were all gender-bending, we were grandmothers, some were married. We were all of those things. [...] And a lot of the stuff we thought was racist. And a lot of the stuff, we thought, was classist. (Miguel in Haugo, 2002: 228)

In this sense, the foundation of Spiderwoman Theater was based on a shared desire to speak out against the lived experience of oppression and forms of prejudice in different ways. The founding members of the company collectively engaged in creating theatre as an act of resistance that would address their subjugated lived experience of being women and the intersectional perspectives and identities that were connected with this. Central to their theatre processes was story weaving, a narrative-cum-devising approach that was rooted in indigenous culture.

The concept of story weaving is in fact tied into the name of the company. 'Spiderwoman' references the 'Hopi goddess who taught her people to weave' and was chosen by the founding members of the company to honour a close friend and collaborator of Muriel Miguel and Lois Weaver, Josephine Mofsie (Hopi), who 'died tragically in a car accident' (Haugo, 2013: 47). It was this concept of 'weaving' that became a constitutive element of the company's creative methodology. 'Story weaving' is a creative story-telling process whereby personal and communal narratives become layered upon each other, working together in an interconnected process in order to enact a collective story. It is, I argue, an approach that is resonant of practices of *testimonio*: by layering different narratives together, in this way, a collective story emerges that speaks out against different power structures and forms of injustice, while speaking *for* a collective.

For Muriel Miguel, this story-weaving approach is an identity forming process, where personal and collective truths are woven together in a circular motion, allowing for the exploration of the interconnections between personal, tribal and community truths. She says:

> Storytelling is the way you feel and know where you are within your family, your clan, your tribal affiliations, and from there into the history of how you fit into the world. Storytelling starts at the kitchen table, on your parent's lap, on your aunt's and uncle's laps. Storytelling begins there, about who you are .... Then it continues from there about who you are in the family; of where you are as a tribal member, as part of that particular nation; then where that nation is in the community; and where that community belongs in the world. There's always circles upon circles upon circles. And that's how Spiderwoman approaches theatre, through circles upon circles upon circles. (Miguel in Haugo, 2002: 225)

The centrality of story weaving to the company's process is signalled within their production, *Persistence of Memory*, and in other Spiderwoman performances through the presence of the Spiderwoman quilt, which is used as a background to the performance. It is made from collected textiles, a 'huge mola' that belonged to Gloria Miguel (Miguel in Haugo, 2002: 225), as well as pieces of calico and other quilts given to Muriel Miguel when the company was being formed. Describing it as being part of their shared 'history' (Miguel in Haugo, 2002: 225), Muriel Miguel's account of the quilt captures the collective spirit of the witnessing process underpinning much of the company's work as she draws attention to those who have contributed to the quilt by adding bits to it as they have worked with the company. In this way, the quilt becomes a collective receptacle of the different personal narratives that are interwoven together in the development of each new play and that also bears witness, in some way, to the historical evolution of the company itself. The story-weaving approach could arguably be understood, then, as a form of collective witnessing, where personal, community, and tribal narratives and truths become woven together to form a collective whole.

In *Persistence of Memory*, these personal and communal memories are performed to attest to the historical development and enduring legacy of Spiderwoman Theater itself. The play incorporates extracts from earlier productions that are re-presented alongside imagined scenes, which become woven together to forge a collective testimony that bears witness not only to the enduring successes of the company, but also to its ongoing confrontation of the systematic oppression of women in general and indigenous women specifically. For underpinning much of the theatre work created by Spiderwoman Theater is a desire to challenge audiences and to initiate a reconsideration of how audiences position themselves in relation to the stories the plays explore and the narratives of race, gender and cultural oppression explored in them. As Ann Haugo argues, 'whether Spiderwoman celebrates Native identity with you or asks that you peel away the layers of false knowledge about Native people gained through popular culture, whether you are Native or non-Native, Spider-woman insists that you walk away from a performance with a fuller perspective' (Haugo, 2002: 220–1).

The choice of *Persistence of Memory* as the title of the play and the story of the play's evolution reveal something of the political intentions of this production. According to Lisa Mayo, the title was chosen by the company after they attended a conference in Sweden which was called 'Persistence of Memory' (see Lisa Mayo in Haugo, 2009: 62). It also refer-ences a Salvador Dali painting from 1931, which depicts the image of several 'melted' clock faces in a dark landscape that is lit up by the sun in the distance. The title 'Persistence of Memory' both in relation to the painting, and the Spiderwoman play, seems to point not only to what from the past is easily lost and forgotten, but also to how acts of remember-ing can resist erasure and keep the past alive and potentially change the present in some way. In the context of Spiderwoman's production, it also seems to suggest that collective narratives can operate to remember and honour certain histories, identities and stories. Describing her initial experience of the *Persistence of Memory* conference in Sweden, Gloria Miguel describes the sense of solidarity and connectedness the company encountered when watching other indigenous women performing their stories at this event. It was a moment, it seems, that evoked a sense of interconnection both in relation to everyday lived experiences of oppression and to the history of indigenous communities and indigenous women in particular. As Gloria Miguel explains:

> There was a Sami woman who did perform her show, and it was called *Persistence of Memory* ... and then an African woman performed her show ... and the women from Greenland performed their show, and we performed ours, and we were aware that each time each performer performed, she set out in a circle. [...] We were saying that as Indigenous people we had something in common that came from waaaaayyyyy back and that also included the *Persistence of Memory*, of doing whatever it was it was in a circle [*sic*]. (Muriel Miguel in Spiderwoman Theater, 2009: 62)

This sense of shared but heterogeneous collective memories is performed in *Persistence of Memory* through the use of personal and collective stories adopted to generate a mode of performed witnessing that weaves a story through the past, the present and towards the future of the company. The narratives are conceived as testimonial accounts of personal lived experience, but like the practices of *testimonio*, they address truths that exceed a personal biographical memory. A moment that exemplifies this approach emerges in a scene that explores the birth of Muriel Miguel. Drawing on traditional story-telling patterns, Muriel witnesses her own birth by telling the story of it using ritualised structures of repetition and evoking call and response traditions. In so doing, she not only addresses the past in the retelling of this story, but draws attention to the story's future as she reflects on the importance of retelling stories that bear witness to certain Native histories and identities and to the centrality of traditional forms of story telling within Native communal life.

> MURIEL: I was born in a white room.
> Not in a white sheeted bed
> But on a white floor
> I almost had a white doctor
> No, no I had a white doctor
> 'Til my grandmother took over.
>
> (*Muriel on hands and knees*)
>
> My mother was on her hands and knees
> In the throes of birthing
> I was told this story
> Many, many times
> I can tell this story like I was there.
> The doctor arrived and said.

'No, no this will never do.
What kind of a women are you?
Putting your daughter on her knees and hands'
The word 'savage' hung heavy in the air.

I was told this story
Many, many times.

They put my mother on her back
That's the right way to do it
I was told this story
Many, many times.
'Savage' was murmured.
My grandmother, the midwife, said, 'OUT!
OUT!
This is my daughter, my grandchild;
Besides, it's not knees and hands, it's hands and knees!' (Spiderwoman
Theater, 2009: 45)

What is illustrated in this short scene is how personal testimony is reshaped by Spiderwoman Theater, firstly, to become a means of honouring the past and forming a lineage of testimony through family and other tribal affiliations, but secondly, as a means of witnessing and marking the collectively experienced encounter of racism and erasure that occludes Native American identities from mainstream political and cultural hegemony. The racialising of the birthing process in this scene is countered with Muriel's repeated motif, 'I was told this story many, many times'. This draws attention both to the circular process of life and the way stories are passed on from one generation to the next, but also to how the testimonial process itself bears witness both to the structure and domination of white privilege and 'white' value systems in America and the capacity of Native American women to oppose and disrupt this. While the 'whiteness' of American value systems is signified by the references to the 'white room', the 'white sheeted bed' and the 'white floor', the word 'savage' stands out against this. Contrasting sharply to the natural image of a mother 'in the throes of birthing', it is a term that reminds the audience of the way Native lives are constantly racialised, misrepresented and denigrated, as well as how the natural experience of birth in the West becomes subjected to forms of regulatory discipline, in the Foucauldian sense, particularly when relocated to institutional and/or clinical settings.

The testimonial stories of everyday lived experience that emerge in *Persistence of Memory*, like many other Spiderwoman productions, attest both to the ongoing presence of Native American people within contemporary American life, and the need to resist the ongoing processes of silencing and erasure that these communities constantly encounter. This erasure and misrepresentation of Native lives in American culture has a long history, and the lack of opportunities for Native communities has meant that very few Native-led companies have emerged to be able to tackle the lack of representation in theatre contexts. As Ann Haugo points out, up until the 1960s and 1970s, there was relatively little drama that included Native American characters at all, and the plays that did exist were 'written by non-Native authors about Native subjects' (Haugo, 2013: 39). As such, representations of Native people in film, television and on stage tended to be framed around stereotypes such as the 'noble savage' or the 'red villain' (Haugo, 2013: 40). Furthermore, these stereotypical cultural narratives of Native people also tended to depict Native culture as belonging in the past, representing Native people as historical beings who have been erased in some way from contemporary life. As Haugo argues, 'Perhaps the most egregious fault lies in the fact that these plays, as well as others, tend to depict American Indians in the past tense (as if they no longer exist) rather than as contemporary, living people with families, homes, jobs, and dreams' (Haugo, 2013: 40).

By bearing witness to the history and continued presence of Spiderwoman Theater, *Persistence of Memory* also bears witness to the enduring existence of the vibrant Native American cultures and traditions that continue to shape contemporary American life. In this sense, the personal stories of racism and shame that are interspersed within *Persistence of Memory* do not simply bear witness to the lives and experiences of those who write and perform them, but instead attest to an ongoing and collective struggle of resistance against the continuing processes of subjugation that delimit Native American histories. These testimonies therefore constitute collective acts of resistance in themselves and enact an enduring struggle that is remembered and passed on from one generation to the next. The continuity of this struggle is captured clearly in an extract that is performed by Lisa Mayo:

> LISA: They called him Wahoo, a stupid Indian
> comic strip character. My father, broad
> shouldered, beautiful smile, glistening
> black hair brought a bright light with him
> When he entered a room. I know my own
> memories. I am an expert for only my own
> memories.
> […]
> Shame, anger, hurt. I must tell the youngest

In my family about this. Elizabeth Ashton, my
Grandmother, hid from anyone who entered
our house, hiding behind parlour curtains
Where everyone could see her bare feet. (Spiderwoman Theater, 2009:
49)

In this mode of witnessing, personal narrative is not tied to a singular
biography, nor is it dramatically structured to address a specific political
issue or perspective. Rather, the presence of the witness him or herself
becomes a form of proof and the testimony that is performed attests to
a plural set of identities and a shared struggle, generating collective
testimonial truths that demand to be heard.

Re-locating witnessing: Towards a decolonising of testimony

Through my identification and examination of these three different models
of witnessing, I have sought to rethink the relationship between the
presence of witness, testimonial dramaturgy and the political and social
context each testimonial play addresses. In each of the three modes of
witnessing discussed in this chapter, the play's dramaturgy, in different
ways, signals a move beyond the Euro-American conceptualisations of
trauma. As such, the narratives and structural form of these plays relocate
and rethink the conceptualisations of witnessing that have dominated
theatre's engagement with trauma, memory and witnessing since the
inauguration of trauma studies in the 1980s. These new decolonised
engagements with testimony foreground the lived experience of the witness
and place testimony centrally within the dramaturgical process. Consequently, it is the witness who drives the action forward by becoming the
agent as opposed to the object of the narrative explored within the play.

As such, in these forms of contemporary testimonial dramaturgies,
the witness is no longer constructed as seeking to retrieve a singular past
narrative; nor is she (or he) conceptualised as retrieving a past memory
in order to come to terms with a past trauma. Rather, through an engagement with collective and shared acts of witnessing, these decolonised
forms of testimonial theatre have sought to address on-going suffering
by acknowledging and engaging with the legacy of the past and using
testimonial practices to address the structures of oppression that continue
to dominate and subjugate those who are deemed 'other'. By moving

witnessing beyond the recuperation of an unsayable and traumatic past event, these dramaturgical processes also reveal the political dimension of testimonial practices. For the act of witnessing can be understood as a performance of alliance with others, where remembering the past and acknowledging present suffering opens up moments of potential solidarity with others.

In the final chapter of the book, I further examine the political potency of testimonial theatre by looking at how testimonial performance can enact a speaking out against structures of power. Here, I position some testimonial narratives as performing what Michel Foucault (2001) describes as acts of *parrhesia*, a form of speech that takes a risk and speaks truth 'to someone who exercises power over him [or her]' (Foucault, 2001: 17). This leads me to examine how testimonial theatre not only exposes certain processes of erasure and silencing, but how it can intervene within discourses of oppression by speaking out against hegemonic structures and disclose certain overlooked narratives and the truths they reveal. Drawing on three different plays that deal with contemporary racism, I examine how testimonial performance can activate certain truth-telling processes and how different testimonial-based dramaturgical practices elicit a commitment to action through a process of speaking out on behalf of those who endure the insidious injustices of racism. This discussion then leads me to consider how the testimonial subject comes to be structured politically and ethically within this form of dramaturgy and, finally, how the ethical demand of testimony might be understood as determining the structure and approach of this form of theatre making.

Notes

1 See my 2011 article "'That's Who I'd Be, If I Could Sing": Reflections on a Verbatim Project with Mothers of Sexually Abused Children', *Studies in Theatre and Performance*, 31(2) for a more extended discussion of writing this verbatim play.
2 Of course, Frantz Fanon's philosophical engagement with the internal landscape of colonialism and racism also had a psychoanalytic dimension to it, and this is, therefore, potentially problematic. However, I am inclined to agree with Craps's assertion that psychoanalysis is not necessarily 'doomed to assist in the repression of the colonized' (Craps, 2015: 35). Rather, following the work of Ranjana Khanna in this area, psychoanalysis can arguably be repositioned as becoming 'the means through which contingent postcolonial futures can be imagined ethically' (Khanna 2003 quoted in Craps, 2015: 35).
3 *Shoot* is the title of a short film piece by performance artist Chris Burden, who in 1971, at F-Space, Santa Ana in California, staged a shooting of himself by a friend who, standing fifteen feet away, shot Burden in the arm with a rifle.

4 A limit-experience is a term used in phenomenological philosophy, particularly Heidegger, to describe the encounter of the self with its own most finitude (Heidegger, 2008). It describes a response to an event or action that is so intense and seemingly impossible that the subject's existential sense of self is radically disrupted and is no longer recognisable. In his essay, 'The Limit-Experience', Maurice Blanchot, drawing on the work of George Bataille, describes the limit-experience as 'the response that man encounters when he has decided to put himself radically into question' (Blanchot, 2003: 203).

5 Lois Weaver together with Peggy Shaw would, in 1980, go on to form Split Britches, one of America's most longstanding and well-known feminist performance companies.

4

Testimony as speaking out: performing the ethico-political imperatives of witnessing

I knew when they told my mom, when the school called her, they were gonna say, 'Niya got in something that didn't involve her'. And that's exactly what they did. So I knew her mind-set was gonna be, 'Oh, Niya! Why didn't you be quiet?' You know, because that's the response I got in third grade. You know, and 'Mind your business, it didn't have nothin' to do with you'. […] And then, *they're* telling me: 'Mind your business, this don't have nothing to do with you'. 'But he just threw a whole girl across a classroom!' How can you mind your business? Like, that's somethin' you need to *make* your business. (Smith, 2019: 75–6)[1]

In a section simply entitled 'The Shakara Story' in *Notes from the Field*, Anna Deavere Smith enacts Niya Kenny, a black eighteen-year-old woman who, in 2015, witnessed a white police officer enter her classroom at Spring Valley High School and violently tip a classmate off her chair, drag her across the floor, before pinning her down and putting her in handcuffs. According to Erik Eckholm in the *New York Times* (2016), the deputy sheriff had been called to the classroom that day because Shakara had 'refused a teacher's order to put away her cellphone then refused an order to leave the classroom' (Eckholm, 2016). Shocked by the violence she witnessed, Kenny intervened and shouted out at the police officer to stop, encouraging other students in the class to film the incident '*to record this! Put it on Snapchat!*' (Smith, 2019: 72, original emphasis). This decision to speak out against what she saw as an injustice would have severe repercussions for Kenny. Shortly after the deputy sheriff had removed Shakara from the classroom, he returned to arrest Kenny herself who was subsequently also handcuffed and taken into custody. Since she was eighteen and considered an adult by the legal system she was then placed in an adult jail where she was later charged before finally being released. Footage of the events that took place in the classroom that day soon went viral, prompting 'an unsettling national discussion' in the United States about whether black students in public high schools were being 'disproportionally punished' and raising questions about the role of the police in high schools (Fausset, Pérez-Peña and Blinder, 2015). In the performance of *Notes from the Field* that I saw at the Royal Court in June 2018, mobile phone footage of Shakara being thrown off her chair and dragged across the room was projected onto the back wall of the stage, providing a disturbing accompaniment to Smith's performance of Kenny.

The 'Shakara Story' was certainly one of the most shocking stories told in *Notes from the Field* and has been a part of the performance that I have found myself discussing most often with others who also saw the play in London in 2018. The violence with which the young, diminutive Shakara is tipped out of her chair and thrown across the room is extremely unsettling; incongruent with the quiet atmosphere of the maths class. The replaying of the filmed footage in the play was highly evocative, adding potency to Smith's portrayal of Niya whose voice is evident in the filmed footage shouting out in horror at what she sees. The 'Shakara Story' powerfully draws attention to the central themes of *Notes from the Field*, reminding us not only that this is a play is about the real lived experience of people of colour in America today, but that the performance itself is also about the act of speaking out against the injustice and the discrimination encountered by these communities in the USA. This importance of speaking out is highlighted further by the incorporation of the mobile phone footage. The use of filmed phone footage as a means of evidencing police violence and the discriminatory practices endured by people of colour has become a familiar tactic of resistance in the United States and beyond and is often used by minoritarian communities to highlight and expose the injustices and violence these communities are subjected to by state agencies, such as the police.

Smith's enactment of Niya is carefully and skilfully undertaken, producing a compelling performance of an angry young woman who is determined to call out the injustice she observes. In her enactment, Smith positions Niya not only as a witness to this event, but as someone performing what Michel Foucault describes as *parrhesia*; a mode of truth telling in which the *parrhesiastes*, the speaker, risks everything to speak out freely and openly about an injustice. Foucault conceptualises *parrhesia* as a politicising process, describing it as the 'truth-telling of the political man' (Foucault, 2010: 159), in which the *parrhesiastes* speaks truth to power. When testimonial performance enacts a mode of *parrhesia*, a politics of witnessing emerges that foregrounds the witness centrally within the narrative as a political subject. In the process of speaking out, the act of bearing witness as *parrhesia* becomes political, enacting a commitment to testimonial truths, while also staging a mode of resistance to hegemonic narratives that supress certain perspectives from being heard or being recognised. Borrowing from Kay Schaffer and Sidonie Smith's writing on the political acuity of life narratives and story telling, *parrhesiastic* forms of testimonial narratives have the potential to 'intervene in the public sphere, contesting social norms, exposing the fictions of official history, and prompting resistance beyond the provenance of the story' (Schaffer and Smith, 2004: 4). By performing the witness as *parrhesiastes*, the theatre maker transforms the testimonial process into a political act, reconfiguring witnessing as an act of resistance.

To develop these ideas in this chapter I examine three plays, each of which addresses police racism and racialised social injustice. In the first section, I begin with an example of what I consider to be a missed opportunity for the restaging of an act of *parrhesia*. In *The Colour of Justice*, a tribunal play that received a very positive critical response when it opened at the Tricycle Theatre in 1999, the restaging of a public inquiry raises some important political questions about institutional police racism but also stops short of representing a protagonist who speaks a truth to power. While the play certainly represents a series of witnesses whose testimony evidences some serious failings within the London Metropolitan Police force, the political agency of those witnesses who were so active in the campaign that led to the inquiry being initiated by the government are ultimately dis-abled by the narrative structure of the play and its strict adherence to the tribunal form. Conversely, in the *Hounding of David Oluwale* (2009), a contrasting approach is adopted and by turning away from verbatim theatre, Oladipo Agboluaje draws on a poetics of witnessing to establish a dramaturgical approach in which David Oluwale re-emerges from the dead to embody a mode of *parrhesia* and speaks out about his death and the racist violence he endured when alive. Through this use of the revenant as *parrhesiastes*, Agboluaje moves the audience beyond an empathic engagement with a victim of crime and instead reconstructs a witness who speaks truth to power in a dramaturgy that resists the erasure of the murdered black subject. This leads me to a third example of testimony as *parrhesia* and to an examination of Smith's *Notes from the Field*, which draws on different testimonies by multiple witnesses who speak truth to power. Smith developed her play by drawing directly on interviews she undertook with numerous people from different communities across the United States. The play tells the story of racialised poverty in the United States, the criminalisation of young people of colour and the trauma endured as a result of this. It also draws attention to the risks of speaking out about this injustice and the personal costs of *parrhesiastic* gestures. In the final section of this chapter, I turn to consider the ethical implications of making theatre that incorporates acts of *parrhesia* and the political and ethical dimensions of theatrical acts of attestation that draw on real lived experience and real witnesses. In order to think through the responsibility that frames the re-enactment of other people's testimonial accounts of the past, I draw on the philosophy of Simon Critchley (2007) and theorisation developed by the Danish philosopher Knud Ejler Løgstrup (1997) to argue that relationships of trust are a necessary element of any dramaturgical process that stages other people's testimony and which engages with the riskiness of *parrhesiastic* acts of witnessing. Importing some of the ethical theories developed by these two philosophers into my engagement with testimonial performance, I develop an account of what I describe as the 'ethical demand of testimonial practice', a framework that establishes the key co-ordinates of a collaborative testimonial practice that is both ethically and politically nuanced.

Performing *parrhesia*: The dramaturgy of speaking truth to power

In his account of the act of *parrhesia*, Foucault positions riskiness as a distinguishing element of speaking truth to power. Describing the *parrhesiastes* as one 'who stands up, speaks, tells the truth to a tyrant, and risks his life' (Foucault, 2010: 61) Foucault characterises *parrhesia* as an act that implicates the speaker at the profoundest level, requiring the *parrhesiastes* to take a great risk and venture into the unknown when speaking out. It is, in fact, this sense of risk taking that leads Foucault to argue that the act of *parrhesia* should be understood as being in an oppositional relationship to the performative utterance of a speech act, as theorised by J. L. Austin ([1962] 2018) and John Searle ([1969] 1999). While the speech act is a performative mode of truth telling in which the utterance enacts a truth, bringing about some form of change in the world (e.g. in speech acts such as: *I name this ship, I pronounce you husband and wife*), in the act of *parrhesia*, Foucault argues, change occurs in a much more open, fluid and undetermined context. A speech act is performed to produce what Foucault describes as a 'codified effect' (Foucault, 2010: 62), because the speaker performing a speech act knows in advance what sort of change will be enacted as a result of this utterance. Yet the act of *parrhesia* 'opens up an unspecified risk' (Foucault, 2010: 62) and, as such, cannot pre-empt the dangers the *parrhesiastes* will face as a result. In this sense, as Foucault suggests, *parrhesia* could be understood as a truth-telling process that is constitutively risky. Through this act of speaking out, a 'fracture' is produced '[opening] up the risk: a possibility, a field of dangers, or at any rate, an undefined eventuality' (Foucault, 2010: 63), and it is this element of risk that arguably opens up the ethical dimensions of *parrhesiastic* testimonial practice.

In a testimonial dramaturgy in which the witness speaks truth to power, the testimonial subject places his or her testimony in the hands of the theatre maker and, in so doing, becomes participant within a process of theatre making that is framed around an act of appropriation. By turning an act of witnessing into a play, the theatre maker must act on behalf of the witness, navigating the risks of betrayal or exploitation of this act of attestation as the testimony is transformed into a play text. To take responsibility for the testimonial subject, who participates within such a testimonial process as a *parrhesiastes*, requires not only care in engaging with the witness, but a recognition of how the ethical demand of such a relationship must inform the dramaturgical structure of the play itself. In other words, in order for a testimonial play to enact a form of *parrhesia*, the witness must be granted a degree of autonomy and be able to speak freely about what has been lived through and the injustices that have been endured. However, this autonomy must also be navigated alongside the need for editorial intervention and the shaping of the dramatic material. In a process that foregrounds the testimonial subject as *parrhesiastes*, the play's dramaturgy must also be configured to work alongside the act of bearing witness and be structured so as to facilitate as opposed to renarrating this process of truth telling. In this sense, for a testimonial play to re-enact *parrhesia*, the dramaturgical structure must serve to position the witness as an agent of their own narrative, where they retain the capacity to speak openly and freely about the events they seek to attest to.

The act of speaking truth to power in testimonial theatre places both ethical and political pressure on a play's dramaturgical structure and, in the context of tribunal theatre, as I will go on to argue, this can take on a somewhat paradoxical quality. For while witnesses are introduced into the play in order to interrogate the truth of the events examined, the dramaturgical text of the play is always tightly predetermined by the format and content of the inquiry itself. In tribunal theatre, in other words, it is the procedural structure of the inquiry as opposed to the truth telling of the witnesses that ultimately determines the dramaturgical shaping of the play. By adopting the tribunal approach, the playwright commits him or herself to a particular ethics of practice, determined by the tribunal form and is therefore confined to using only material from the inquiry upon which the play is based. In so doing, however, the play foregrounds certain narratives and political perspectives that do not always coalesce with the act of witnessing itself, and sometimes the dramaturgy of the tribunal play can overlook the testimonial truth that the witness is trying to express. In the case of *The Colour of Justice*, which I now go on to discuss, the dramatic action of the play is structured to align closely with the inquiry upon which the play was based. As a result however, the play also has little capacity to move beyond the structure of the inquiry nor, for that matter, can it easily critique it. As such, the political potential of *The Colour of Justice* comes to be predetermined by the values of the inquiry itself, and this limits its capacity to give expression to any of the testimonial truths with which it engages.

The Colour of Justice: The absent *parrhesiastes*

The Colour of Justice opened at the Tricycle Theatre on 6 January 1999, a month prior to the publication of the Stephen Lawrence inquiry, a public investigation ordered by the UK's Home Secretary at the time, Jack Straw. Led by Sir William Macpherson, the inquiry examined the murder of the black teenager Stephen Lawrence, the police's mishandling of the investigation and the accusations that the management of the case had been impeded by the racism of the officers involved. In writing *The Colour of Justice*, Richard Norton-Taylor edited together material from '69 days of public hearings' (Norton-Taylor, 1999: 7), creating a tribunal play that draws out some of the key elements of the inquiry and which examines the accusations of racism that were levelled against the Metropolitan Police. Through the reanimation of the interrogation of various police officers, the play reconstructs the events of the 22 April 1993, when eighteen-year-old Stephen Lawrence and his friend Duwayne Brooks were waiting at a bus stop in Eltham, South East London, where they were approached by a group of 'about six white boys' (Norton-Taylor, 1999: 39) shouting explicitly racist abuse at them. Duwayne Brooks called out to his friend to run, however, on turning back he saw that Stephen had been surrounded and had been struck by something that knocked him to the floor. As Stephen got up to try to run again, he collapsed as a result of what was later revealed to be two large knife wounds 'on both sides of his body' that had 'severed major arteries' (Lawrence, 2006: 73). The first emergency unit to arrive at the scene were two police officers, both of whom failed to attend to Stephen's injuries, apply basic first aid or do anything to staunch the flow of blood from the wounds he had received. These significant failures became one of the first of many accusations of incompetence and racism levelled against the Metropolitan Police force, because, as the play makes clear, the decision not to provide any first aid care was viewed by many as evidence of 'police officers not wishing to dirty their hands with a black man's blood' (Norton-Taylor, 1999: 27). Through the re-enactment of the testimony from various police officers involved in the case, the audience learns of further failings that hampered the investigation into Stephen's murder, such as the inadequate support provided to the Lawrence family and the poor and disrespectful treatment of Duwayne Brooks, who initially, at least, was viewed not as a witness or a potential victim, but as adversarial and potentially culpable in some way.

The play was highly political at the time it was premiered at the Tricycle, not least because of what Joe Kelleher refers to as its 'topicality' (Kelleher, 2009: 21). *The Colour of Justice* was '"about" something going on in the world that should not be happening, that should be preventable' (Kelleher, 2009: 21). In this sense, one of the key successes of the play was its capacity to open up the findings of the Stephen Lawrence inquiry to public debate by making a legalistic process more directly accessible and relatable. Certainly, the play played an important role in disseminating the outcomes of the inquiry. By opening a month before the inquiry published its findings, it was the play and not the Macpherson Report that first made the key findings in the report public. However, notwithstanding these successes, I would argue the play also missed an important opportunity to engage directly with the campaign for justice for Stephen Lawrence that played such a critical role in raising awareness of the racism that had impacted so significantly upon this investigation and which ultimately led to the government calling for this inquiry. The campaign was largely led by Doreen and Neville Lawrence, Stephen's parents, who were supported by other key leaders in the black community who, in the years following Stephen Lawrence's murder, fought vociferously for justice and public recognition of the prejudicial attitudes that had marred the police investigation. This side-lining of the Lawrences, and the Lawrence campaign within the play, is significant, I suggest, firstly because it appears to reduce the role the Lawrences played in the fight for justice for their son, and secondly, but just as importantly, because it overlooks their role as *parrhesiastes* in this campaign. For the Lawrences's fight for justice for their son was essentially a *parrhesiastic* campaign, in which the Lawrences and their supporters sought to speak truth to power by exposing the police racism that hindered the investigation into their son's death and insisting that the inability to apprehend and charge anyone was ultimately a result of the police's discriminatory practices and their partiality towards those who were suspected of the murder. These acts of *parrhesia* required the key protagonists to take great personal risks, opening them up to public scrutiny and criticism. As Doreen Lawrence makes clear in her book about her son's death, when she explains that in the course of campaigning to bring the 'state to admit that terrible wrongs had been done to [her] son and to [her] family', she was 'ignored and derided for protesting too much' (Lawrence, 2006: x).

At the time of writing this book, some twenty-six years after the murder, the UK has just celebrated its first ever Stephen Lawrence Day commemorating the life of the murdered teenager. In an article in *The Guardian* newspaper to mark this occasion, Doreen Lawrence spoke out not only of the work being done to commemorate her son, but also of the need to 'admit our communities are still unequal', leading her to call for an acknowledgment that racism in Britain is still a battle that needs to be fought (Lawrence, 2019). The Lawrences's long and very public campaign is, of course, one of the reasons that the name of Stephen Lawrence is imprinted into public memory in a way that is not the case for so many other young black men who were also murdered on the streets. Yet, while the play effectively contributed to this process of memorialising, not least by transferring to the West End and being televised by the BBC, it also failed to capture the importance of the Lawrence campaign and what it achieved politically. Furthermore, Doreen and Neville Lawrence and the black community who supported their campaign are largely absent from the play itself. This absence is heightened further by the lack of black actors who appear in the play. As Robert Butler pointed out in an article in *The Independent* newspaper at the time, the production included only 'a handful of black performers', with Doreen Lawrence being allocated only 'five lines' and with Mr Lawrence getting 'none' (Butler, 1999). In this sense, while the campaign for justice for Stephen Lawrence was founded on acts of *parrhesia* and was undertaken predominantly by the Lawrence family and the black community, the debates of police racism and racial injustice explored in the play do not focus on this struggle. Instead, the dramaturgy of the play is framed around a narrative of hegemonic institutional critique with the action of the drama being developed by white establishment figures, such as Sir William MacPherson, Edmund Lawson, Michael Mansfield and Jeremy Gompertz. The absence of black characters is all the more significant because, of course, the issue of race was critical both to the murder of Stephen Lawrence and the proceedings of the inquiry. The Lawrences's insistence that their son's murder was racially motivated and the refusal of the police to acknowledge this became a key thematic in both the inquiry and the play. However, while Norton-Taylor's faithful replication of the inquiry process certainly ties the dramaturgy of the play closely to the inquiry proceedings, this approach also meant that the perspective of key black protagonists, such as Doreen and Neville Lawrence or Duwayne Brooks, Stephen's friend, is relegated to the side-lines of the play's narrative.

One example where this absence becomes particularly significant relates to Mrs Lawrence's sense of anger at the government's reluctance to hold an inquiry. While this is hinted at points in the play, it is somewhat side-lined by a dramaturgy that is more interested in a narrative focusing on the culpability of individual police officers. In one of the few scenes when Doreen Lawrence gets to speak, we sense her frustration with the way she is being positioned within the inquiry. It is a scene that occurs near the end of the play and depicts Mrs Lawrence's interrogation by Jeremy Gompertz, the QC Counsel for the Commissioner of the Metropolitan Police:

> GOMPERTZ: Can I ask you about something quite different now: your journey home from the hospital on the night in question. You went, did you not, to the Welcome Inn?
> MRS LAWRENCE: No.
> GOMPERTZ: Where did you go then?
> MRS LAWRENCE: Can I ask a question here? Am I on trial here or something here? I mean, from the time of my son's murder I have been treated not as a victim. Now I can only tell you or put into my statements what I know of [what] went on that night. And for me to be questioned in this way, I do not appreciate it. (Norton-Taylor, 1999: 115)

The short exchange between Gompertz and Doreen Lawrence is over quickly and soon the action moves on to another scene. As a consequence, Doreen Lawrence's criticisms of the inquiry remain undeveloped and her perspective is somewhat erased from the play. In part, this is a result of Norton-Taylor's perspective and his own editorial decisions. However, it is also because the play makes use of a tribunal form that relies entirely on the use of transcribed material. As a consequence, Norton-Taylor can only draw on what was directly said, and the play therefore simply repeats and replicates any points of erasure that emerged as a result of the structure and format of the inquiry itself.

This is not to say that the play did not perform an important function in disseminating the findings of the inquiry, not least because it was able to make this public before the report was published by Macpherson. As theatre scholar Janelle Reinelt aptly points out, the timeliness of *The Colour of Justice* contributed to the public's engagement with the Stephen Lawrence inquiry and events it addresses. She also goes on to argue that by enacting a truth-telling process, the play not only intervened in the way the public thought about the case, but how it psychologically came to terms with Stephen Lawrence's murder: 'coming shortly before the dramatic conclusions of the Macpherson Report, the initial performances repeated and rehearsed the facts, reclaimed their undeniability at a time when the public was wanting "closure" – to be comforted even, by this reassertion of the "truth"' (Reinelt, 2006: 80). While I think Reinelt is right to argue that the play helped raise a general awareness of the findings of inquiry, at least among the theatre going public, to interpret the play in the way she does here risks perceiving this sense of closure as something that was experienced by the multiple communities in Britain, and I am not convinced this is the case. This perspective certainly does not seem to resonate with the viewpoint of Doreen Lawrence who, in 2018, argued that the treatment of those who have been stabbed on the streets of London is still largely influenced by the ethnicity of the victim, leading her to say recently, 'the government needs to get a grip. It comes under the race issue again – look who's dying. If that was the amount of kids who were in the white community that were dying, do you think that something would have been done?' (Lawrence in Greenfield, 2018).

Any sense of comfort communicated by the play should therefore be understood as being directed towards a white community who are to be reassured that the Metropolitan Police is capable of dealing with its own shortcomings and are still a trustworthy institution, able to acknowledge its own tendencies and biases. Yet of course, while *The Colour of Justice* disseminated and 'rehearsed the facts' of the Stephen Lawrence case (Lawrence in Greenfield, 2018), these truths had also been addressed by the Lawrences's campaign some years earlier, which in 1994 led to a private prosecution that ultimately failed to secure any convictions. In this sense, I would suggest that another way of interpreting the truth-telling function of *The Colour of Justice* is to say that it examined how the Metropolitan Police, as a state institution, was being forced to acknowledge its own inadequacies and racist tendencies as a result of the Stephen Lawrence campaign. However, the play was unable to foreground the political work of the campaign. The tribunal form meant that the dramaturgy of the play ultimately ended up caught in a narrative of institutional self-critique, where the murder of Stephen Lawrence became a sub-plot or an inciting incident to a different drama: one that exposed a series of corrupt police officers and forced an institution to reflect on its own discriminatory practices.

If we view *The Colour of Justice* as a play, rather than an extension of a highly political juridical process, it becomes possible to recognise the limitations of the tribunal form to enact a form of politics. For while the play successfully disseminates the political processes of the Stephen Lawrence inquiry, the focus on the re-enactment of transcribed material means that the dramaturgy itself remains entangled within a replaying of the internal politics of this state-led initiative and unable to offer any critique of this. In this sense, the tribunal form relegates the play to a position within the hegemonic apparatus where it can disseminate but not interrogate or critique the juridical processes it represents. This complicity with the hegemonic apparatus of the state is made clear in the opening scene of the play where Sir William Macpherson addresses the audience to explain the function of the inquiry, moving on to directly address the parents of Stephen Lawrence and the 'dreadful' suffering they have endured (Norton-Taylor, 1999: 19). In his somewhat prosaic statement, Macpherson neatly positions Mr and Mrs Lawrence not within a political context but within a discourse of victimhood saying:

> MACPHERSON: To Mr and Mrs Lawrence, these years must have been dreadful. We hope sincerely that while nothing can alleviate the pain and loss which they have suffered, they may accept that all of us have done our best to establish what was done so that the future may not see repetition of any errors which may be uncovered during our hearings. (Norton-Taylor, 1999: 19)

The use of Macpherson's opening speech to open the play subtly frames the dramatic action within the institutional perspective of Macpherson, who is established as the one who will preside over the truth-telling processes that follow. As such, we do not, for example, find out that, prior to the inauguration of the inquiry, the Lawrence family raised serious objections with the Home Secretary about the appointment of William Macpherson, nor do we hear of the 'indignation in the black press' or *The Observer* newspaper stating that 'Macpherson was insensitive on issues of race' (Lawrence, 2006: 180). Furthermore, by omitting the black character Dr John Sentamu from the play, who was one of the inquiry's advisors, Norton-Taylor could not include his opening comments to the inquiry, which were differently nuanced to Macpherson's and served to acknowledge the struggle of the Lawrences. Doreen Lawrence reports him as saying:

> Words, arguments and counter-arguments are going to be vigorously offered throughout this inquiry. Let us not forget in that combat the really hurting ones: Neville and Doreen Lawrence and Stephen's brother and sister, Stuart and Georgina. For five years they have laboured hard to see the truth and justice prevail since Stephen was brutally murdered on 22nd April 1993. (Lawrence, 2006: 183)

The narrative of victimhood that comes to be allocated to Mr and Mrs Lawrence could be viewed as also being extended to the way Stephen Lawrence himself is positioned within the play. Encountered in the course of the drama only through his absence, Stephen Lawrence emerges as an almost mythic presence and victim who represents the tragedy of lost potential. This is further established through the play's dramaturgical form. For the tribunal structure does not allow for metaphorical or figurative truths, and by rooting itself firmly in a re-enactment of the proceedings of the inquiry itself, the play includes very few characters who knew Stephen personally. As a consequence, the reality of Stephen remains only loosely sketched out, and he is represented as an almost symbolic, iconic figure.

While statements from Mr and Mrs Lawrence and Duwayne Brooks were presented to the inquiry, in the course of the play, presumably in order to factually replicate the format of the inquiry itself, these statements are read not by the witnesses themselves, but are presented by their legal representatives and this ultimately further removes any sense of a direct engagement with the real 'Stephen'. This dramaturgical approach stands in contrast to the way the character Jamie Acourt is constructed. Acourt was one of the suspects initially identified by Duwayne Brooks, who was arrested in the months following the murder, but was then released. Acourt appears in the play in a highly dramatic scene that takes place near the end where he is cross-examined by Michael Mansfield, a QC for the Lawrence family. Although Acourt says very little, the scene is dramatic because while the rest of the play has focused predominantly on the police investigation of the murder, here the audience comes face-to-face with someone who may have been present when Stephen was killed or who may even be one of the perpetrators of the murder. In the terse exchanges with Mansfield, Acourt refuses to be drawn into a dialogue, despite the compelling evidence he's presented with that has been taken from police surveillance footage of him and his brothers. While the other witnesses in the play, most of whom are members of the police force, present carefully worded responses when cross-examined, Acourt responds with largely one word answers and seems less prepared. As such the scene takes on a more naturalistic quality and would seem to require a degree of psychologically nuanced acting, not least because the short 'no' and 'yes' answers uttered by Acourt require some actorly intervention in their enactment. The scene is made all the more unsettling because the crude racism, adopted by Acourt's associates and captured on the surveillance footage, is repeated verbatim back to him by Lawson, QC counsel to the inquiry within the scene. However, despite this, Acourt remains undeterred and continues to say little, appearing calm and almost triumphant in the face of these accusations, thus further implicating himself.

The dramaturgical construction of Acourt in this scene stands in marked contrast to the discourse of victimhood that determines the construction of Doreen and Neville Lawrence. By being presented as essentially passive characters who have no agency, the play's dramaturgy transforms Doreen and Neville Lawrence from political subjects, who have been wronged in some fundamental way and who are antagonistically and forcefully demanding justice, into what Luc Boltanski (2004) describes as 'unfortunates'; those who come to be viewed through their positioning as victims. In this sense, the play radically shifts audience engagement with the narrative surrounding the murder of Stephen Lawrence away from the acts of *parrhesia* that marked out the Lawrence's campaign for justice and instead frames Stephen and the Lawrences in a dramaturgy underpinned by a 'politics of pity' (Boltanski, 2004: 3). Developing his interrogation of the spectacle of the suffering of others through an engagement with Hannah Arendt's essay 'On Revolution', Boltanski distinguishes the 'politics of pity' from what he describes as 'a politics of justice' (Boltanski, 2004: 3). In the politics of pity, he argues, 'good fortune and misfortune are conditions that define separate groups' (Boltanski, 2004: 4) and, as a consequence, such a politics 'regards the unfortunate together *en masse*' as objects of pity (Boltanski, 2004: 4), instead of individuals who have agency. Such a formulation regards the unfortunate as a victim of suffering, and any call for change does not therefore entail a call for political action but instead becomes driven by a desire 'to bring an end to the suffering' (Boltanski, 2004: 4). In *The Colour of Justice*, the dedicated commitment to the tribunal form, I suggest, restages a politics of pity where Stephen Lawrence comes to be viewed as an unlucky 'unfortunate' whose murder led to a process of important institutional self-critique on the part of the police and juridical establishment. While, without a doubt, the inquiry itself brought about changes in police procedure, there is little to suggest that it was sufficient to inaugurate a sense of closure to the black community who continue to experience the day-to-day impact of unchecked racism on the streets of London. As such, while the play engages with the politics of race, it also shifts the debate away from the lived experience of racism and resistance to it. In this sense, by adopting the tribunal form and centring the dramaturgy around the identification of the few 'bad' racist police officers who were culpable for the mistakes in the investigation of Stephen's murder, the play misses the opportunity to restage the form of *parrhesiastic* speaking out that propelled the campaign that fought for justice for him. As a consequence the play ultimately diminishes the agency of the Lawrence family both in the play's dramatic structure and in its depiction of them as political subjects, despite the fact that the campaign was efficacious and ultimately provoked the government to call for an inquiry.

The Hounding of David Oluwale: The revenant as *parrhesiastes*

In the writing of *The Hounding of David Oluwale*, written ten years prior to *The Colour of Justice*, playwright Oladipo Agboluaje made the conscious decision *not* to adopt a verbatim/tribunal writing approach. In Agboluaje's play, which examines the death of Nigerian born David Oluwale, who was relentlessly and repeatedly assaulted by two members of the Leeds police force, David Oluwale is brought back to life as a ghostly presence to speak out about the injustice and racism he endured during his life in Britain. By approaching the story in this way, Agboluaje moves his play beyond a narrative of victimhood, repositioning David Oluwale as a political character who can speak out from his own lived experience and tell his own story.

Produced by Eclipse, a black-led Sheffield-based production company, *The Hounding of David Oluwale* opened in 2009 at the West Yorkshire Playhouse in Leeds, some forty years after the body of David Oluwale was pulled out of the river Aire, near Leeds Bridge. Adapted from a book of the same name by Kester Aspden (2008), Agboluaje's play tells the story of David Oluwale who, in 1949, arrived as a stowaway in the UK, aged just nineteen, on board the *Temple Bar* cargo ship from Lagos, Nigeria. For many migrants from West African colonies at that time, the United Kingdom represented the possibility for new opportunities and a chance to play a part in the British post-war industrial context, rebuilding Britain after the war. After arriving in Hull, Oluwale, or 'David' as he is known in Agboluaje's play, spent his first month in the UK in Armley prison in Leeds, serving a 'twenty-eight-day sentence' (Aspden, 2008:

22) for entering Britain as a stowaway. After his release, he was able to use his training in tailoring to find employment in the city's clothing industry. However, life in the UK proved hard. Racism was rife, money hard to come by and employment opportunities somewhat sporadic. The reality of Britain for David was far removed from the promises sold by white British colonialists back in Nigeria, where 'the grass was always greener elsewhere. And the grass was greenest in the UK' (Agboluaje, 2009: 49). Following several difficult years in and out of employment, between 1953 and 1969 David fell into what Kester Aspden describes as his 'lost years', where 'he fell off the map – the social, physical and moral map' (Aspden, 2008: 50), living either as an inmate within a mental asylum, on the streets or in prison. It was soon after his release from Menston psychiatric hospital that David became something of a 'problem' for the local police force. The increasingly negative attitudes towards issues of race and immigration that blighted Britain at the time was extended to the police, and, having spent eight years of his life in hospital, David found himself living on the streets in Leeds where he was repeatedly arrested for disorderly conduct. As Aspden argues, this was an era when 'urban policing was becoming more anonymous, more impersonal', and, soon, David became 'the object of a highly personalised campaign' (Aspden, 2008: 176) by two police officers, Ellerker and Kitching, who subjected him to a series of violent attacks. Eventually, in the early hours of 18 April 1969, the two police officers 'hounded' David to his death and he drowned in the river Aire. There followed an investigation where both Ellerker and Kitching were charged with manslaughter and received custodial sentences, with Ellerker serving 'a three-year sentence' and Kitching 'twenty-seven months inside' (Aspden, 2008: 176). These convictions were remarkable not least because, as Agboluaje points out, 'it is the only case in the history of Great Britain that policemen have been tried for the death of a man of African origin' (Agboluaje, 2009: 17).

   Despite the historical precedence of this conviction, unlike that of Stephen Lawrence, the story of David Oluwale has been subjected to what Aspden describes as a form of cultural 'amnesia' (Aspden, 2008: 13), and there has been little or no civic-based attempts to memorialise David Oluwale's life or his tragic death. As a result, the memory of David appears almost to have been eradicated from the history of Leeds. This sense of a historical erasure is also evident in the treatment David received by the state support systems he encountered when he was alive and explains something of the paucity of evidential facts about David in official archival resources from the time. As Aspden's research so poignantly illustrates, far from being recognised as a vulnerable individual with

mental health problems, who was homeless, David was persistently
subjected to racist-fuelled encounters with the very agencies that should
have offered him support but who instead perpetually mis-documented
and mis-recognised him, negating and erasing his lived experience from
the archive. David was also forced to change his name on a number of
occasions, in a bid to conceal a Nigerian heritage that proved to be such
a stumbling block for potential British employers. In addition to this, his
name was also constantly inaccurately recorded in the various bureaucratic
documentation that evidences his time in the UK. It was this enduring
erasure of David's personhood that became what Agboluaje describes as
'the point of attack' when approaching the process of adapting Aspden's
book into a play (Agboluaje, 2009: 17). It is also what led him to focus on
a dramaturgical approach that would 'rediscover David' and 'recuperate
him as a person' (Agboluaje, 2009: 17). As a consequence, in the writing of
the play, Agboluaje decided against the use of a documentary or verbatim
theatre techniques because, he argues, 'a verbatim account would mean
David's story being told by others' (Agboluaje, 2009: 17). Instead, the
play is constructed as a form of a testimonial text, producing what I have
described in Chapter 3 as a poetics of witnessing, a dramaturgical approach
in which David himself becomes represented as a revenant who returns
from the dead in order to attest to the injustices that tormented him
in life.

In Agboluaje's play, as Victor Ukaegbu argues, character becomes a
'politicized site' (Ukaegbu, 2015: 204) where the ghostly David is constructed as a post-colonial subject whose life and death epitomise the
injustices of the colonial system and the failed promises of the Empire.
In this way, I suggest, Agboluaje reconstructs David not as a *victim* of
racism, but as a *parrhesiastes*; someone who speaks truth to power by
directly confronting the injustices of racism he encountered during his
life in Britain and the corrupting discourses of colonialism that framed
his formative years in Nigeria. One of the moments in this play where
this emerges most clearly is in the second act where David confronts
how his personal situation is connected with the failed promises of the
colonial context in Nigeria:

> DAVID: In history they taught us about the British Empire and the Empire
> Boys. You were our heroes. You civilised us. And for that it was your
> right to eat the best of my country because that was how you lived in the
> UK, like kings. You told us that you lived in Jerusalem. And I swallowed
> it. I could be a man of my own making. Then I came here. For the first
> time I saw poor white people. I saw rationing. When I think of how I
> struggled to get here, the family and friends I felt behind. (Agboluaje,
> 2009: 81)

Through his construction as a post-colonial subject and by positioning him not as an absent figure, but as a figure who is present, albeit as a revenant, Agboluaje stages an act of bearing witness in which David attests not only to the injustices he suffered in the UK, but to the colonial history of Nigeria. In so doing, David's act of *parrhesia* stages a rupturing of the colonial narrative, opening up a moment where, in Gomez-Pena's terms, the colonised subject '[slides] into the space of the coloniser' (Gomez-Pena quoted in Ukaegbu, 2015: 205) as a revenant, a witness that exists both in the present and the past.

The dramatic function of the ghost enables Agboluaje to move *The Hounding of David Oluwale* away from the restaging of the absence of David that persists so strongly in Aspden's book, where the historical process of piecing together an account of David Oluwale's life is continually hindered by the failure of the historical record to accurately document his life. By positioning David as a witness as opposed to a victim, Agboluaje reconstructs him as a subject who can speak for himself and in so doing it is David, and not the white police officer investigating his murder, who speaks out about the injustices that blighted his life and the racism that so brutally ended it. As David illustrates at one point in the play:

> DAVID: I walked six miles back from the middle of nowhere. I couldn't ask for directions because people stared at me as if I was some kind of animal […] When they saw me back in town they beat me up so badly. I was crying like a baby. They wouldn't stop so I bit Ellerker's hand and held on. Kitching came at me. I got a piece of him too. (Agboluaje, 2009: 88)

The figure of the ghost also allows Agboluaje to bring the audience into David's present lived experience. Unlike *The Colour of Justice*, where the action of the play is centred around events occurring four years after Stephen Lawrence's murder, Agboluaje locates his play in May 1969, with the opening scene depicting the moment in which David's body is pulled from the river Aire. As such, the play shows instead of tells the audience the police racism that marked David's lived experience when he was alive. We see this clearly in the opening scene of the play:

> POLICEMAN: By God. It is. Poor old Uggy.
> FROGMAN: I always called him George.
> POLICEMAN: What was his real name?
> FROGMAN: David. David. Allywally, Allywalla …
> *Policeman rummages through the evidence bag. He picks out a bible with documents inside.*
> POLICEMAN: (*Reads a document. Attempts to pronounce David's surname.*) David … ( ) Knew him well then? (Agboluaje, 2009: 23–4)

The poignant opening of the play serves to reveal that while David was a familiar figure in Leeds, he was also ultimately viewed as radically 'other' to the white police officers he encountered there, who refused to remember his name. In the same scene, just after the policeman exits, David, the revenant, stirs into life to observe these police officers attending to his dead body. In this way, the play establishes a direct encounter with David and by positioning him as a *parrhesiastes* rather than as an object of other people's narratives, the play stages David speaking out, addressing the audience directly:

> DAVID: I shared a pauper's grave, my misspelt name on the tombstone. Abandoned in death in a land I called him for twenty years, longing for Lagos that was really no more than a dusty memory. (Agboluaje, 2009: 102)

David becomes a guide for DC Perkins, who is responsible for investigating David's death and who emerges in the play as an ethical character who delves into past events in order to reveal the truth. Significantly, however, David's relationship with Perkins is constructed as being a somewhat antagonistic one, and David views Perkins, initially at least, with some suspicion. In this sense, the revenant David is not presented as a compliant, open witness; on the contrary, he emerges as a more complex character whose past is not a story he easily shares with DC Perkins, who after all is a representative of the very institution that brutalised David in life. In this sense, David is not constructed as a psychoanalytical witness and therefore DC Perkins does not emerge as a therapeutic listener who has the power to heal David or even to help David retrieve or remember the past. Although David's life is clearly marked out by traumatic events, he is not configured by Agboluaje as a traumatised subject. The ghostly David does not seek a listener who will identify him as a victim, nor does he adopt a confessionary form of attestation that elicits an audience response of empathy or sympathy. Rather, in Agboluaje's construction of David, he becomes a political character whose act of bearing witness is rooted in a political, as opposed to a psychological, dimension. To understand the witness this way requires shift away from the act of witnessing being interpreted as a psychological process and viewing it instead as a political act, where the witness him or herself speaks out to address injustice.

In Agboluaje's play, witnessing also becomes a way of recuperating the selfhood of David and conceptualising him as a truth teller and an agent of change, as he reveals the processes that erased and oppressed him. In this sense, Agboluaje's dramaturgy illustrates how the act of *parrhesia* is not simply a matter of communicating or exposing a truth; instead it is about *who* speaks out and how the person who speaks truth to power becomes implicated in the retelling of the injustices that precipitated subjection in life. In David's case, this means not only speaking of the violence he suffered at the hands of the police but also addressing the way he was betrayed by the English people, who brutalised him when he was at his most vulnerable. This resonates with the way Foucault distinguishes acts of *parrhesia* from the performative speech act. For the *parrhesiastes*, Foucault argues, does not speak with status or from a predetermined position that is validated by codified determinates. Rather, as Foucault explains, 'What characterises the *parrhesia*stic utterance is precisely that, apart from status and anything that could codify and define the situation, the *parrhesiates* is someone who emphasises his own freedom as an individual speaking' (Foucault, 2010: 65). Of course, in Agboluaje's play, the act of *parrhesia* is performed by a fictive character, the ghost of David. Yet, the use of the device of the ghost, I suggest, does not detract from the politics of this dramaturgical decision. After all, as Lynette Goddard (2018) suggests, the dramaturgical choices adopted in plays such as *The Hounding of David Oluwale* frame the way past injustices are remembered and how black lives are memorialised. As Goddard goes on to argue, plays such as *The Hounding of David Oluwale* become 'tools of social engagement', demonstrating 'the ways in which British playwrights contribute to showing that black lives matter' (Goddard, 2018: 85). Arguably, then, the dramaturgical choices that construct the performance of witnessing in Agboluaje's play not only determine what audiences know about the events surrounding the life and death of David Oluwale, but how the spectatorship of these narratives is encountered. Performing witnessing, then, is not simply about acts of truth telling, but about a process of political engagement with the past, and such dramaturgical projects can reconfigure who can speak out and how past events can be remembered.

Anna Deavere Smith's *Notes from the Field*: Multiple voices of political alliance

Like *The Colour of Justice* and *The Hounding of David Oluwale*, which both engage with the racism of the police force, in Anna Deavere Smith's *Notes from the Field*, the criminalisation of race and poverty is examined. In my discussion of Smith's play, I consider how her use of different narrators enacts multiple forms of *parrhesia*, allowing Smith to become a surrogate witness who speaks out against the injustices that are endured by many people of colour within the many multi-racial communities across America.

The dramaturgy of *Notes from the Field* draws on 250 interviews conducted by Smith with a range of people from different communities across America. These different narratives are woven together and tell seventeen different stories where each character is enacted by Smith herself. The play initially opened in New York in November 2016, where it received very positive reviews and was subsequently presented at the Royal Court Theatre in London in 2018, where I saw it as part of the London International Festival of Theatre (LIFT) season. In 2018 it was also adapted into a film by HBO. The play forms part of a broader social justice initiative led by Smith called 'The Pipeline Project', which aims to draw attention to the school-to-prison pipeline; a social problematic impacting on communities from economically deprived parts of America where young people of colour are criminalised at a young age and then find themselves caught up in the prison system.[2] This phenomenon was revealed in recent years when statistical data emerged proving that, compared to their richer, whiter counterparts, young people of colour in America were more likely to be excluded from school and to be in prison at some point in their lives: 'the US Justice Department released statistics that show that poor black, brown and Native American children are suspended and expelled more frequently than their middle-class and white counterparts, and that these suspensions and expulsions are directly linked to the likelihood that they will be incarcerated at some point in their lives' (Smith, 2019).

Within the various communities she visited, Smith interviewed a wide range of different people, such as 'students, teachers, principals, mentors, advocates, judges, inmates, government officials, and more' (Solomon, 2019), enabling her to gather different kinds of material from differing perspectives. When performed collectively in the course of the play, these different testimonies bear witness to the school-to-prison phenomenon and to America's unjust criminal justice system. These different viewpoints are brought to life through the central performance of Smith herself, who adopts a unique performance style to embody seventeen characters and enact a range of different identities, ethnicities and genders. Smith's approach to characterisation is based on a close observation of the other person, enabling her to carefully replicate the voice, gestures and body language of her interviewees. It is a mode of performance she has adopted in previous productions and generates a hyper-real style of enactment, producing what Alison Forsyth describes as a 'multi-vocal performance' where different testimonies are placed together in a careful 'hermeneutically-charged juxtaposition' (Forsyth, 2011: 142).

Like her other plays, *Notes From the Field* eschews any sense of a linear narrative, opting instead for an interweaving of different stories from multiple protagonists who, in different ways, all speak out against the unjust situations they have had to endure both at school and at the hands of the police. Collectively these narratives attest to an ongoing struggle of people of colour across the United States, who find themselves persistently caught up within a 'cursed intersection of two American institutions, the school and the prison, in a racially divided nation' (Brantley, 2016). Their experiences are further illuminated in *Notes from the Field* through the presentation of selected clips of television, archive and phone-filmed footage projected onto the wall at the back of the theatre stage that depicts shocking live in-the-moment scenes of violence of police against young people of colour. Smith's performance is punctuated poignantly by a haunting jazz-based accompaniment, performed by Marcus Shelby, the only person to share the stage with Smith throughout the play.

In a review about the production for *The Guardian* newspaper, Arifa Akbar describes *Notes from the Field* as a 'harrowing and extraordinary verbatim production' in which the different voices in the play 'form a palimpsest of "broken people" living in a "broken system" that fast tracks black men into a pipeline from school to prison' (Akbar, 2018). While I agree with Akbar's assessment of the potency of *Notes from the Field*, I would suggest that the play's dramaturgy and the particular form of characterisation adopted by Smith is substantially different from those that are adopted in verbatim theatre. As discussed in Chapter 2, verbatim theatre makers tend to construct the dramaturgy of the play by undertaking interviews and using this material either to reproduce two dimensional characters who become emblematic in some way, standing in for particular political perspectives, or to generate characters that fit a form of social realism and who seem psychologically coherent and fully rounded. Often the authenticity of the verbatim material is used to generate characterisation that is determined by a psychological motivation and clear wants and desires determined by the actor. As Tom Cantrell's and Bella Merlin's writing on the process of enacting real people reveals, many actors in British verbatim theatre use Stanislavskian approaches to generate this form of psychologically truthful forms of characterisation (see Merlin, 2007; Cantrell, 2013). However, while Smith draws on interview material for the basis of her performance text, her dramaturgical and performative approach to characterisation is very different.

Like her other work, *Notes from the Field* is structured as a solo performance and draws on a very specific form of characterisation. Smith's decision to enact each and every character in the play, regardless of race, culture, nationality, age or gender, enables her to move seamlessly from one character to the next, while presenting an ongoing dialogic engagement with the presence of Anna as an actor herself. In her performance of these very different people, characterisation is not generated by an acting approach rooted in the unified and transformative mode of approaches advocated by Stanislavski and his proponents. Smith's performance style is constructed so that it preserves and performs the gaps, spaces and elisions between herself as an actor and the characters being portrayed. The effect of maintaining, rather than overcoming these spaces is that Smith's performance redirects the audience's attention away from an expectation of an innate psychological motivation within these characters and instead points towards the external factors and socio-political and economic determinants that have impacted on each subject's life experiences. In so doing, Smith unsettles any notion of individualised psychological drive and other essentialist markers of identity and, as Dorinne Kondo argues, Smith 'problematises notions of stable subject-positions, highlighting instead the forging of those positions in matrices of power and history' (Kondo, 2000: 98). This approach refocuses the action of the play away from the representational work of the actor and towards the social and political issues that have predetermined the choices available to the young people Smith depicts. Furthermore, through the adoption of an inter-racial approach to characterisation, the play 'casts into relief the way our essentialist notions of race and other social forces are in part enacted through intonation, gesture, movement, and accent' (Kondo, 2000: 83), and this both challenges racially nuanced stereotyping, while exposing the political and social forces that regulate and govern these young people's lives. This approach, which self-consciously keeps open the gaps between self and other, serves to reframe the re-enactment of the witness as a *political* endeavour, where, in the moment of performance, the actor acknowledges the differences between self and other, actor and enacted, as opposed to subsuming the other person's identity within a seamless act of representation. For Smith, it seems, this mode of performance is born out of the desire to acknowledge the distinctiveness and difference of each individual person she enacts; it is adopted to actively resist 'mushes of identity' (Smith quoted in Kondo, 2000: 96) in which generic types of character are reproduced in order to represent certain views or perspectives – her approach instead allows her to 'reach' for the other. Describing this mode of enactment, she says:

> I don't believe that when I play someone in my work, that I 'am' the character. I want the audience to experience the gap, because I know if they experience

the gap, they will appreciate my reach for the other. This reach is what moves them, not a mush of me and the other, not a presumption that I can play everything and everybody, but more a desire to reach for something that is very clearly not me – my deep feeling of my separateness from everything, not my ability to pass for everything. Race is also not arbitrary here. Race, gender, size, beauty, etc., are all extremely, extremely significant. We live in a society of visual rhetoric. For better or for worse, for most people what you see is what you get. ... For me, the minute a certain race is put on certain material, it is significant. I believe my work onstage carries with it a racialization which is significant. (Smith quoted in Kondo, 2000: 96)

What Smith highlights here is the potency of bringing these particular narratives and identities together and then being able to explore the impact of this dialogical encounter of different perspectives through embodied performance. By adopting a form of acting that allows for fluid and different forms of characterisation, Smith herself, as an actor, bears witness to the multiple stories she performs. It is an approach that demonstrates a deep respect of the distinctiveness of each individual she portrays, thereby generating a performance process that pivots around a reaching out and acknowledgment of these differences and a recognition of the shared injustices that underpin different lived experience. The political and ethical dimensions of these re-enactments become all the more heightened by the fact that these stories are being told in a theatrical context, for, as Kondo points out, 'theatre is a privileged site in which to examine these issues' (Kondo, 2000: 82). The testimonial truths enacted by Smith also take on a deeper meaning and significance because of the way Smith enacts each of the characters who appear in the play. In this sense, while the play stages re-enactments of *parrhesiastic* gestures of speaking truth to power, it is the way Smith performs each of the subjects she represents that is so potent and which ultimately generates new ways of thinking about the issues examined by the play. While in his account of *parrhesia*, Foucault examined the power of speech and the action of speaking out, Smith's performance reminds us that bearing witness is also an embodied, performative action. It is a way of *doing something*, in which the corporeality of the witness becomes implicated within the testimonial act and becomes a means of generating new knowledge and understanding. As such, it is both the *parrhesiastic* text of the witnesses and Smith's performance of the subjects she represents that change the way audiences think about the various issues and events encountered in the course of the play. While these issues may have some familiarity to some members of the audience, due to the media coverage they received at the time, Smith's performance reimagines and re-embodies these events and, as such, audiences are invited to think them through afresh. In this sense, the performance also provides a new way of remembering and memorialising the young people of colour who lost their lives at the hands of the police as well as *parrhesiastes*, such as Niya Kenny, whose existence was shaped by her decision to speak out to challenge the injustice and violence she witnessed being wrought on others.

In this sense, through the re-enactment of testimonial text and the embodiment of the people interviewed, *Notes from the Field* remembers and bears witness to the traumatic, but everyday lived experience of racism and, as such, attests to the 'insidious trauma due to systemic oppression and discrimination' (Craps, 2015: 29). However, it is worth noting that Smith refuses to position these acts of witnessing within the realm of psychological trauma and, while the events depicted in the course of the play are infused with the 'affect' of the traumatic, Smith does not allow this to be transferred onto the individual characterisation as she performs it. By this I mean, that the witnesses re-enacted by Smith are not presented as traumatised subjects who seek to remember and retrieve a past event in order to heal and move on. Instead, these witnesses are constructed as subjects who are involved in an active and ongoing process of speaking out, in order to resist the unjust hegemonic and racially inscribed structures that continue to oppress and subjugate them and their communities.

By making visible the elisions and spaces between herself and the characters she embodies, Smith performs a mode of witnessing in which she does not simply replace or replicate the witness, instead she and the witness emerge as co-existing within a dialogical encounter. This ultimately redirects the audience's attention away from the suffering and trauma of the individual and towards the systems of oppression and subjugation that have predetermined the situations being narrated. In this sense, as Smith herself argues, her mode of performance is not constructed upon 'psychological realism' (Smith in Martin, 1993: 51). Rather, it addresses what Smith refers to as 'the struggle' (Smith in Martin, 1993: 52), by which I think she means the struggle for these witnesses to speak out against the discrimination they encounter on a daily basis and the challenge of finding a way of putting this into words, or in Smith's terms, 'the struggle he or she has to sift through language to come through' (Smith in Martin, 1993: 52) when speaking out. The sense of a struggle to find a language and a means of speaking out resonates with Foucault's account of *parrhesia*, which he describes as being contingent on risk taking and for some being potentially dangerous. In Foucault's terms, 'someone is said to use *parrhesia* and merit consideration as a *parrhesiastes* only if there is a risk of danger for him in telling the truth' (Foucault, 2001: 16).

After all, as Foucault goes on to argue, the act of speaking truth to power risks not only being disbelieved or being over-ruled or out-argued by the rhetoric of others, but it also risks the violence of others and the possibility 'that the words one utters fail to persuade and the crowd turn against you' (Foucault, 2010: 105). This risk of incurring the antagonism of others underpins elements of Smith's performance. For in some of the characters she portrays, she addresses the visceral risks of speaking out to those in power, such as the police. One of the moments when this emerges most clearly in *Notes from the Field* is in Smith's portrayal of Allen Bullock, a young black teenager who was arrested for his participation in the Baltimore protests, which sprung up in reaction to the death of Freddie Gray, a young black man who died as a result of injuries sustained from being transported within a police van in April 2015. Through her re-enactment of Allen, Smith draws attention to the risks of speaking out, highlighting the well-known taboo that forbids young black men from looking a police officer directly in the eye. In a talk Smith gave about the play in 2016, she explained that Freddie Gray 'had made eye contact with one of the police officers and this had started the interaction' (Smith, 2016). In her enactment of Bullock, Smith emphasises the importance of not looking directly at a police officer, exploring the unspoken threat of violence that Bullock reports impacting on all young black men from his community when in the presence of a police officer. Describing him as 'a kind of ethnographer of his community' (Smith, 2016), Smith performs Bullock as a reluctant *parrhesiastes* who recognises the risk of speaking out about the police, struggles to find the words but commits to the act of *parrhesia* all the same. When in role as Bullock, in the performance I attended at the Royal Court in London, Smith's voice became barely audible, and she delivered a lot of the monologue with her face turned away and her eyes averted from audience. It was an evocative moment that drew attention to Allen's desire to speak but also to his anxiety and unease about doing so:

> ALLEN BULLOCK: Because if you look at a police so hard or so straight – I don't know, like see how he was, Freddie Gray, you feel me, <u>in</u> the <u>way</u>, like he was around his neighbourhood, if the neighbourhood police they don't <u>care</u>, they -do- not care bout <u>none o'that</u> you – If they *know* you in that neighbourhood, they gonna *do* some t' – I don't care what neighbour-hood you in, it could be a quiet neighbourhood, anything, the police know, you from … *bein'bad,* or not even being' bad, but bein' around the area, anything, hanging with somebody, that that they know, that's bad, they gonna *harass* you – *and* if they gon' harass you – 'Why you lookin at me like that?' – They will *ask* you 'Why you looking at me like that',

like, in a <u>smart</u> way you feel me jump out the car, pulling their stick, all
that, you feel me. (Smith, 2019: 18–19; original emphasis)[3]

In her representation of Bullock, and as a result of the careful attention
to detail and the sensitivity she exhibits towards her characterisation,
Smith's performance bears witness to the unspoken threat of police violence
confronting Bullock and his community on a daily basis.

When acting Allen Bullock, like many of the other characters Smith
embodies, it is Smith's dramaturgical approach itself and the questions
she asks during her research process that ultimately make the acts of
parrhesia a possibility within the play. Smith's performance and the creative
approach that generates it re-cognises Allen Bullock as a political subject,
framing him as someone to whom we need to listen and who has the
expertise and experience to speak out against the kinds of police action
that tragically ended Freddie Gray's life and which also corrode the black
community's trust in the integrity of the police force as a whole. As
such, Smith's performance, I suggest, does not seek to elicit a sense of
pity for her enacted subjects, instead, *Notes from the Field* offers 'a way
to rethink enduring political inequalities and the possibility for political alliance and social justice for minoritarian subjects' (Kondo, 2000:
82). In this way, the incorporation of witnessing within the play serves
to remind audiences why we need to critically engage with initiatives
such as *#blacklivesmatter*, inviting us to reflect on our own privilege and
our positioning as allies or advocates in relation to the issues the play
explores.

The political potency of Smith's performance relies primarily on the
way Smith reconstructs the testimonial subject within her dramaturgical
process and within the performances she enacts. In this sense, *Notes from
the Field* has a political dimension to it, not only because it represents
certain *parrhesiastic* subjects, but because, through the incorporation
of acts of *parrhesia*, the play is able to engage responsibly with the
political subject matter it addresses. In order to fully understand the
ethical implications of making political theatre by drawing on real
people's lived experience, then, it is important to understand the responsibility that comes with speaking on behalf of others and the ethical
demands of telling other people's stories in this way. In the final section
of this chapter, I move on to examine what I call the 'ethical demand
of testimonial practice', where I formulate some proposals about how
dramaturgical processes might responsibly engage with the testimonial
subject and how the relationship between the theatre maker and testimonial subject might be forged upon an expectation of responsibility
and care.

The ethical demand of testimonial practice: Repositioning the witness in theatre making

In her seminal article, 'The Problem of Speaking for Others' (1991), feminist philosopher Linda Alcoff effectively lays out some of the problematics of speaking on behalf of others and adopting identity positions that are not one's own. Writing about a body of thought emerging in feminism and anthropology in the 1980s, Alcoff draws attention to 'a strong, albeit contested, current within feminism which holds that speaking for others is arrogant, vain, unethical, and politically illegitimate' (Alcoff, 1991: 6). While Alcoff addresses her analysis to discursive practices, primarily adopted in areas such as anthropology, ethnography and literary studies, her argument is also pertinent to practices in theatre and performance studies where real people's stories and lived experience are co-opted as the basis for the dramaturgy of a performance. The ethical trickiness of speaking on behalf of others is, as Alcoff argues, formed by two interconnected problematics. Firstly, there is the question of the identity and location of the speaker and the one who is being spoken of – and the difficulty of speaking from a position that is not one's own – since 'where one speaks from affects the meaning and truth of what one says [… and] one cannot assume an ability to transcend one's location' (Alcoff, 1991: 7). The second element of this problematic acknowledges the role of power and privilege inherent within acts of speaking for others and the potential harm this can do. Alcoff examines the dangers of appropriating other people's stories as our own and points out that 'the practice of privileged persons speaking for or on behalf of less privileged persons has culturally resulted (in many cases) in increasing or reinforcing the oppression of the group spoken for' (Alcoff, 1991: 7).

This viewpoint holds a particular significance for theatre practitioners who seek to use testimonial practices to disrupt and trouble dominant narratives and who seek to harness story-telling processes to challenge or confront situations of oppression.

Arguably, in the context of theatre making, the act of narrating and representing others is a constituent element of the representational function of the art form. Yet, I would argue that the ethical problematics of who speaks for whom and how the privilege of being a narrator for others is negotiated and designed frames and determines the ethical demand of testimonial practice. Of course, one response is to opt for an approach where the theatre maker only speaks for themselves, creating work that always focuses on characters drawn from their own community or location.

Yet, this opens up other ethical problems, and not least because it means limiting the theatre maker's cultural engagement with the world solely to one perspective and restricting the possibility for theatre to enact a form of political alliance with others. While speaking on behalf of those who are less privileged than ourselves can be tricky and problematic, then, such acts are also critical to the staging of political theatre and to the possibility of engaging with wider socio-political issues that impact on the lived experience of others. This need to establish a form of alliance is also acknowledged by Alcoff herself, who argues for the importance of political responsibility, writing that:

> we might ask, if I don't speak for those less privileged than myself, am I abandoning my political responsibility to speak out against oppression, a responsibility incurred by the very fact of my privilege? If I should not speak for others, should I restrict myself to following their lead uncritically? Is my greatest contribution to *move over and get out of the way*? And if so, what is the best way to do this – to keep silent or to deconstruct my discourse? (Alcoff, 1991: 8; original emphasis)

For the testimonial theatre maker who does not feel able to '*move over and get out of the way*' and who feels compelled to support the struggle of those who are less privileged or who are vulnerable in some way, and unable to speak out, the theatre-making process becomes underpinned by an important sense of responsibility that is both political and ethical. For it is undeniable that within the privileged site of theatre, it is the theatre maker and not the person who is being enacted that ultimately gets to determine whose story is being narrated and what stories are to be told. To some degree, of course, all theatre making is always entangled with this power relationship, and not least because theatre is a representational art form where one group of people are represented by another. However, for verbatim and testimonial theatre makers, who use real people and real personal narrative to generate a play, promising to enact a narrative that is rooted in truth telling, the question of authorial privilege and responsibility become all the more acute. As I have argued in the first part of this book, verbatim and testimonial theatre making are structured around the promise of truth telling and therefore construct an implicit contract formed with the audience that promises a degree of authenticity and verity. As such, audiences of verbatim or testimonial theatre expect a degree of veracity that exceeds the fictional frame of a play. For example, when Allen Bullock, in Smith's *Notes from the Field*, tells us about his experience of the police as a young black man, the audience will believe that this is what the real Allen Bullock actually said or actually believed. In testimonial, verbatim and documentary theatre practices, then, there is always also some expectation of a correlation between actual lived experience and those experiences represented in the play – and so it matters how the play represents these lived experiences through its content and dramaturgical structure. It is this dramaturgical and methodological formation, I suggest, that forms the relationship between the theatre maker and the testimonial subject as one that is underpinned by the ethical imperative of responsibility, a responsibility that ultimately places certain demands upon the theatre maker. To understand how the ethical demand of testimonial practice impacts on the methodological process of a practice, I turn first to examine what ethical experience might mean in this context and do so by drawing on the philosophy of Simon Critchley, who was influenced in his thinking in this area by the ideas of the Danish theological philosopher Knud Ejler Løgstrup. Critchley's engagement with ethical experience is useful here because he provides a way of thinking about ethics that moves beyond a singular and universal concept of the good. In his book *Infinitely Demanding: Ethics of Commitment, Politics of Resistance* (2007), Critchley offers a structure of ethics that helps us think about how an ethical demand can be framed by and rooted within in the specific events of each and every situation in which we encounter other people.

Critchley formulates his account of ethical experience as a response to a demand that emerges from a situation 'to which I give my approval' (Critchley, 2007: 14). Instead of developing a virtue-based ethics structured around a predetermined formulation of the good, Critchley develops the 'approval and demand' structure as a means of accounting for the way an ethical experience is encountered, where ethical action emerges directly from a specific situation and the unspoken demands that occur as a result of our relationship with another person and the acute sense of responsibility that accompanies this. In this formulation of ethics, the good does not pre-exist the situation; rather, it 'comes into view through approval' and, as such, it is a response to an ontological demand, 'a demand that requires approval' (Critchley, 2007: 16). The ethical demand, therefore, is not predetermined nor is it 'somehow objectively given in the state of affairs'; on the contrary, as Critchley argues, it is 'only felt as a demand for the self who approves it' (Critchley, 2007: 18). This resonates with the ethical philosophy of Løgstrup who understands the ethical demand as an unspoken and 'anonymous' call upon us to 'take care of the life which trust has placed in our hands' (Løgstrup, 1997: 18). Underpinning Løgstrup's work in this area is a recognition that our existence is framed by relationships of interdependence that bind us to one another. This relational existence is not something of our choosing; instead, as Løgstrup suggests, it is simply the way our lives are ordered. As a consequence, we are always called upon to take responsibility and care for those who place their trust in us and to whom we are bound through interrelated connections of co-existence. As Løgstrup explains:

> It is not within our power to determine whether we wish to live in responsible relationships of not; we find ourselves in them simply because we exist [...]. We are born into a life that is already ordered in a very definite way, and this order lays claim upon us in such a manner that as we grow up we find ourselves bound to other people and forced into responsible relationships with them. (Løgstrup, 2007: 107)

For Løgstrup, it is the relationships of trust and responsibility that bind us to others and that determine the basis of our existence, requiring us to respond with care. Ethical experience emerges as a result of this relational existence and from an acknowledgment that such relationships are structured around an axis of power and trust, for when another person trusts us with their life, or, in the context of testimonial theatre, with their life story, this opens up a relationship of both power and responsibility. As philosopher, Robert Stern explains:

> According to Løgstrup [...] the fate of the other person is placed in your hands thereby giving you power over their life; it is then your responsibility to do what is best for them, and it is this need that should be your reason for acting, not a sense of duty or obligation or responsibility as such, which only arises when you have already failed to see the situation in the right way. (Stern, 2019: 5)

As Stern points out, for Løgstrup, the concept of the ethical demand is radically different from the idea of honouring a duty or a law. Instead of being framed around a law, the ethical demand reveals a mode of comportment to others that sits beyond any legal imperative that might frame our responsibility to others. Løgstrup frames the ethical demand not as an *a priori* duty but as an existential call upon the self, where the requirement to act emerges as a response to the needs of another. This is a 'silent demand' (Løgstrup, 1997: 8) that crucially is not encountered as an articulated need or want that is expressed directly to us by another person. Nor is the content of what ought to be done in response to this demand fixed or conditioned by any predetermined rule, code or law; rather, the ethical demand is a call to care, and the relevant action is revealed by the situation itself – as Stern puts it, 'the obligation itself comes from what is required to care for the other, and the directive power of their needs in the situation' (Stern, 2019: 5).

Importing Løgstrup's concept of ethical demand into an exploration of testimonial theatre usefully illuminates how the ethical responsibility of dramatising or enacting another person's story can be understood in relation to the methodological decisions and commitments that determine the structure of this theatre-making process. Central to both the ethical demand and the act of making testimonial theatre is the relational quality of trust, a mode of being with another person configured around the ethical experience that binds us to others. For Løgstrup, trust is a constitutive element of the everyday relationships that form part of daily life, leading him to suggest that it is 'characteristic of human life that we normally encounter one another with trust' (Løgstrup, 1997: 8). This grounding sense of trust is significant not only because we are born into relationships with other people but because, as Løgstrup suggests, human existence is determined by a capacity for self-surrender and our need to, on occasion, place ourselves in the hands of others. The trust we feel towards other people, then, is not chosen by us, however, it forms the essence of our existence and our interactions with others. In Løgstrup's terms, 'Trust is not of our making; it is given. Our life is so constituted that it cannot be lived except as one person lays him or herself open to another person and puts her or himself into that person's hands either by showing or claiming trust' (Løgstrup, 1997: 18). Løgstrup's account of trust and the ethical demand therefore enables us to think through the ethical demands of testimonial theatre practice and how a theatre maker negotiates the challenges of telling other people's stories. Following Løgstrup, I would argue that the ethical demands of this form of theatre making are grounded in the securing and upholding of trusting relationships between the testimonial subject and the theatre maker. The importance of these relationships and what they demand of the practitioner emerges as three interconnected areas of concern. Firstly, it determines the quality of the relationship forged between the theatre maker and the testimonial subject, framing an encounter by which the witness trusts their testimony to the theatre maker. By agreeing for their story to become the basis of a play's dramaturgy, the witness, in Løgstrup's terms, 'lays him or herself open' (Løgstrup, 1997: 18) to the theatre maker and places their own integrity and subjecthood at the centre of a dramaturgical process, which is designed to honour and facilitate the testimonial act itself. In taking up this testimony and forging it into a play, the theatre maker becomes a surrogate for the witness, implicitly taking responsibility for their testimony and, in some deferred sense, taking on the act of witnessing; in so doing, they also bear witness to the events being attested to. The relationship of trust between the theatre maker and the witness, then, becomes one framed around a structure of demand and approval, where the theatre maker must respond to the testimonial truth-telling process and the truth claims that emerge as a result.

The second concern of the ethical demand of testimonial practice relates to the way the testimonial subject's integrity and their truth-telling process is validated and attended to, both by the structure of the creative process and the play's dramaturgy. By this I mean that if a play's dramaturgy is configured to tell a witness's story then the play's structure and content should operate together to honour both the process of truth telling and the witness's status as a testimonial subject. When a witness engages with a creative process and contributes his or her testimony, this is undertaken in good faith and with the firm belief that these testimonial truths will be honoured – or, to draw on Critchley's terms, will be 'approved' – by the theatre maker who, in this moment, becomes a witness to the act of witnessing. Løgstrup understands this sense of taking another's word as 'truth' as being a cornerstone of the trusting relationship we rely upon in our engagement with other people. He says:

> Under normal circumstances [...] we accept the stranger's word and do not mistrust him until we have some particular reason to do so. We never suspect a person of falsehood until after we have caught him in a lie. If we enter into conversation on the train with a person whom we have never met before and about whom we know nothing, we assume that what he says is true and do not become suspicious of him unless he begins to indulge in wild exaggerations. (Løgstrup, 1997: 8)

In this sense, the witness approaches a testimonial theatre-making process trusting that he or she will be believed and that his or her truth process will be approved by the process. The theatre maker then supports the emergence of this testimony and approaches the witness committed to the belief that what is attested to corresponds to what the witness believes to be true. In other words, an ethical testimonial process does not seek to frame the witness in the dramaturgy of the play as an object of suspicion or mistrust, unless the theatre maker is given cause to doubt the testifying subject's integrity or to suspect some falsehood. If this then becomes the case, then the performance of attestation no longer has the status of a testimonial act. When the theatre maker holds the testimonial subject in good faith then the dramaturgical process must facilitate and support the testimonial act rather than contradict it, even if, at times, this might be felt to be factually incongruent. Of course, this is not to suggest that sometimes testimony might be used as evidence or to either validate or disprove certain facts and truths asserted by another witness. However, arguably, when a dramaturgical process uses testimony simply to evidence and support particular narratives, in so doing, it ultimately subsumes testimony back into the verbatim form, where it loses its testimonial status and becomes simply a personal narrative that represents a particular perspective or form of evidence within a play.

The third element of the ethical demand of testimonial practice relates to the role of the audience in the testimonial encounter. When coming to see a testimonial play, as indicated above, audiences expect there to be some kind of tangible correlation between the real, actual witness and the witness's testimony, as presented by the theatre maker. There is also an assumption that what is said in the course of the play corresponds to what the witness believes to be true and what he or she has actually said, or alluded to, outside the context of the dramaturgical process. As a consequence, the truth-telling process of a testimonial play implicates both the witness and the audience in an ethico-political encounter, where the truth of an event and the witness's testimony to this is presented and can be either believed or disbelieved by an audience. If the witness is disbelieved, then he or she ultimately loses the status of being a testimonial subject. As such, the approval or denial of the testimony presented in the play then becomes directly tied to the integrity of the witness him or herself, how the witness is viewed by the audience and how the events discussed in the play are portrayed and understood. The audience do not expect to be lied to and approach the forms of truth-telling processes of the play with the expectation that these are grounded in an adherence to the unspoken contract, established by the theatre maker, between the witness and the audience. This contract is framed around promises that address the relationship between the creative process, that of course is not present in the moment of performance, and the development of the play text itself. For example, such a contract might affirm that all the characters in the play are based directly on real testimonial subjects, or it might designate a process by which individual and real testimonies were used and amalgamated together into a series of composite characters that appear in the play.

The ethical experience that shapes the development of an ethically responsive testimonial play, then, positions the witness at the centre of the play's dramaturgy, while also establishing a contract determining the relationship between real witnesses and real events and the representations that appear in the play. The witness's centrality in the dramaturgical process is then drawn upon to produce a narrative structure that supports the testimonial process, enabling the witness to become an agent of their own narrative and generating an act of witnessing that ultimately underpins and directs the play's structural components. The relationship between the testimonial subject and the play's dramaturgy therefore becomes a distinctive element of testimonial theatre, distinguishing it from other dramaturgical approaches where testimony is used only as evidence to verify or refute other types of truth claim. An example of this contrasting dramaturgical approach is described by David Hare in his account of the process of writing *The Permanent Way* (2003). Here Hare explains that he 'had no interest in writing a play purely about the railways' (Hare in Hare and Stafford-Clark, 2008: 58). Instead, what he was looking for, he explains, was a central 'metaphor of the play', which, in *The Permanent Way*, emerged as 'deciding what is necessary suffering and what is unnecessary suffering' (Hare in Hare and Stafford-Clark, 2008: 58). Within this dramaturgical approach, as Hare himself suggests, there is little difference between writing a play based on real people and writing a fictional play because the participation and presence of real people in the creative process make little call upon the dramaturgical direction of the play itself. Hare further emphasises this point, when he goes on to argue that there is 'absolutely no difference between the writing of a good documentary play and the writing of a wholly imagined play, because it's about the same thing, which is wanting to create something in the space between what the audience is feeling and what's going on on stage' (Hare in Hare and Stafford-Clark, 2008: 61). Through the establishment of a dramaturgical process that ultimately overlooks any demand emerging from the testimonial subjects who participated in the dramaturgical process, Hare's play might be 'a very artful piece of writing' (Stafford-Clark in Hare and Stafford-Clark, 2008: 60) but rather than being testimonial, it 'just happens to use lines that [he has] been given by other people' (Hare in Hare and Stafford-Clark, 2008: 60).

By contrast, the centrality of the witness in the dramaturgical process and the ethical demands this places upon the theatre maker, and ultimately on the audience, not only becomes one of the key challenges of making testimonial theatre, but also one of its defining features. In this sense, it is the ethical demand of testimonial practice that ultimately constitutes the foundation of testimonial performance. As a consequence, testimonial theatre is intrinsically concerned with the ethical dimensions of its own construction. For when it operates well, it can become a potent form of political theatre that highlights injustice and exposes perspectives and subject positions that are often over-looked or erased by the power structures of hegemony and the concerns and viewpoint of the majority.

Notes

1 This extract is taken from the published script of the HBO film version of Smith's *Notes from the Field* (2019), which is not always exactly the same script

as the stage version of the play. However, Smith certainly performed Niya Kenny in the stage version of the play at the Royal Court, and my memory of her performance corresponds closely to what is recorded in the HBO script.

2 For more information about Smith's Pipeline Project, please refer to the Anna Deavere Smith Projects website, www.annadeaveresmith.org/ (accessed 25/07/2019).

3 This excerpt has been taken from the script produced for the HBO film of *Notes from the Field* (2019). While the script differs in places from the play performed in the theatre, the character Allen Bullock was also performed by Smith in the stage version of the play.

Conclusion: Performing witnessing in a post-truth era

When delivering a lecture on testimonial theatre to some first-year undergraduate students in 2017, I began by asking the class to tell me how they understood the term 'testimony', what it meant and what importance it held for society today. One of the students put his hand up and asked whether, in fact, testimony today had any relevance at all, since, he pointed out, we were now in an era of post-truth. The student's question was both important and relevant; it also highlighted some of the confusion that proliferates within current discourses of truth, falsity and post-truth, not least because it was not entirely clear whether this student viewed the post-truth context as a *de facto* state of affairs or a tendency that needed to be critiqued and resisted. Regardless of this, the student's question was, of course, very timely. For in 2016, the Oxford Dictionary named 'post-truth' as its word of the year. This came at a time when the UK was in the first phase of the political turmoil following the Brexit referendum, won by a political campaign constructed around a factual untruth, written on the side of a bus.[1] It also followed the controversial presidential election of Donald Trump in the US, following a campaign rooted in right-wing populist values and the factually inaccurate claims made by Trump and his supporters before and afterwards (see Leonhardt, 2016). However, while Trump continues to decry certain facts as being 'fake news' and while his supporters, such as Kellyanne Conway, have asked for him to be judged by what's in his heart, rather than 'what's come out of his mouth' (Blake, 2017), to describe the current era as being framed by a post-truth context is not to suggest that truth and truth telling no longer matter. As the Oxford Dictionary's definition makes clear, 'post-truth' does not denote a redundancy of truth. As Lee McIntyre (2018) argues, it is a term that is in fact 'irreducibly normative' (McIntyre, 2018: 6), pointing not to a belief that facts and the truth no longer have relevance, but rather to a concern over the way that truth is being deployed and re-authored to manipulate the opinion of others. The term 'post-truth', in other words, reveals 'an expression of concern by those who care about the concept of truth and feel that it is under attack' (McIntyre, 2018: 6). It is this denotation of the word that emerges in the Oxford Dictionary's account of the term, which reads as:

> POST-TRUTH: Relating to or denoting circumstances in which objective facts are less influential in shaping public opinion than appeals to emotion and personal belief.
> *'in this era of post-truth politics, it's easy to cherry-pick data and come to whatever conclusion you desire'*
> *'some commentators have observed that we are living in a post-truth age'.*
> (Oxford University Press, 2019)

As McIntyre points out, 'the prefix "post" is meant to indicate not so much the idea that we are "post" truth in a temporal sense (as in "postwar")' but rather, 'that truth has been eclipsed – that it is irrelevant' (McIntyre, 2018: 5). In this sense, post-truth – certainly as it is understood by many commentators – is conceptualised not as an inevitable consequence of the way we now understand what truth is. Rather, it is a term that reflects a growing unease at the way truth has been eroded and has lost value in certain sectors of social, political and civic life. Of course, debates around what constitutes the truth are not new and can be traced back to philosophical thought that existed in Ancient Greece – for example, in Plato's critique of the Sophists. However, the claims of 'fake news' or 'alternative facts' that underpin the emergence of terms such as 'post-truth' today come from a very different form of discourse, drawn not from philosophical analysis or epistemological insight but from the rhetoric of politicians and media figures who seek to control how certain issues are to be debated and understood. The political evocation of post-truth or fake news tends to be adopted as a way of closing down, rather than expanding debates. As such, some of the most deleterious impacts of the current discourse of post-truth are in the way these concepts are being used to control political debate and to regulate what the public knows and how they understand certain political perspectives. As McIntyre argues, 'the idea of post-truth is not just that truth is being challenged, *but that it is being challenged as a mechanism for asserting political domination*' (McIntyre, 2018: xvi; original emphasis). Within this current context of post-truth public discourse, the role of theatre as a mode of truth telling becomes ever more critical – in particular, I argue that testimonial theatre, which aims to expose and interrogate the kinds of truths that are being re-authored or erased by today's politicians, can play a central role.

After all, determining my conceptualisation of the ethics and politics of testimonial practice is a recognition of the ways in which testimonial theatre moves beyond a dramaturgy rooted in practices that impose a predetermined narrative or juridical process on the dramatic text of a play. Instead of reiterating pre-existing texts or structures, like tribunal theatre, testimonial theatre generates new forms of truth telling that emerge out of a dramaturgical process that is itself structured around different modes of witnessing and the truth of the *parresiastes*-witness. This foregrounding of the witness is a distinguishing element of testimonial performance and is also an approach that underpins the ethics of practice and the political imperatives that frame this mode of theatre making. The formation of dramaturgical processes that are designed to be led and informed by the act of attestation becomes all the more acute in a context of post-truth politics, where public faith in the truth telling of politicians is constantly being eroded and denigrated by the populist tendencies of an increasingly right-wing political context. Furthermore, while the discourses of fake news and post-truth debates have gained currency within political and public life, so has the denigration and oppression of minoritarian subjects. According to recent statistics published by the Home Office in the UK in 2019, for example, hate crimes against gay, lesbian and trans people have risen significantly since 2014 and, since 2016, as a result of the discourses that circulated around the Brexit campaign, there has also been an increase in 'racism and race-related hate crime' (BBC, 2019). The foregrounding of identity politics both in the media and upon the stage has therefore become increasingly urgent, with new forms of testimonial theatre emerging not only to address the side-lining and denigration of certain subject positions but to bear witness to the continued presence of difference and diversity within society. In this sense, the shifting political landscape opens up new and innovative modes of performance and as a consequence, testimonial practices are themselves evolving and changing. One such example of the innovative use of testimony in performance is *And the Rest of Me Floats* by Outbox Theatre, a play presented at the Bush Theatre in 2019, which explores the testimony of a group of young people about their experiences of growing up and finding a place within the trans, non-binary, queer community.

Through its use of testimonial text and the incorporation of dance, music and song, the play does not simply tell the story of being trans or queer. Rather, it generates a mode of corporeal witnessing, in which the presence of the actor's bodies combines with their stories to performatively attest both to their presence before us on stage, but also to the visceral experiences of living as a trans or queer subject within the heteronormative and regulatory structures of social life. The motif of being present and being seen or acknowledged is repeated throughout and is examined most directly in the following testimonial moment, that appears in the second half of the play:

> JOSH-SUSAN: Do you see me?
> I mean, beyond the fabulous figure-hugging
> Frock and the mismatched baritone.
> Do you really see me?
> [...]
> I'm the kid who danced his way
> out of chaos, like a brown Billy Elliot.
> Except I never got to swim in Swan Lake.
> Cos places like that weren't for people like
> me. Or so I was told. But I kept moving.
> When they told me to straighten my spine
> and ground my hips. I grooved through,
> around and between their pronouns. Never
> quite settling for one, letting my body do the talking. (Outbox, *And the Rest of Me Floats*, 2019).

Created by Outbox Theatre, a London-based company dedicated to '[making] theatre queerly' (Outbox, 2019), the play explores the 'messiness of gender' (Buratta, 2019), drawing on stylised movement, pop songs and moments of dress-up to create a celebratory and anarchic performance 'built around the performers' identity and relationship to their gender' (Buratta, 2019). While the extracts of testimonial text that emerge in the course of the play poignantly explore experiences of discrimination and oppression, ultimately it is the performers on stage, the presence of their bodies before the audience and the way they relate to the stories that we are told that most potently bear witness. Throughout the play, Josh-Susan's question quoted above, 'Do you see me? [...] Do you really see me?' (Outbox, 2019) is repeated, serving as a provocation to the audience as well as a form of attestation. Like the other actors in the play who also ask this same question, Josh-Susan challenges the audience to look beyond the factual details of the testimonial narrative that is being told, inviting audiences to recognise a fluid subjectivity, a self who slips and slides 'between their pronouns' and who refuses to remain within one fixed gender norm. The performed presence of Josh-Susan, like the other performers in the play, collectively attests to a non-normative subjectivity, disrupting any expectation of 'causal narratives that see trans and queer people' as victims of trauma (Buratta, 2019). In so doing, the performance repositons the actors as agents of their own narrative, generating an approach where they become the subject rather than the object of theatre's representational process. In this way, *And the Rest of Me Floats* reimagines trans and queer subjectivity, opening up new ways of thinking about the interconnections between gender and identity and how processes of self-identification are founded and experienced.

The use of testimonial practices in *And the Rest of Me Floats* has much in common with what I describe in Chapter 3 as 'witnessing as resistance'. While the play foregrounds the actors' experiences of gender and sexuality, it also moves beyond a predetermined process of reiteration found in verbatim theatre. Consequently, the testimonial accounts of the actors' lived experiences combine with the effect of their bodies in the space, operating together to explore a way of speaking out against the oppressive social and medical structures that have sought to oppress or regulate these young people's sense of self. Through the adoption of music and dance and the conscious dismantling of the markers of normative bio-graphical chronology, the play engages with what Buratta describes as the 'queering of time' (Buratta, 2019). As such, testimonial text is used rather like an orchestral score that emerges as one of many other performa-tive elements of the play, combining and dialoguing with the other elements to explore the intricacies of gender, sexuality and identity. In this sense, *And the Rest of Me Floats* is an example of a burgeoning new form of performance work that seeks to uncouple performed testimony and verbatim text from individualised accounts of past events, producing new dramaturgical approaches in which testimony of lived experience becomes more fluid, malleable and choreographic. Elements of this type of approach have also been adopted, albeit in very different ways, by companies such as DV8, in their verbatim-based dance pieces, such as *John* (2014), *Can We Talk About This* (2011) and *To Be Straight With You* (2007), where verbatim text of personal testimony becomes a musical score that is interpreted, or in Jess McCormack's terms, 'translated', by the dancer/performer (McCormack, 2018).

What these different contemporary engagements with the act of witness-ing begin to reveal is the diverse ways in which testimony is being adopted within many performance practices to explore different lived experience and identities. Within these new performances, testimony has been loosened from its framing as an act that retrieves a past event through a narrative form. Rather, it emerges as a dramaturgical element that interweaves with the presence of the actor's body, dialogically working together to debate and explore the issues the production examines. By disrupting the narrative structure and chronology of testimony, the performance text draws attention to the normative assumptions that frame any engagement with another person's life narrative and invites the audiences to recognise the testimonial subject afresh.

The fluid and responsive quality of testimonial performance means it is well placed to respond to new and challenging political and ethical contexts. By foregrounding the witness and placing the truth telling at the heart of the dramaturgical process, new testimonial performance work develops that can be responsive to each new situation or event that emerges. While the era of post-truth discourse will continue to place increasing pressures on those whose lived experience cannot be easily located within the hegemony of normative structures, testimonial theatre continues to provide theatre makers, particularly those from minoritarian contexts, with the means of having a voice with which to articulate their own truths that dominant discourse increasingly seeks to discount or erase. By drawing out misrepresented narratives and highlighting lived experiences that are erased or silenced by the populist ideologies of the time, testimonial performance can expose injustices and lay the groundwork for moments of potential alliance and *communitas* that are configured around newly forged acts of solidarity.

As I have argued over the course of this book, it is the capacity for truth telling that distinguished the new forms of verbatim and testimonial plays that emerged in the last decades of the twentieth century from the documentary theatre that preceded it. Rather than drawing on different forms of factual evidence, verbatim and testimonial theatre centres on the presence and utterance of the witness, incorporating testimony and using this to authenticate and ground the testimonial truths that are asserted in the course of the play. In order to fully understand how testimony and witnessing are reconfigured in this type of theatre work, it is important then to move beyond the discourses of the real that have tended to dominate the critical engagements with verbatim and documentary theatre work. In order to do this, I have returned to an examination of some of the influential documentary plays that emerged in Germany in the post-war period. Written by a new generation of playwrights who were seeking to make sense of the events of the Holocaust and Second World War and Germany's involvement in this, these plays established new dramaturgical strategies that moved documentary theatre away from representations of social reality and towards an interrogation of personal culpability and truth telling.

In the contemporary verbatim and testimonial theatre that emerged some thirty years later, this focus on truthfulness re-emerged but the form evolved and changed considerably, leading to the development of new dramaturgical approaches that reimagined the relationship between personal testimony and the event and establishing new ways of conceptualising the performance of witnessing. The renewed interest in verbatim and testimonial theatre that took place at this time had a global reach, and different forms of theatre making, drawing on personal testimony, emerged across the world in Australia, Africa, America, Europe, Russia and Latin America. As I have argued, in order to respond to each event and each situation it addresses, testimonial theatre attends to the particular truth claims and the lived experiences of the witnesses whose stories it tells. As such, these contemporary engagements with performed testimony have reimagined not only the dramaturgical process of creating theatre from lived experience but how witnessing itself is configured within the dramaturgical process. In many of these contemporary testimonial plays, the act of witnessing does not address the retrieval of a past event; nor therefore is the act of attestation conceptualised around an event-based trauma. Instead, in many of these plays, the performance of testimony addresses ongoing situations of injustice and suffering. It is the presence of the witnesses as well as the narrative of the testimony that become a generative force within the dramaturgical structure of the play. The reimagining of witnessing which emerges in these plays coalesces with recent thinking around the decolonising of trauma theory that has been developed in the humanities and in other disciplines (see Andermahr, 2016a) – and as I have suggested, this act of decolonising testimony has been usefully explored in testimonial theatre forms. In this sense, the types of witnessing being explored in contemporary testimonial performance constitute a fluid and expansive category, shifting and changing in order to respond to each situation that is addressed in each play. As such, in the course of this book I have not sought to determine a finite definition of what constitutes testimonial theatre. Rather, I have identified three modes of witnessing in order to conceptualise some of the particular demands and structures of attestation that are adopted in this form of theatre. In my exploration of what I have called the 'poetics of witnessing', the 'witness-narrator' and 'witnessing as resistance', I have developed an account of three different modes of witnessing that enable us to think through what the genealogical development of these practices reveals regarding the ethico-political imperatives that constitute each of these modes of witnessing and the dramaturgical structures that determine them.

The performance of witnessing has great political potential because it can stage what Foucault describes as acts of *parrhesia*, where the witness speaks truth to power and speaks out about the injustices he or she has suffered or endured. However, as with all theatre making, testimonial theatre is constituted through representational processes, where testimony and acts of witnessing performed in one context are appropriated and reused in another. In this sense, while the performance of witnesses can stage a form of politics, it is also constituted through processes that are ethically challenging and complex. When engaging in a dramaturgical process, the testimonial subject places their story and their testimonial truth in the hands of the theatre maker, and the play that ultimately emerges then comes to stand in, in some fundamental way, for this testimonial truth and for the integrity of the witness him or herself. The ethical and political demands of this kind of practice both shape the dramaturgical development of the play and determine the relationships of trust that underpin the formulation of the creative process. To think through the ethical framework of these transactions, I have drawn on the ethical theory developed by philosophers Simon Critchley and Knud Ejler Løgstrup. Importing their theorisation on the structure of ethical experience and the ethical demand in particular into my engagement with testimonial theatre making, I have developed a conceptualisation of what I describe as the 'ethical demand of testimonial practice'. This, then, becomes a means of thinking through the challenges and opportunities of developing ethical relationships of trust between the theatre maker and testimonial subject when developing the dramaturgical processes of testimonial performance. While the era of post-truth discourse will continue to place increasing pressures on those whose lived experience cannot be easily located within the hegemony of normative structures, testimonial performance has the means to intervene in these situations and challenge the moments of re-authoring wrought by increasingly populist discourses that seek to close down or erase dissenting voices. In this sense, testimonial performance offers theatre makers an important range of strategies that can lay the groundwork for critical forms of ethico-political resistance and solidarity with others.

Notes

1 This refers to the Vote Leave campaign where a slogan was displayed on the side of a bus claiming that Britain was currently paying £350 million to the European Union (EU) weekly, which would be diverted to the National Health Service if the country were to leave the EU. The campaign was supported by a number of leave-supporting senior Conservative and some Labour MPs but was later dropped when it became evident that this was not factually correct (see Travis, 2016).

BIBLIOGRAPHY

Adorno, T. (1983) Cultural Criticism and Society. In: Adorno, T. *Prisms*. Cambridge, MA: The MIT Press. pp. 17–35.

Adorno, T. (1986) What Does Coming to Terms with the Past Mean? In: Hartman, G. (ed.) *Bitburg in Moral and Political Perspective*. Bloomington, IN: Indiana University Press. pp. 114–29.

Agamben, G. (1999) *Remnants of Auschwitz: The Witness and the Archive*. Translated by D. Heller-Roazen. New York: Zone Books.

Agboluaje, O. (2009) *The Hounding of David Oluwale*. London: Oberon Books.

Akbar, A. (2018) Notes from the Field Review – Searing Exposé of the School-to-Jail Pipeline. *The Guardian*, 17 June. Available at: www.theguardian.com/stage/2018/jun/17/notes-from-the-field-review-royal-court-london-anna-deavere-smith (accessed: 25/07/2019).

Alcoff, L. (1991) The Problem of Speaking for Others. *Cultural Critique*. 20, pp. 5–32.

Andermahr, S. (ed.) (2016a) *Decolonizing Trauma Studies: Trauma and Postcolonialism*. Basel: MDPI.

Andermahr, S. (2016b) Decolonizing Trauma Studies: Trauma and Postcolonialism – Introduction. In: Andermahr, S. (ed.) *Decolonizing Trauma Studies: Trauma and Postcolonialism*. Basel: MDPI. pp. 1–7.

Anderson, M. and Wilkinson, L. (2007) A Resurgence of Verbatim Theatre: Authenticity, Empathy and Transformation. *Australasian Drama Studies*. 50, pp. 153–69.

Anthony, A. (2017) Minefield: Two Sides of the Falklands War – on One Stage. *The Guardian*, 12 November. Available at: www.theguardian.com/stage/2017/nov/12/two-sides-falklands-war-one-stage-minefield-veterans-stories (accessed: 18/11/2018).

Arendt, H. (1964) The Deputy: Guilt by Silence? In: Bentley, E. (ed.) *The Storm Over The Deputy*. New York: Grove Press. pp. 85–94.

Arendt, H. (2006) *Eichmann in Jerusalem: A Report on the Banality of Evil*. New York and London: Penguin Books.

Arias, L. (2017) *Minefield*. Translated by D. Tunnard. London: Oberon Books.

Aristotle (1987) *The Poetics*. Translated by R. Janko. Indianapolis, IN: Hackett Publishing Company.

Arjomand, M. (2016) Performing Catastrophe: Erwin Piscator's Documentary Theatre. *Modern Drama*. 59(1), pp. 49–74.

Aspden, K. (2008) *The Hounding of David Oluwale*. London: Vintage Books.

Austin, J. L. ([1962] 2018) *How to Do Things with Words*. Edited by J. O. Urmson. Eastford, CT: Martino Fine Books.

Australian Human Rights and Equal Opportunities Commission (1997) *Bringing Them Home: National Inquiry into the Separation of Aboriginal and Torres Straits Islander Children from Their Families*. Available at: www.humanrights.gov.au/sites/default/files/content/pdf/social_justice/bringing_them_home_report.pdf (accessed: 25/07/2019).

Barnett, D. (2014) *Brecht in Practice*. London and New York: Bloomsbury Methuen Drama.

BBC2 (2006) The Original BBC Radio Ballads – History. Available at: www.bbc.co.uk/radio2/radioballads/original/orig_history.shtml (accessed: 24/07/2019).

BBC (2019) Brexit 'Major Influence' in Racism and Hate Crime Rise. BBC Wales, 20 June. Available at: www.bbc.co.uk/news/uk-wales-48692863 (accessed: 25/07/2019).

Bennett, J. and Kennedy, R. (2003) *World Memory: Personal Trajectories in Global Time*. Basingstoke and New York: Palgrave Macmillan.

Bennett, S. (1997) *Theatre Audiences: A Theory of Production and Reception*. Abingdon: Routledge.

Bentley, E. (1964) Forward. In: Bentley, E. (ed.) *The Storm Over The Deputy*. New York: Grove Press. pp. 8–10.

Bentley, E. (1971) *Are You Now or Have You Ever Been: The Investigation of Show Business by the Un-American Activities Committee, 1947–1958*. New York: Harper and Row.

Berwald, O. (2003) *An Introduction to the Works of Peter Weiss*. New York and Woodbridge: Camden House.

Beverley, J. (1996) The Margin at the Centre: On Testimonio. In: Gugelberger, G. (ed.) *The Real Thing: Testimonial Discourse and Latin America*. Durham, NC: Duke University Press. pp. 23–42.

Billington, M. (2005a) My Name Is Rachel Corrie: Review. *The Guardian*, 14 April. Available at: www.theguardian.com/stage/2005/apr/14/theatre.politicaltheatre (accessed: 24/07/2019).

Billington, M. (2005b) 'Talking to Terrorists'. *The Guardian*, 6 July. Available at: www.theguardian.com/stage/2005/jul/06/theatre (accessed: 12/11/2018).

Billington, M. (2012) V is for Verbatim Theatre. *The Guardian*, 8 May. Available at: www.theguardian.com/stage/2012/may/08/michael-billington-verbatim-theatre (accessed: 28/03/2019).

Blake, A. (2017) Donald Trump's Fake Case Against the 'Fake News Media'. *Washington Post*, 24 February. Available at: www.washingtonpost.com/news/the-fix/wp/2017/02/24/donald-trumps-fake-case-against-the-fake-news-media/?utm_term=.90564de560a7 (accessed: 25/07/2019).

Blake, N. (2006) *The Deepcut Review*. Available at: www.gov.uk/government/publications/the-deepcut-review (accessed: 26/01/2020).

Blanchot, M. (2003) *The Infinite Conversation*. Translated by S. Hanson. London and Minneapolis, MN: University of Minnesota Press.

Blank, J. and Jensen, E. (2002) *The Exonerated*. London: Faber and Faber.

Bloodworth, A. (2017) Minefield, Royal Court, Review: Grim Tales of War Become a Creative Feast Thanks to Imaginative Staging. *Metro*, 4 December. Available at: https://metro.co.uk/2017/11/04/minefield-royal-court-review-grim-tales-of-war-become-a-creative-feast-thanks-to-imaginative-staging-7053792/?ito=cbshare (accessed: 12/11/2018).

Blythe, A. (2008) Alecky Blythe. In: Hammond, W. and Steward, D. *Verbatim Verbatim*. London: Oberon Books. pp. 77–103.

Boltanski, L. (2004) *Distant Suffering: Morality, Media and Politics*. Cambridge: Cambridge University Press.

Botham, P. (2008) From Deconstruction to Reconstruction: A Habermasian Framework for Contemporary Political Theatre. *Contemporary Theatre Review*. 18(3), pp. 307–17.

Bottoms, S. (2006) Putting the Document into Documentary. *TDR*. 50(3), pp. 56–68.

Brantley, B. (2016) Review: Anna Deavere Smith's 'Notes from the Field' Delivers Voices of Despair and Hope. *New York Times*, 2 November. Available at: www.nytimes.com/2016/11/03/theater/notes-from-the-field-review-anna-deavere-smith.html (accessed: 25/07/2019).

Brecht, B. ([1940] 1964) Short Description of a New technique of Acting which Produces an Alienation Effect. In: Willet, J. (ed.) *Brecht on Theatre: The Development of an Aesthetic.* Translated by J. Willet. London: Methuen. pp. 136–47.

Brecht, B. (2015a) Notes on The Threepenny Opera. In: Silberman, M., Giles, S. and Kuhn, T. (eds) *Brecht on Theatre* (3rd edn). London: Bloomsbury Methuen Drama. pp. 71–80.

Brecht, B. (2015b) On Experimental Theatre. In: Silberman, M., Giles, S. and Kuhn, T. (eds) *Brecht on Theatre* (3rd edn). London: Bloomsbury Methuen Drama. pp. 133–6.

Brecht, B. (2015c) The Street Scene: A Basic Model for an Epic Theatre. In: Silberman, M., Giles, S. and Kuhn, T. (eds) *Brecht on Theatre* (3rd edn). London: Bloomsbury Methuen Drama. pp. 176–84.

Brittain, V. and Slovo, G. (2004) *Guantanamo: 'Honor Bound to Defend Freedom'.* London: Oberon Modern Plays.

Brittain, V., Kent, N., Norton-Taylor, R. and Slovo, G. (eds) (2014) *The Tricycle Collected Tribunal Plays: 1994–2012.* London: Oberon Books.

Brown, P. (1993) *Aftershocks: A Project of the Newcastle Workers Cultural Action Committee.* Sydney: Currency Press.

Buratta, B. (2019) A Note on the Play. In: Outbox, *And the Rest of Me Floats.* London: Oberon Modern Plays. (unpaginated).

Butler, R. (1999) Trial by Tricycle Theatre. *The Independent*, 17 January. Available at: www.independent.co.uk/arts-entertainment/trial-by-tricycle-theatre-1074415.html (accessed: 23/04/2019).

Cantrell, T. (2013) *Acting in Documentary Theatre.* Basingstoke and New York: Palgrave Macmillan.

Carlson, M. (2018) *Shattering Hamlet's Mirror.* Michigan: University of Michigan Press.

Carman, T. (2003) *Heidegger's Analytic: Interpretation, Discourse, and Authenticity in Being and Time.* Cambridge: Cambridge University Press.

Caruth, C. (1995) Introduction. In: Caruth, C. (ed.) *Trauma: Explorations in Memory.* Baltimore, MD: John Hopkins University Press. pp. 3–13.

Caruth, C. (1996) *Unclaimed Experience: Trauma, Narrative, and History.* Baltimore, MD and London: John Hopkins University Press.

Cheeseman, P. (1970) Introduction: Documentary Theatre at Stoke-On-Trent. In: Cheeseman, P. *The Knotty: A Musical Documentary.* London: Methuen and Co Ltd. pp. vi–xx.

Cheeseman, P. (2005) On Documentary Theatre. In: Soans, R. *Talking to Terrorists.* London: Oberon Books. pp. 104–7.

Chouliaraki, L. (2006) *Spectatorship of Suffering.* London and Delhi: Sage Publications.

Cohen, R. (1998) The Political Aesthetics of Holocaust Literature: Peter Weiss's The Investigation and its Critics. *History and Memory.* 10(2), pp. 43–67.

Craps, S. (2015) *Postcolonial Witnessing: Trauma Out of Bounds.* Basingstoke: Palgrave Macmillan.

Critchley, S. (2007) *Infinitely Demanding: Ethics of Commitment, Politics of Resistance.* London: Verso.

Derrida, J. (2000) *Demeure: Fiction and Testimony.* Translated by E. Rottenberg. Stanford, CA: Stanford University Press.

Derrida, J. (2005) Poetics and Politics of Witnessing. In: Dutoit, T. and Pasanen, O. (eds) *Sovereignties in Question: The Poetics of Paul Celan.* Translated by T. Dutoit and O. Pasanen. New York: Fordham University Press. pp. 65–97.

Dodgson, E. (1995) Background to the International Programme at the Royal Court. In: Pohl, K. *Waiting Room Germany.* Translated by D. Tushingham. London: Nick Hern Books (unpaginated).

Duggan, P. (2013) Others, Spectatorship, and the Ethics of Verbatim Performance. *New Theatre Quarterly.* 29(2), pp. 146–58.

Durrheim, K., Mtose, X. and Brown, L. (2011) *Race Trouble: Race, Identity, and Inequality in Post-apartheid South Africa.* Pietermaritzburg: University of KwaZulu-Natal Press.

Eckholm, E. (2016) South Carolina Law on Disrupting School Faces Legal Challenge. *New York Times*, 11 August. Available at: www.nytimes.com/2016/08/12/us/south-carolina-schools.html (accessed: 23/04/2019).

Edgar, D. (2008) Dram and Doc. *The Guardian*, 27 September. Available at: www.theguardian.com/stage/2008/sep/27/theatre.davidedgar (accessed: 20/06/2019).

Ellis, R. (1987) *Peter Weiss in Exile: A Critical Study of His Works*. Ann Arbor, MI: UMI Research Press.

Elvgren, G. (1974) Documentary Theatre at Stoke-On-Trent. *Educational Theatre Journal*. 16(1), pp. 86–98.

Enright, H. (2011) Theatre of Testimony: A Practice-led Investigation into the Role of Staging Testimony in Contemporary Theatre. PhD Thesis. University of Exeter. Available at: https://ore.exeter.ac.uk/repository/handle/10036/3639 (accessed: 25/07/2019).

Etchells, T. (1999) *Certain Fragments: Contemporary Performance and Forced Entertainment*. Abingdon and New York: Routledge.

Farber, Y. (2008a) *Theatre as Witness: Three Testimonial Plays from South Africa*. London: Oberon Books.

Farber, Y. (2008b) Interviewed by Amanda Stuart Fisher. In: Farber, Y. (2008) *Theatre as Witness: Three Testimonial Plays from South Africa*. London: Oberon Books. pp. 19–28.

Farber, Y. with Mtshali-Jones, T. (2008c) *A Woman in Waiting*. In: Farber, Y. *Theatre as Witness: Three Testimonial Plays from South Africa*. London: Oberon Books. pp. 29–85.

Fausset, R., Pérez-Peña, R. and Blinder, A. (2015) Race and Discipline in Spotlight after South Carolina Officer Drags Student. *New York Times*, 27 October. Available at: www.nytimes.com/2015/10/28/us/spring-valley-high-school-sc-officer-arrest.html (accessed: 25/07/2019).

Favorini, A. (1995) *Voicings: Ten Plays from the Documentary Theatre*. Hopewell, NJ: The Ecco Press.

Favorini, A. (2011) History, Memory and Trauma in the Documentary Plays of Emily Mann. In: Forsyth, A. and Megson, C. (eds) *Get Real: Documentary Theatre Past and Present* (2nd edn). Basingstoke and New York: Palgrave MacMillan. pp. 151–67.

Felman, S. (1992) Education and Crisis, Or the Vicissitudes of Teaching. In: Felman, S. and Laub, D. (eds) *Testimony: Crises of Witnessing in Literature, Psychoanalysis, and History*. Abingdon and New York: Routledge. pp. 1–57.

Felman, S. and Laub, D. (eds) *Testimony: Crises of Witnessing in Literature, Psychoanalysis, and History*. Abingdon and New York: Routledge.

Filewod, A. (2011) The Documentary Body: Theatre Workshop to Banner Theatre. In: Forsyth, A. and Megson, C. (eds) *Get Real: Documentary Theatre Past and Present*. (2nd edn). Basingstoke and New York: Palgrave MacMillan. pp. 55–73.

Forsyth, A. (2011) Performing Trauma: Race Riots and Beyond in the Work of Anna Deavere Smith. In: Forsyth, A. and Megson, C. (eds) *Get Real: Documentary Theatre Past and Present* (2nd edn) Basingstoke and New York: Palgrave MacMillan. pp. 140–51.

Forsyth, A. and Megson, C. (2011) Introduction. In: Forsyth, A. and Megson, C. (eds) *Get Real: Documentary Theatre Past and Present* (2nd edn) Basingstoke and New York: Palgrave MacMillan. pp. 1–6.

Foucault, M. (1991) Nietzsche, Genealogy, History. In: *The Foucault Reader: An Introduction to Foucault's Thought*. Edited by P. Rabinow. London: Penguin Books. pp. 76–101.

Foucault, M. (2001) *Fearless Speech*. Edited by J. Pearson. Los Angeles, CA: Semiotext[e].

Foucault, M. (2010) *The Government of Self and Others: Lecturers at the Collège de France 1982–1983*. Translated by G. Burchell. Basingstoke and New York: Palgrave Macmillan.

Freud, S. ([1914] 2006) Remembering, Repeating and Working Through. In: Philips, A. (ed.) *The Penguin Freud Reader*. London: Penguin. pp. 391–402.

Fuchs, E. (1996) *The Death of Character: Perspectives on Theatre after Modernism*. Bloomington, IN: Indiana University Press.

Fugard, A. (1997) Introduction. In: Mann, E. *Testimonies: Four Plays by Emily Mann*. New York: Theatre Communications Group. pp. ix–xi.

Gale, M. and Deeney, J. (2010) Early Political Theatres: Introduction. In: Gale, M. and Deeney, J. (eds) *The Routledge Drama Anthology and Sourcebook: From Modernism to Contemporary Performance.* Abingdon and New York: Routledge. pp. 290–310.

Garde, U., Mumford, M. and Wake, C. (2010) A Short History of Verbatim Theatre. In: Brown, P. (ed.) *Verbatim: Staging Memory and Community.* Sydney: Currency Press. pp. 9–18.

Goddard, L. (2018) #Blacklivesmatter: Remembering Mark Duggan and David Oluwale in Contemporary British Plays. *Journal in Contemporary Drama in English.* 6(1), pp. 69–86.

Goodman, D. M. and Severson, E. R. (eds) (2016) *The Ethical Turn: Otherness and Subjectivity in Contemporary Pyschoanalysis.* Abingdon and New York: Routledge.

Greenfield, P. (2018) Doreen Lawrence: If Stab Victims Were White, MPs Would Care More. *The Guardian,* 26 January. Available at: www.theguardian.com/uk-news/2018/jan/26/doreen-lawrence-if-stab-victims-were-white-mps-would-care-more (accessed: 25/07/2019).

Grochala, S. (2017) *The Contemporary Political Play: Rethinking Dramaturgical Structure.* London: Bloomsbury Methuen Drama.

Gugelberger, G. and Kearney, M. (1991) Voices for the Voiceless: Testimonial Literature in Latin America. *Latin American Perspectives.* 18(3), pp. 3–14.

Guignon, C. (2004) *On Being Authentic.* London and New York: Routledge.

Hare, D. (2003) *The Permanent Way.* London: Faber and Faber.

Hare, D. (2005) On Factual Theatre. In: Soans, R. *Talking to Terrorists.* London: Oberon Books. pp. 111–13.

Hare, D. (2007) *Obedience, Struggle and Revolt.* London: Faber and Faber.

Hare, D. and Stafford-Clark, M. (2008) David Hare and Max Stafford-Clark. In: Hammond, W. and Steward, D. (eds) *Verbatim Verbatim: Contemporary Documentary Theatre.* London: Oberon Books. pp. 45–77.

Hartman, G. (1996) *The Longest Shadow: In the Aftermath of the Holocaust.* Bloomington, IN: Indiana University Press.

Haugo, A. (2002) Weaving a Legacy: An Interview with Muriel Miguel of the Spiderwoman Theater. In: Uno, R. and Burns, L. M. S. P. *The Colour of Theater: Race, Culture, and Contemporary Performance.* London and New York: Continuum. pp. 219–37.

Haugo, A. (2009) Persistent Memories: An Interview with Spiderwoman Theater In: Armstrong, A., Johnson, K. and Wortman, W. (eds) *Performing Worlds into Being: Native American Women's Theatre.* Oxford, OH: Miami University Press. pp. 60–75.

Haugo, A. (2013) Native America Drama: A Historical Survey. In: Dawes, B. (ed.) *Indigenous North America Drama: A Multivocal History.* New York: Suny Press. pp. 39–63.

Heddon, D. (2008) *Autobiography and Performance.* Basingstoke and New York: Palgrave Macmillan.

Heddon, D. (2009) To Absent Friends: Ethics in the Field of Auto-Biography. In: Haedicke, S., Heddon, D., Oz, A. and Westlake, E. *Political Performances: Theory and Practice.* The Netherlands: IFTR and Rodopi. pp. 111–37.

Heidegger, M. (2010) *Being and Time.* Translated by J. Stambaugh. New York: State University of New York Press.

Herzfeld-Sander, M. (2001) *Contemporary German Plays 1: Rolf Hochhuth, Heinar Kiddhardt, Heiner Müller.* New York: Continuum.

Higson, R. (2007) Home Girls Have Their Say. In: Valentine, A. *Parramatta Girls and Eyes to the Floor.* Sydney: Currency Press. pp. 3–6.

Hilton, I. (1970) *Peter Weiss: A Search for Affinities.* London: Oswald Wolf.

Hirsch, J. (2003) *Shakespeare and the History of Soliloquies.* Madison, NJ and London: Fairleigh Dickinson University Press.

Hobsbawm, E. (1995) *Age of Extremes: The Short Twentieth Century 1914–1991.* London: Abacus Books.

Hochhuth, R. (1964) *The Deputy.* Translated by R. Winston and C. Winston. New York: Grove Press.

Horsman, Y. (2011) *Theatres of Justice: Judging, Staging and Working Through in Arendt, Brecht, and Delbo.* Stanford, CA: Stanford University Press.

Hutchison, Y. (2011) Verbatim Theatre in South Africa: 'Living History in a Person's Performative'. In: Forsyth, A. and Megson, C. (eds) *Get Real: Documentary Theatre Past and Present* (2nd edn). Basingstoke and New York: Palgrave MacMillan. pp. 209–24.

Huyssen, A. (1980) The Politics of Identification: "Holocaust" and West German Drama. *New German Critique*. 19, pp. 117–36.

Huyssen, A. (1995) *Twilight Memories: Marking Tome in a Culture of Amnesia*. New York and Abingdon: Routledge.

Innes, C. (1972) *Erwin Piscator's Political Theatre: The Development of Modern German Drama*. Cambridge: Cambridge University Press.

Irmer, T. (2006) A Search for New Realities: Documentary Theatre in Germany. *TDR*. 50(3), pp. 16–28.

Isaac, D. (1971) Theatre of Fact. *TDR*. 15(3), pp. 109–35.

Janko, R. (1987) Notes to *Poetics* I. In: Aristotle, *The Poetics*. Translated by R. Janko. Indianapolis, IN: Hackett Publishing Company. pp. 66–159.

Jestrovic, S. (2005) The Theatrical Memory of Space: From Piscator and Brecht to Belgrade. *New Theatre Quarterly*. 21(4), pp. 358–66.

Kelleher, J. (2009) *Theatre and Politics*. Basingstoke: Palgrave Macmillan.

Kelly, D. (2007) *Taking Care of Baby*. London: Oberon Books.

Kennedy, R. (1997) Autobiography: The Narrator as Witness. Testimony, Trauma and Narrative Form in *My Place*. *Meridan*. 16(2), pp. 235–60.

Kennedy, R. and Wilson, T. (2003) Constructing Shared Histories: Stolen Generations Testimony, Narrative Therapy and Address. In: Bennett, J. and Kennedy, R. (2003) *World Memory: Personal Trajectories in Global Time*. Basingstoke and New York: Palgrave Macmillan. pp. 119–41.

Kennedy, R., Bell, L. and Emberley, J. (2009) Decolonizing Testimony: On the possibilities and limits of witnessing. *Humanities Research*. 15(3), pp. 1–10.

Kent, N. (2014) *Srebrenica*. In: Brittain, V., Kent, N., Norton-Taylor, R. and Slovo, G. *The Tricycle: Collected Tribunal Plays 1994-2012*. London: Oberon Books. pp. 195–291.

Kent, N., Norton-Taylor, R., Slovo, G. and Edgar, D. (2014) Verbatim Theatre (Verbatim). In Brittain, V., Kent, N., Norton-Taylor, R. and Slovo, G. *The Tricycle: Collected Tribunal Plays 1994-2012*. London: Oberon Books. pp. 4–39.

Kipphardt, H. (1968) *In the Matter of J. Robert Oppenheimer*. New York: Farrar, Straus and Giroux.

Knaller, S. (2012) Authenticity as an Aesthetic Notion: Normative and Non-Normative Concepts in Modern and Contemporary Politics. In: Funk, W., Gross, F. and Huber, I. (eds) *The Aesthetics of Authenticity: Medial Construction of the Real*. Germany, New York and London: Transaction Publishers. pp. 25–41.

Kondo, D. (2000) (Re)Visions of Race: Contemporary Race Theory and the Cultural Politics of Racial Crossover in Documentary Theatre. *Theatre Journal*. 52(1), pp. 81–107.

Kruger, L. (1999) *The Drama of South Africa: Plays, Pageants and Publics since 1910*. London and New York: Routledge.

LaCapra, D. (2001) *Writing History, Writing Trauma*. Baltimore, MD and London: John Hopkins University Press.

Lane, D. (2010) *Contemporary British Drama*. Edinburgh: Edinburgh University Press.

Langer, L. (1995) *Admitting the Holocaust*. Oxford: Oxford University Press,

Laub, D. (1992) An Event Without a Witness: Truth, Testimony and Survival. In: Felman, S. and Laub, D. (eds) *Testimony: Crises of Witnessing in Literature, Psychoanalysis, and History*. Abingdon and New York: Routledge. pp. 75–93.

Lawrence, D. (2006) *And Still I Rise: A Mother's Search for Justice*. London: Faber and Faber.

Lawrence, D. (2019) On the First Stephen Lawrence Day, Let's Admit Our Communities Are Still Unequal. *The Guardian*, 22 April. Available at: www.theguardian.com/commentisfree/2019/apr/22/stephen-lawrence-day-british-society-doreen-lawrence (accessed: 29/01/2020).

Lehmann, H. (2006) *Postdramatic Theatre*. Translated by K. Jürs-Munby. Abingdon and New York: Routledge.

Leonhardt, D. (2016) The Lies Trump Told. *New York Times*, 27 September. Available at: www.nytimes.com/2016/09/27/opinion/campaign-stops/the-lies-trump-told.html (accessed: 25/07/2019).

Leys, R. (2000) *Trauma: A Genealogy.* Chicago, IL: University of Chicago Press.

Lipovetsky, M. and Beumers, B. (2008) Reality Performance: Documentary Trends in Post-Soviet Russian Theatre. *Contemporary Theatre Review.* 18(3), pp. 293–306.

Løgstrup, K. E. (1997) *The Ethical Demand.* Notre Dame, IN: University of Notre Dame Press.

Løgstrup, K. E. (2007) *Beyond The Ethical Demand.* Translated by S. Dew and H. Flegal. Notre Dame, IN: University of Notre Dame Press.

Luckhurst, M. (2010) Ethical Stress and Performing Real People. *Performing Ethos.* 1(2), pp. 135–52.

Maedza, P. (2017) *Performing Asylum: Theatre of Testimony in South Africa.* The Netherlands: African Studies Centre.

Malina, J. (2012) *The Piscator Notebook.* Abingdon and New York: Routledge.

Mann, E. ([1988] 1997) *Annulla: An Autobiography.* In: Mann, E. (ed.) *Testimonies: Four Plays by Emily Mann.* New York: Theatre Communications Group. pp. 1–31.

Martin, C. (1993) Anna Deavere Smith: The Word Becomes You. An Interview by Carol Martin. *TDR.* 37(4) (T140), pp. 45–62.

Martin, C. (2006) Bodies of Evidence. *TDR.* 50(3), pp. 8–15.

Martin, C. (2013) *Theatre of the Real.* Basingstoke and New York: Palgrave Macmillan.

McCormack, J. (2018) *Choreography and Verbatim Theatre: Dancing Words.* Basingstoke and New York: Palgrave Macmillan.

McIntyre, L. (2018) *Post-Truth.* Cambridge, MA: The MIT Press.

Megson, C. (2011) Half the Picture: 'A Certain Frisson' at the Tricycle Theatre. In: Forsyth, A. and Megson, C. (eds) *Get Real: Documentary Theatre Past and Present* (2nd edn) Basingstoke and New York: Palgrave MacMillan. pp. 195–209.

Mengel, E. and Borgzaga, M. (2012) Introduction. In: Mengel, E. and Borgzaga, M. *Trauma, Memory, and Narrative in the Cotemporary South African Novel.* The Netherlands: Rodopi.

Merlin, B. (2007) *The Permanent Way* and the Impermanent Muse. *Contemporary Theatre Review.* 17(1), pp. 41–9.

Munk, E., Weiss, P. and Gray, P. (1966) A Living World. In Interview with Peter Weiss. *The Tulane Drama Review.* 11(1), pp. 106–14.

Nelson, R. (2013) *Practice as Research in the Arts: Principles, Protocols, Pedagogies, Resistances.* Basingstoke and New York: Palgrave.

Nicholson, S. (2012) *Modern British Playwriting: The 1960s: Voices, Documents, New Interpretations.* London: Methuen Drama.

Norton-Taylor, R. (1999) *The Colour of Justice.* London: Oberon Books.

Nussbaum, L. (1981) The German Documentary Theater of the Sixties: A Stereopsis of Contemporary History. *German Studies Review.* 4(2), pp. 237–55.

Oades, R. (2010) Creating a Headphone-Verbatim Performance: Workshop by Roslyn Oades. In: Brown, P. (ed.) *Verbatim: Staging Memory and Community.* Sydney: Currency Press. pp. 84–7.

Oades, R. (2010) Parramatta Girls: Verbatim Theatre about the Forgotten Australians. In: Brown, P. (ed.) *Verbatim: Staging Memory and Community.* Sydney: Currency Press. pp. 59–66.

Outbox (2019) *And the Rest of Me Floats.* London: Oberon Modern Plays.

Oxford University Press (2019). 'Post-Truth'. Available at: www.lexico.com/en/definition/post-truth (accessed: 25/07/2019).

Paget, D. (1987) 'Verbatim Theatre': Oral History and Documentary Techniques. *New Theatre Quarterly.* 3(12), pp. 317–36.

Paget, D. (1990) *True Stories? Documentary Drama on Radio, Screen and Stage.* Manchester and New York: Manchester University Press.

Paget, D. (2008) New Documentarism on Stage: Documentary Theatre in New Times. *ZAA.* 56(2), pp. 129–41.

Paget, D. (2010) Acts of Commitment: Activist Arts, the Rehearsed Reading and Documentary Theatre. *New Theatre Quarterly.* 26(2), pp. 173–93.

Paget, D. (2011) The 'Broken Tradition' of Documentary Theatre and Its Continued Powers of Endurance. Forsyth, A. and Megson, C. (eds) *Get Real: Documentary Theatre Past and Present* (2nd edn). Basingstoke and New York: Palgrave MacMillan. pp. 224–39.

Parragirls (Parramatta Female Factory Precinct Assoc. Inc.). Website. Available at: www.parragirls.org.au/ (accessed: 25/07/2019).

Peters, S. (2016) Acting in Verbatim Theatre: An Australian Case Study. *Australasian Drama Studies.* 68, pp. 143–67.

Phelan, P. (1993) *Unmarked: The Politics of Performance.* Abingdon and New York: Routledge.

Phelan, P. (1999) Forward. In: Etchells, T. *Certain Fragments: Contemporary Performance and Forced Entertainment.* Abingdon and New York: Routledge. pp. 9–14.

Piscator, E. (1964) Introduction to The Deputy. In: Bentley, E. (ed.) *The Storm Over The Deputy.* New York: Grove Press. pp. 11–15.

Piscator, E. (2014) The Documentary Play. In: Holdsworth, N. and Willcocks, G. (eds) *European Theatre: Performing Practice, 1900 to the Present.* Farnham and Burlington, VT: Ashgate Publishing Company. pp. 272–8.

Plunka, G. (2009) *Holocaust Drama: The Theatre of Atrocity.* Cambridge: Cambridge University Press.

Pohl, K. (1995) *Waiting Room Germany.* Translated by D. Tushingham. London: Nick Hern Books.

Radosavljević, D. (2013) *Theatre Making: Interplay Between Text and Performance in the 21st Century.* Basingstoke and New York: Palgrave Macmillan.

Ralph, P. (2008) *Deep Cut.* London: Oberon Books.

Rebellato, D. (2007) Denis Kelly. *Contemporary Theatre Review.* 17(4), pp. 596–608.

Reinelt, J. (2006) Toward a Poetics of Theatre and Public Events. *TDR.* 50(3), pp. 69–87.

Reinelt, J. and Hewitt, G. (2011) *The Political Theatre of David Edgar: Negotiation and Retrieval.* Cambridge: Cambridge University Press.

Rickman, A. and Viner, K. (2005) *My Name Is Rachel Corrie.* London: Nick Hern Books.

Robbins Dudeck, T. (2013) *Keith Johnstone: A Critical Biography.* London: Bloomsbury.

Rothberg, M. (2008) Decolonizing Trauma Studies: A Response. *Studies in the Novel.* 40(1 and 2), pp. 224–34.

Ruff, M. E. (2017) *The Battle for the Catholic Past in Germany, 1945–1980.* Cambridge: Cambridge University Press.

Schaffer, K. and Smith, S. (2004) *Human Rights and Narrated Lives: The Ethics of Recognition.* Basingstoke and New York: Palgrave Macmillan.

Schechner, R. (1993) Anna Deavere Smith: Acting as Incorporation. *TDR.* 37(4), pp. 63–4.

Schulze, D. (2017) *Authenticity in Contemporary Theatre and Performance: Make It Real.* London: Bloomsbury.

Searle, J. R. ([1969] 1999) *Speech Acts: An Essay in the Philosophy of Language* (new edn). Cambridge: Cambridge University Press.

Slovo, G. (2011) *The Riots: From Spoken Evidence.* London: Oberon Modern Plays.

Smith, S. (2014) *Parramatta Girls* by Alana Valentine. Teachers Notes, Education at Riverside. Available at: https://riversideparramatta.com.au/wp-content/uploads/Parramatta-Girls-Teachers-Notes-2014.pdf (accessed: 20/01/2020).

Smith, A. D. (2016) Check it Out: Anna Deavere Smith's *Notes from the Field. Revolution Newspaper,* 8 November. Available at: https://revcom.us/a/464/check-it-out-anna-deavere-smiths-notes-from-the-field-en.html (accessed: 29/01/2020).

Smith, A. D. (2018a) *Fires in the Mirror: Crown Heights, Brooklyn, and Other Identities.* New York: Bantam Doubleday Dell Publishing Group.

Smith, A. D. (2018b) *Twilight: Los Angeles.* New York: Anchor Publishing

Smith, A. D. (2019) *Notes from the Field.* New York: Penguin Random House.

Soans, R. (2005) *Talking to Terrorists.* London: Oberon Books.

Soans, R. (2008) Robin Soans. In: Hammond, W. and Steward, D. (eds) *Verbatim Verbatim.* London: Oberon Books. pp. 17–34

Solomon, A. (2019) Digging Up the Pipeline. *Anna Deavere Smith Projects* website. Available at: www.annadeaveresmith.org/ (accessed: 25/07/2019).

Sontag, S. (1964) Reflections on *The Deputy*. Bentley, E. (ed.) *The Storm Over The Deputy*. New York: Grove Press. pp. 117–23.

Sosa, C. (2014) *Queering Acts of Mourning in the Aftermath of Argentina's Dictatorship: The Performances of Blood*. New York and Woodbridge: Tamesis Books.

Spencer, C. (2005) Chilling, Moving and Mesmerising: Review. *The Telegraph*, 30 April. Available at: www.telegraph.co.uk/culture/theatre/drama/3641278/Chilling-moving-and-mesmerising.html/ (accessed: 23/07/2019).

Spiderwoman Theater (2009) *Persistence of Memory*. In: Armstrong, A., Johnson, K. and Wortman, W. (eds) *Performing Worlds into Being: Native American Women's Theatre*. Oxford, OH: Miami University Press. pp. 42–57.

Stafford-Clark, M. (1983) Untitled Introduction. In: Stafford-Clark, M. *Falkland Sound*. London: Royal Court Theatre.

Steinicke, O. (1995) Proletarian Agitation Theatre: The Performance in the Großes Schauspiel-haus. In: Favorini, A. (ed.) *Voicings: Ten Plays from the Documentary Theatre*. Hopewell, NJ: The Ecco Press. pp. 12–13.

Stern, R. (2019) *The Radical Demand in Løgstrup's Ethics*. Oxford: Oxford University Press.

Straub, J. (2012) *Paradoxes of Authenticity*. New York: Cambridge University Press.

Stuart Fisher, A. (2011) 'That's Who I'd Be, If I Could Sing': Reflections on a Verbatim Project with Mothers of Sexually Abused Children. *Studies in Theatre and Performance*. 31(2), pp. 193–208.

Stuart Fisher, A. (2011) Trauma, Authenticity and the Limits of Verbatim. *Performance Research*. 16(1), pp. 112–24.

Stuart Fisher, A. (2013) *From the Mouths of Mothers*. Twickenham: Aurora Metro Books.

Taylor, D. (1997) *Disappearing Acts: Spectacles of Gender and Nationalism in Argentina's 'Dirty War'*. Durham, NC: Duke University Press.

Taylor, P. (2005) Talking To Terrorists, Playhouse, Oxford. *The Independent*, 2 May. Available at: www.independent.co.uk/arts-entertainment/theatre-dance/reviews/talking-to-terrorists-playhouse-oxford-222420.html (accessed: 13/11/2018).

Tinker, H. (ed.) (1983) *A Message From the Falklands: The Life and Gallant Death of David Tinker Lieut., R.N. From His Letters and Poems*. London: Penguin.

Travis, A. (2016) The Leave Campaign Made Three Key Promises – Are They Keeping Them? *The Guardian*, 27 June. Available at: www.theguardian.com/politics/2016/jun/27/eu-referendum-reality-check-leave-campaign-promises (accessed: 25/07/2019).

Turner, C. and Behrndt, S. (2008) *Dramaturgy and Performance*. Basingstoke and New York: Palgrave Macmillan.

Tushingham, D. (1995) A Note on the Text. In: Pohl, K. *Waiting Room Germany*. Translated by D. Tushingham. London: Nick Hern Books. p. 1.

Ukaegbu, V. (2015) Witnessing to, in, and from the Centre: Oladipo Agboluaje's Theatre of Dialogic Centrism. In: Brewer, M., Goddard, L. and Osborne, D. (eds) *Modern and Contemporary Black British Drama*. Basingstoke and New York: Palgrave Macmillan. pp. 194–209.

Valentine, A. (2007) *Parramatta Girls and Eyes to the Floor*. Sydney: Currency Press.

Valentine, A. (2010) Interviewed by Roslyn Oades. In: Brown, P. (ed.) *Verbatim: Staging Memory and Community*. Sydney: Currency Press. pp. 107–8.

Wake, C. (2010) Verbatim Theatre within a Spectrum of Practices. In: Brown, P.(ed.) *Verbatim: Staging Memory and Community*. Sydney: Currency Press. pp. 6–8.

Wake, C. (2013a) Headphone Verbatim Theatre: Methods, Histories, Genres, Theatres. *NTQ*. 29, pp. 321–35.

Wake, C. (2013b) The Accident and the Account: Towards a Taxonomy of Spectorial Witness in Theatre and Performance. In: Trezise, B. and Wake, C. (eds) *Visions and Revisions: Performance, Memory, Trauma*. Copenhagen: Museum Tusculanum Press. pp. 33–57.

Wake, C. (2014) The Complexity of Courage: Roslyn Oades' Headphone Verbatim Trilogy. In: Oades, R. *Acts of Courage: Three Headphone Verbatim Plays*. Sydney: Currency Press. pp. vii–xviii.

Weiss, P. ([1968] 1995) Fourteen Propositions for a Documentary Theatre. In: Favorini, A. (ed.) *Voicings: Ten Plays from the Documentary Theatre*. Hopewell, NJ: The Ecco Press. pp. 139–43.

Weiss, P. (2010) *The Investigation: Oratorio in 11 Cantos*. Translated by A. Gross. London and New York: Marion Boyers.

Wicker, T. (2017) Minefield director and writer Lola Arias: 'My shows are living creatures that evolve'. *The Stage*, 27 October. Available at: www.thestage.co.uk/features/interviews/2017/minefield-director-writer-lola-arias-my-shows-living-creatures-that-evolve/ (accessed: 13/11/2018).

Wilde, F. (2013) Divided They Fell: The German Left and the Rise of Hitler'. *International Socialism*. 137. Available at: http://isj.org.uk/divided-they-fell-the-german-left-and-the-rise-of-hitler/ (accessed: 8/10/2018).

Winston, C. (1964) The Matter of 'The Deputy'. *The Massachusetts Review*. 5(3), pp. 423–36.

Wittgenstein, L. (2009) *Philosophical Investigations* (4th edn). Edited by P. M. S. Hacker and J. Schulte. Hoboken, NJ: Wiley-Blackwell.

Worrall, N. (1996) *The Moscow Arts Theatre*. Abingdon: Routledge.

INDEX

Milton Keynes UK
Ingram Content Group UK Ltd.
UKHW021456050923
428092UK00041B/599